Lili Marlene

Lili Marlene

THE SOLDIERS' SONG
OF WORLD WAR II

Liel Leibovitz and Matthew Miller

W • W • Norton & Company　　New York　London

Copyright © 2009 by Liel Leibovitz and Matthew Miller

For information about permission to reproduce selections from this book,
write to Permissions, W. W. Norton & Company, Inc.,
500 Fifth Avenue, New York, NY 10110

For information about special discounts for bulk purchases, please contact
W. W. Norton Special Sales at specialsales@wwnorton.com or 800-233-4830

Manufacturing by RR Donnelley Bloomsburg
Book design by Margaret M. Wagner
Production manager: Julia Druskin

Library of Congress Cataloging-in-Publication Data

Leibovitz, Liel.
Lili Marlene : the soldiers' song of World War II / Liel Leibovitz and
Matthew Miller. — 1st ed.
p. cm.
Includes bibliographical references and index.
ISBN 978-0-393-06584-8 (hardcover)
1. Schultze, Norbert, 1911–2002. Lili Marleen. 2. Leip, Hans, 1893–1983.
3. Schultze, Norbert, 1911–2002. 4. Andersen, Lale. I. Miller, Matthew
I., 1979– II. Title.
ML385.L397 2008
782.42164—dc22

2008024113

W. W. Norton & Company, Inc.
500 Fifth Avenue, New York, N.Y. 10110
www.wwnorton.com

W. W. Norton & Company Ltd.
Castle House, 75/76 Wells Street, London W1T 3QT

1 2 3 4 5 6 7 8 9 0

For Lisa,
L.L.

For MT
MM

Contents

Lili Marlene

Note on Translation and Sources

As THERE are many ways in which the name Lili Marlene can be spelled, and as differences in spelling abound between German and English sources, we have decided, for the sake of convenience and ease, to alter every variation and use instead the spelling suggested above. The same is true for the song's many existing translations: in various points in the plot, various versions are presented, according to the way the song was experienced by its respective listeners.

Also, as numerous events described in the book are of a contentious and personal nature, several conflicting accounts exist for a few of the narrative's key points. Unless we have been able to verify one version beyond any doubt, we have relayed the most credible alternative in the book, addressing the other versions in the endnotes.

Prologue

FITZROY MACLEAN brought his vehicle to a stop and stepped onto the spacious Libyan desert. He and his small raiding party, deep behind the German and Italian lines, were making their way as quietly and discreetly as possible toward the Axis port installations at Benghazi, where they were to plant explosives, sow chaos, and otherwise disrupt the enemy armies moving out there, somewhere, in the desert. By nighttime, Maclean knew, the scalding, rocky expanse of sand that surrounded him would cool down considerably and the entire landscape, from Benghazi to distant Cairo, would feel like icy glass.

Yet as he stood in the afternoon heat aside his battered, open-topped Ford, Maclean was dressed in his familiar drill shorts, sandals, and an Arab headdress worn as much for the allure of the look as for protection against the desert sun. Such were the practical limits of a daytime wardrobe in North Africa; even a shirt would have been too cumbersome. Maclean, a graduate of Eton and Cambridge, the son of one of Scotland's finest families, truly relished the freedom afforded by army life. In the desert, there was little need for decorum, no use for formalities, and he, a former diplomat accustomed to parties at Parisian embassies and the mysterious workings of Soviet government ministries, now found himself living in a vast open space alongside fellow adventurers with whom he could share the thrill of the unknown.

Maclean had fought hard for the privilege of being a soldier, as he was not permitted to leave the diplomatic corps for any reason excluding pursuit of public office. Thus, Maclean, though no lover of politics, ran for a seat in the House of Commons and, to his astonishment and good fortune, won. His career as a parliamentary representative was short-lived, however: shortly after his election Maclean abandoned his constituents and made his way to the army, North Africa, and the Special Air Service, the elite, newly formed unit which was given some of the war's most dangerous and daring missions.

Undertaking long-range raids in the hazy days of 1942, Maclean spent most of his waking hours driving across the desert with his comrades, stopping briefly for noontime lunches of tinned salmon, sardines, and canned fruit. In the evenings, the group's grueling advance would be brought to a standstill as the men, trudging through ground that was at times flat and at others hilly, began, with the night's frost already in descent, to set up camp under the starry skies. They would pour a bit of petrol into a tin filled with sand, producing an impromptu campfire. Huddling around it for warmth, the men would cook supper: a hot beef stew accompanied by tea and a drop of rum, a meal that the men ate with gusto and deliberation. They then filled their water bottles in preparation for the following day, wired whatever messages they had to far-off headquarters, threw their greatcoats over their shoulders and once again took their seats by the fire. By this time, it would be nearly ten o'clock, and the men, exhausted, would sit and wait for their one true joy in the lonely desert. It was a song, relayed every night at 9:57 by Radio Belgrade, a German army station. It began with a bugle call, the sort that signaled the day's end to generations of soldiers. Then, gently, a sweet melody, simple to hum and impossible to forget, started to play. Over it, a woman's voice, harsh and compelling:

Vor der Kaserne
Vor dem grossen Tor . . .

Maclean and his men understood little of the German lyrics, their poetry and notes of longing. And yet, something about the foreign song made it irresistible, meaningful, their own. Maclean, writing later in his memoirs, noted that the singer's voice, "husky, sensuous, nostalgic, sugar-sweet . . . seemed to reach out to you, as she lingered over the catchy tune, the sickly sentimental words."

This siren's song made Maclean ponder what the war had in store for him, for Scotland and the world. He was curious about faraway Yugoslavia, where this strange tune was being broadcast to the enemy armies with whom he shared the yawning desert.

"Belgrade," he wrote, "the continent of Europe seemed a long way away. I wondered when I would see it again and what it would be like by the time we got there."

Maclean's wartime experiences were filled with danger, color, and intrigue. They would eventually inspire a friend of his, the budding writer Ian Fleming, to create a character based largely on his personality and exploits. Fitzroy Maclean, then, would come to be known as the dashing James Bond, the resourceful and elegant secret agent.

But even more wondrous than Maclean's journey from civil servant to superspy, though, was the one undertaken by the song that meant so much to him in the empty wastes of Libya, that

German tune which had captured the hearts of fighting men on both sides of the trenches, defied governments, and transcended ideologies. In a war remembered mostly for its stark divides and brutal, dehumanizing crimes, this song emerged from the ashes as a tiny reminder of unity, hope, and brotherhood. Eventually, it would become one of the world's most recorded tunes. And yet it began its life at the dawn of the First World War, in the lonely and romantic mind of a young Prussian soldier hoping for peace and thinking of love.

I

Underneath the Lantern

FOR the first time in his short and unhappy military career, Hans Leip was late for duty. It was April 3, 1915, and the gaunt young man was running as fast as he could, rushing from his cozy apartment on Chausseestrasse to the army barracks a few blocks away. Off-barracks residence was a privilege awarded only to a few in the rigid hierarchy of his Prussian Guard unit, and Leip, a candidate for the officers' course, feared, as he finally arrived at his post and caught a glimpse of a displeased Herr Feldwebel, the sergeant of the guard, that his happy days in the spacious apartment were over. Leip muttered a few breathless words of apology. Feldwebel twirled his mustache and barked some words at him. The crisis was averted.

Leip, however, was far from relieved. He could think of nothing but the long hours ahead of him, with the thick stench of the nearby sewage canal and the banshee screams of the hulking trains transporting men to and from the front. Ever since arriving in Berlin a few months before to begin his military service, Leip came to detest the sound of locomotives. For him, the syncopated din of turning wheels, the clatter of men and metal tossed together at great velocity, and the shrieks of pulled brakes were the sounds of death. From his position next to the barracks, he saw trains carry off loads of fresh-faced young men into battle and then, months later, return with a harvest of invalids—burned, maimed, and disfigured beyond recognition—headed to the military hospital with nothing but agony to look forward to. Irrational as it might have been, Leip blamed it all on the trains, as if they were not merely the instrument but the cause of such misery. With every whistle of an engine, he shuddered.

To expel the war from his mind, Leip, as he often did at the beginning of the night, before the fog and the stench and sheer exhaustion sent him into a grey, numb paralysis, began to think of his life and the strange turns it had taken in the past few months. Exactly one year before, on Easter of 1914, Leip took a job as an arts teacher at a respectable school for boys in his native Hamburg. Never much of a student himself, he nonetheless excelled in the arts, earning some distinction both as a singer in a local church choir and as a poet. This was enough to bring him to the attention of Alfred Lichtwark, the director of Hamburg's principal art museum, the Kunsthalle. Having single-handedly worked to elevate the Kunsthalle into a mini-Mecca for art enthusiasts—purchasing for the museum anything from Caspar David Friedrich and other German Romantics to the still-obscure French Impressionists—Lichtwark took pleasure in helping young men of modest backgrounds channel their passion into careers in education and public service, and Leip, he thought, was a perfect candidate for his tutelage. A few introductions were made, and Leip, a recent graduate of a teachers' seminar, was awarded the comfortable, if dull, teaching position.

Then, there was Lina Stellmann. This auburn-haired beauty

was Leip's first love, and the two had been dating since both were in their early teens. But now that they were getting older, Stellmann's tone began to change. Previously amorous and carefree, she was becoming steadily more concerned about the future. She began to pressure Leip for a commitment: if not for a marriage, then at least an engagement. Such talk made him nervous; shortly before accepting the position at the boys' school, he traveled with his father to England, where he became enchanted with foreign culture, the idea of travel, and the freedom of the sea. This is how he saw his life, a stream of adventure and worldly affairs, a life, he realized, that would not be possible with a wife and a family. But Stellmann was adamant, and his love for her was genuine. Begrudgingly, Hans Leip settled down.

And then came the war. The son of an old soldier, Leip grew up listening to his father tell heroic stories about the Franco-Prussian War of 1870, a war that crushed the French and brought the Fatherland both glory and wide swaths of captured land, including the lush region of Alsace-Lorraine. Leip always imagined war as a dangerous but noble pursuit, the purview of men with horses and bayonets and impeccable morals. Given his infatuation with all things nautical, a plan began to emerge: if he had to enlist, he would join the navy, thus extricating himself both from an undesirable marriage and an unexciting job.

Merely a month after England declared war on Germany as a result of the latter's invasion of Belgium, the newly created German submarine fleet had its first major victory: on September 5, 1914, after weeks of trailing British ships, a submarine commanded by Lieutenant Otto Hersing set its sights on the British Royal Navy light cruiser *Pathfinder*. It launched a torpedo, and moments later, the *Pathfinder's* magazine exploded. It took less than four minutes for the ship to sink, and with it the lives of all 259 men on board were lost. It was the first successful combat engagement of the modern submarine, and Leip, intrigued, applied to join the underwater fleet.

Being a poet, however, he soon found himself overlooked because of the other applicants, more virile men with greater military skills. A short while later, he was altogether rejected by the navy. With little choice, he followed in his father's footsteps and joined the Prussian Guard; it wasn't life on the high seas, but it was still, in Leip's mind, better than a life of premature domestication. By the fall of 1914, he was already in Berlin, enrolled in an officers' course and condemned to long evenings of guard duty by the barracks.

It was a routine he deeply despised. Not only was it lonely and cold, miserable conditions for the sociable and outgoing Leip, but it also forced him to witness what he considered a particularly grotesque dissonance brought about by the madness of the war. On one side of the barracks stood a hospital, and, night after night, small bands of men were unloaded into its brick buildings, mutilated beyond recognition, their uniforms tattered and their flesh coated with the slime of open wounds, disinfectants, and the dirt of foreign battlefields. Leip tried his best to avoid these ghoulish sights but, at the same time, couldn't help but think that these broken men were once hopeful and lively like him, were once standing guard and dreaming of young women and the lives they led back home. Such thoughts usually overpowered him, and he tended to walk quickly away from the hospital, toward the other end of the barracks. There, however, he was confronted with an equally disturbing sight: in the elongated officers' quarters, he saw, through windows bathed in the fireplace's reddish glow, young men drinking and laughing, playing songs on the piano and clinking their glasses to toast every occasion. These were his commanders, the men responsible for carrying him into battle, for leading him under fire, and yet there they were, a few yards away from the grim hospital, seemingly oblivious to the true meaning of the war. Leip was as disgusted with the officers as he was with the wounded, perhaps even more so as their decrepitude seemed to him not physical but spiritual, emotional, moral.

Trying his best to avoid both ends of the barracks, he paced restlessly. It was chilly, and the last remnants of a brutal winter did their best to find shelter in the bones of men unlucky enough to be outside. Leip tightened the belt around his coat, increased the pace of his march, and let his thoughts sail off to the one topic he knew would bring him joy and warmth—young women. Two young women, in particular: Lili and Marlene.

When Leip left Hamburg behind to travel to Berlin, he said his goodbyes to Lina Stellmann, his longtime lover, informing her that, with a long war lying ahead, both should be free to seek pleasure and comfort elsewhere. And while the lovelorn woman was left stunned and hurt, Leip himself was relieved; a few weeks into his military tenure, now installed in a big apartment with two spirited roommates, he was anxious to spend every minute not wasted marching up and down the path surrounding the barracks wooing beautiful young women.

His first chance came with Betty, and she was the niece of the widow Stolzenberg, Leip's landlady. She lived with her father, a greengrocer, on the ground floor of the building, and spent many mornings feeding the chickens that roamed the inner courtyard. In a sketch Leip made of her at the time, she appears rather plain: black hair tied in a bun, thick arms, a round, alabaster face. And yet, with her puckered lips, warm eyes, and a welcoming smile, she intrigued many of the young men who took rooms in the building.

First to fall for her charms was Klas Deterts. A roommate of Leip's and a fellow Prussian guard, he was taken with the young woman and saw her as a shining example of German femininity, that strong and sensible type, which, while not as mysterious and alluring as the French, or as passionate and fiery as the Italians, nonetheless stood alone in assuring a fellow a solid, nurturing, and proper home. Together with Leip, Deterts watched Betty as she fed the chickens every day, particularly touched by her gentle manner even in the midst of such a menial task. Rather than throw the feed on the ground for the birds to peck at, Betty sprinkled it gently with smooth, calculated movements—movements that seemed much too delicate for her stocky arms and large, rough hands—all the while sweetly cooing to attract the birds' attention. She would call out "Pipi! Pipi!" and the chickens would gather around, pecking peacefully at their food.

Deterts was infatuated, and so, secretly, was Leip. Inspired by the sound Betty made, the two renamed her Lili. For them, both astute students of German letters, no name stood in higher distinction: Lili was the nickname of Anna Elisabeth Schöne-mann, the one-time fiancée of none other than Goethe himself. Although the great writer called off the engagement—Lili was too young, too sexual, too frivolous for his taste—he remained largely devoted to her. As an octogenarian, nearing his end, Goethe told his friend and confidant Friedrich Soret that "Lili was the first that I loved deeply and truthfully, and perhaps also the last." Deterts, who had never been in love before, designated the charming chicken-feeder as his immortal Lili; Leip, who had a bit more experience, simply went along with the fun.

That evening—April 3, 1915—hurrying to his post, Leip rushed down the stairs and out the building, only to come across Lili standing, as she often did, in the backyard. The fog and the moonlight cast a certain otherworldly glow on her face, and Leip was at once struck with the desire to kiss her. She was his best friend's beloved, although Deterts, being a shy man, had said nothing to her. She was the landlady's niece, and any impropriety, they both knew, could get them expelled from their comfortable apartment. And Leip was running late. Yet, nothing mattered: he walked over to Lili, embraced her, and kissed her lips. To his surprise, she made no attempt to break away, instead returning his embrace, kissing him passionately.

The two stood entwined for a few long moments. Then, the image of his commanding officer, Sergeant Feldwebel, with his steely mustache, took over Leip's mind, and he tore away from Lili and began running toward his post. Without turning back, he could hear Lili's voice struggling against the commotion of buses and the wind, yelling to him "Stay here! Stay here!" But he couldn't. He continued to run.

Naturally, then, it was Lili who was on his mind that evening, her voice still ringing in his ears. He wanted nothing more than to end his sorry shift and rush back to her. He would, of course, have to explain it to Deterts, and the widow Stolzenberg, and intimacy might be hard to come by in an apartment shared by three men, but . . .

His thoughts were interrupted by a grunt, and Herr Feldwebel materialized by his side. He was one of those stereotypical Prussian military men, the kind who considered mirth a punishable offense, who worshiped order, and who cared very little for matters of the heart. He huffed at Leip, asking him how he was doing. Knowing there was no point trying to confide in this disciplinarian, in trying to unfold before him the immense drama of love and peril, Leip curtly replied that all was well and that nothing worth reporting had occurred. The sergeant nodded, pleased. Then, a woman appeared.

She was svelte, with short hair that curled neatly on her forehead, large luscious lips, and a flirtatious gaze. As Leip saw her walking by, he grew pale.

Just a few weeks before, on a frosty Sunday afternoon, Leip had met her at the National Gallery. He was there to look at some works by Jacob de Gheyn, a painter he admired and about whom he was planning to write his university dissertation, once the war was over and normal life resumed. His artistic pursuit, however, came to an abrupt end when a young woman strolled to his side, admiring de Gheyn's work as well. Intrigued, Leip struck up a conversation, learned that the young woman's name was Marlene, that she was from Rostock, that her father was a doctor, and that she herself worked as a doctor's assistant in the military hospital located in Leip's barracks.

Leip asked more and more questions but soon was hushed by the museum's other patrons, who were distracted and miffed by Leip and Marlene's happy chatter. Leip suggested they leave, Marlene asked where to, and Leip, on a whim, suggested the zoo. It was, after all, not only the pride of the city—the first of its kind in Germany and one of the first in the entire European continent—but also afforded a pair of young lovers many discreet and secluded spaces in which to take cover for an hour or two. Marlene agreed, and the two went off to the zoo.

There, Leip used every bit of his poetic skills to court the young woman. She was most impressed with the new nickname he had given her, Meerlan, playfully rearranging her name to include the German word for the sea, *meer*. Her voice, he told her, reminded him of it, so deep and sonorous and full. She laughed. As their time together came to an end, Leip secured a promise to see him again.

In the following days, Leip and Marlene were inseparable. Whenever their often-conflicting schedules permitted, they would get together, take long walks, visit museums, and share hours of conversations. Leip, in short, was falling in love.

And yet he was as interested in the wants of the flesh as he was with the needs of the heart. Furthermore, he suspected that Mar-

hours spent agonizing over words and coming up with suitable rhymes—this one was effortless. The words seemed to ooze from his pen. He wrote the first verse:

In front of the barracks,
In front of the large gate,
There stood a lantern,
And if it stands there still,
Let's meet there once again,
Let's stand underneath the lantern,
Like once before, Lili Marlene.

He put down his pen. He had taken two very different women—the plain and lovely Lili and the seductive Marlene— and turned them into one. In his mind, he was trying to imagine what they might look like put together. Although they were so radically different, they were now forever united in his mind. He continued to write:

Both of our shadows
Looked like they were the same,
We held each other closely,
You'd think that we were one.
And the world will see it again
When we stand underneath the lantern,
Like once before, Lili Marlene.

Yes, the two were one: one woman representing life and love, like Goethe's Lili; one woman who will still be there when the war ends, waiting under that lantern by the barracks gate, waiting to reunite with her man, waiting for the world to be itself again. The war, Leip couldn't ignore it, not even in a love poem. He wrote on:

The sentry calls already,
"Here comes the bugle call.
It can cost us three days."
"Comrade, I'm coming right away."
Then we said goodbye,
How I wanted to go with you instead,
With you, Lili Marlene.

And with that, the poem was over. Leip glanced at it again, satisfied. It had good imagery, he thought, especially the forlorn lovers departing underneath the lantern. And it adequately captured his mood—dreading the war but already focused on what might await him at its end. It was melancholy and hopeful at one and the same time. He scribbled the title on the top of the page: "Lied eines jungen Wachtposten," or "Song of a Young Sentry," a song to himself. He folded the paper and put it in the drawer.

Later that day, as his roommates Müller and Deterts returned home, Leip showed them his new poem. They took to it immediately. A few minutes at the piano, and Leip had a simple and spirited melody. That evening being the trio's night off from guard duties, they decided to stay home and entertain themselves. Cheap beer was procured, and, to save on oil, the three left the apartment dark, lit only by the glow of a theater marquee across the street. Müller, in particular, loved Leip's song; he sang it again and again, each time louder and louder, eventually sweeping his friends into a crescendo of shouting and thumping on the piano's keys. It was the release all three needed, and they collapsed into a deep, uninterrupted sleep. A day or two later, they boarded a train to the front in the Carpathian Mountains.

Almost immediately, Schalli Müller was struck by a bullet and killed. Also killed was a man named Pridat, a former flatmate from the Chausseestrasse. Leip was despondent. On April 12, shortly after arriving at the front, he wrote a letter to his sister Grete: "The whole frontline reeks sweetly of decaying bodies. It smells like Hamburg eel soup."

A few days later, while crossing a makeshift bridge, Leip fell and hurt his spine. Not even a month into combat, his military career was over: He was shipped back to the very same military hospital in Berlin that he so detested and, despite his hopes, did not see Marlene there. From there, he was shipped off to Hamburg, back to his family, back to Lina Stellmann, his childhood sweetheart. By the spring of 1916, the two were married.

Ironically, what struck Leip, only two years before, as a terrible and stifling fate, now seemed to him a fortunate and welcome resolution. His military experience, brief as it was, knocked out of him any sense of adventure he might have had, and he was now perfectly content to settle down, resume his career as a teacher, and start a family.

That feeling, however, was not to last. The life of a teacher was far too ordinary for the young man with the artistic temperament and an appetite for life made even deeper by the deprivations of the war. He forsook the steady salary of school for a more tenuous position as a writer for a newspaper, the *Neue Hamburger Zeitung*—a particularly imprudent move considering the fact that Germany, struggling with the ongoing toll of the war, was experiencing turbulent economic times. Hamburg was hit hard: With most of the city's economy based on its port, and with most of the port's economy based on trade with Germany's far-flung colonies, the war—which robbed the empire of its satellites—was an economic disaster for Hamburg. As the once-bustling port creaked along at half-capacity and the city slowed to a standstill, the sensible Lina had no time for Leip's flights of fancy. The couple found themselves at odds, and soon divorced.

Meanwhile, the end of the war brought major changes for

Germany. As a result of the military defeat at the hands of the Allies, the empire folded, and a parliamentary democracy was built in its stead, announced in the city of Weimar on October 28, 1918. On October 29, the army attempted to revolt, and two months of clashes were unleashed on the already ailing country. Militias on the left and the right battled each other and internal factions in the streets, with opposing forces establishing competing fiefdoms. Finally, in January of 1919, order was once again restored and the Weimar Republic began its short, stellar, and troubled life, a life snuffed out by Hitler and his goons a mere fourteen years later.

These fourteen years, however, were the most eventful of Leip's life. He ravenously set out to fashion for himself a life worthy of his bohemian disposition. Together with a few colleagues at the Hamburg newspaper, he joined a group that met once a week to discuss literature with a passion and emotional involvement reminiscent of the eighteenth-century literary movement of Sturm und Drang. Unlike their chaste predecessors, however, Leip and his friends declared themselves free of the constraints that tethered human sexuality to the rusty fence of morality; whereas Goethe's Werther, the very embodiment of Sturm und Drang, chose to end his life rather than further impose on the marriage of his beloved Lotte and her husband, these young intellectuals had no such qualms.

Leip moved in with Cläre Popp, a young puppeteer, and helped her with the operations of her short-lived puppet theater while he wrote two collections of illustrated short stories about life in Hamburg. Then, as now, neither puppets nor prose provided much in the way of a living, and Popp, a sprightly and attractive woman, soon found herself in the arms of M. H. Wilkens, a wealthy jeweler with a large apartment in one of the better quarters of town. Leip, on his part, opted for the least Wertherian path of all; happily, he moved in with Popp and Wilkens, continuing, by most accounts, his affair with his lover without interruption even as he was supported by her new spouse. The room allotted him in Wilkens's house was a sun-drenched atelier, and Leip named it Himmelsecke, or sky-corner. He lived there for ten years.

The early 1920s were a period of extraordinary creativity for Leip. In 1923, he published his first novel; titled *Der Pful* (*The Waterhole*), it was a bleak, expressionistic account of life in Hamburg in the aftermath of the First World War. The book earned a few positive reviews, and Leip soon began work on his second, a novel, titled *Godekes Knecht* (Godekes's Servant). In early 1925, however, before he even had the chance to complete the book, Leip came across a competition sponsored by the *Köllnische Zeitung* newspaper. The first prize was 10,000 marks, a substantial amount of money, and the judges included such famed writers as Wilhelm Schäfer, Wilhelm Schmidtbonn, and, most importantly, Thomas Mann. Mann, having just published his masterpiece *The Magic Mountain* the year before, enjoyed a stature that transcended the world of letters, and he was as celebrated for his passionate defense of the Weimar Republic and its progressive values as he was for his literary accomplishments. Leip admired Mann and craved his approval just as much as he wanted the prize money. He won both.

His achievement, widely publicized at the time, catapulted Leip into fame and fortune. While he still lived in Wilkens's atelier, he was now free not only to write the kind of literature he had always wanted—he immediately set to work on a host of novels pertaining to life at sea, his first love—but also to cultivate his celebrity. He organized large gatherings, often celebrating a specific theme and requiring elaborate wardrobes. One surviving picture from that era, for example, shows Leip, dressed in a Chinese costume, flanked on both sides by beautiful, bare-breasted women. There was talk, though never substantiated, of orgies. Whatever the case, the intellectual and artistic elites of Hamburg crowned him their prince.

Meanwhile, with Cläre Popp preoccupied with her jeweler, Leip became close with two sisters, Gretl and Ilsa Haalk, who doted on him and vied for his attention. Shortly after winning the prize, he took Gretl on a long trip to Paris and, upon their return, married her. While the couple rented a small apartment in a humbler part of town, they spent most of their time living in Wilkens's atelier, further complicating the geometry of an already odd love triangle.

The rest of the 1920s were spent in a whirlwind. Leip and his small family—Gretl bore him two children—traveled around the world. In 1926, they visited Algiers, Mallorca, Barcelona, Portugal, and the South Tyrol, followed two years later by a lengthy trip to New York. Everywhere he went, he took a pencil and pad, sketching people and buildings and everyday scenes. He also wrote about his experiences at length, publishing a string of successful books. By 1931, he moved his family out of the crowded atelier and into an elegant three-story mansion on the Suellbergstrasse, in the most prestigious part of Hamburg.

Theoretically, the 1930s were supposed to be Leip's time to reap what he had sown: wealthy, prolific, and admired, he was perfectly positioned to become the éminence grise of Hamburg's cultural and intellectual life, wielding influence and exerting power. In reality, Germany's decimated economy propelled fringe thinkers into the realm of respected politics and, after free elections, Adolf Hitler was awarded the chancellorship on January 30, 1933. Less than two months later, on March 23, Hitler's cabinet passed the aptly titled Enabling Act, giving it the mandate to pass laws without the consent of the parliament. German democracy and the freewheeling Weimar Republic were dead.

In the rapidly clouding atmosphere of fear and repression, Leip could no longer continue to lead his carefree life. The parties and soirées came to a sudden halt, their participants fearful of appearing too cosmopolitan in the eyes of the narrow-minded Nazis. Even worse for Leip, literature and journalism were now closely monitored, and soon were regulated by the zealous and watchful state.

For a while, Leip tried to continue pursuing his passions. In 1935, for example, he was appointed as an editor of the widely read newspaper *Hamburger Illustrierte*, but was forced to resign his position a year later after publicly speaking out on behalf of Ernst Bailach, a Jewish friend and colleague who was not approved by the Nazis to work as a journalist. A position of prominence, Leip realized, was no longer possible for him. Yet, any position at all demanded a modicum of collaboration with the new Nazi order. He did so begrudgingly, writing freelance columns and short sketches, focusing mainly on arts and culture reviews, and all the while keeping a low profile.

Few things brought him joy in those times. In 1937, however, he smiled for a brief moment when he came across the poem he had written two decades before. He was editing a collection of his early work for publication and was delighted to rediscover his sweet lines about the soldier and his sweetheart, waiting underneath the lamplight by the barracks' gate. He thought fondly of that evening in Berlin, of Lili and Marlene and Herr Feldwebel, of how easy it was to feel hopeful back then. Reading the poem twenty years later, however, a few additional lines caught his eye; he had written them in 1915, along with the rest of the poem, and yet he had always left them out. There was something ghoulish about them, he thought at the time, something infused with suffering and death. He read:

The lantern knows your steps,
Your graceful movements.
Every evening she burns,
Although she forgot me long ago.
And should I ever have bad luck,
Who would stand underneath the lantern
With you, Lili Marlene?

And then:

Out of the silent spaces,
From the ground of the earth,
Come to me, like in a dream,
Your beloved lips.
When the evening fog swirls,
I will stand by the lantern,
Like once before, Lili Marlene.

His thoughts drifting back to Lili and Marlene, something within Leip told him that this particular poem was too personal to share with the public, filled with too many tender memories, and the mature writer regretfully told his publisher, in love with the sentimental words, that he wasn't interested in seeing this one in print. Leip's publisher, however, would not budge. It was perfect for the compilation, he said, and convinced the skeptical poet to include it. And so, with premonitions of bad luck and silent graves, Lili Marlene was first given to the world.

II

A Harsh, Primitive Voice

As the day dawned in Berlin on November 7, 1931—just a few weeks after Hans Leip had finally abandoned his complicated living arrangements at Wilkens's house—a young, willowy blonde named Liselotte Wilke ran through the streets in an effort to find an open kiosk. The *B. Z.*, the city's premiere tabloid, was rumored to have run a review of her performance in a small cabaret, and she had spent a sleepless night waiting for the newsstands to open. In Berlin, a city so crowded by theaters, cabarets, and clubs, even the smallest glint of recognition could set one apart from the dense mass of hopefuls and mark one as a bona fide talent.

But Wilke also needed a good review, needed to see her name positively in print, for a more complicated set of personal reasons. Unlike some of her fellow entertainers in the troupe, she was no carefree young bohemian. At twenty-six, she was a married woman, a mother of three small children, the youngest of whom was not even three years old. Her husband, a painter named Paul Wilke, was living in what is now known as Bremerhaven, a sleepy seaside town many miles to the northwest, where she herself had grown up and where she had always imagined she would live out the rest of her days. However, from a very early age, Wilke's passions lay with singing, while her town's were given to shipbuilding and fishing.

Marrying an artist, she had hoped, would breathe an air of sophistication into her otherwise provincial life, and, for a while, it did. Paul Wilke was tall and chiseled, his facial features so determined they seemed to have been carved into his skin by the freezing winds that blew over the North Sea. Even though he was a painter, he had that roguish air that seems to forever be associated with men who make their living off the sea, that disdainful rakishness so common among ship captains and smugglers alike. He sometimes wore a hoop earring in his left ear, often a sailor's handkerchief around his neck, and always a lopsided smirk that, somehow, worked wonders on Bremerhaven's young women. Liselotte, the daughter of a pilot-boat captain, was herself no exception; at seventeen, hopelessly tired of a social life that included little else apart from strolls in well-manicured gardens and local church fairs, she said her vows to Wilke, cut her hair, and composed a boyish wardrobe of knee-length socks and short-sleeved blouses with wide collars that gave her the overall appearance of a teenaged ensign.

And yet here she was, not even a decade later, shivering in the predawn dampness of the Kurfürstendamm, Berlin's imperious artery of culture and commerce. She hadn't yet severed any ties to her old life, at least not officially. Still married, she left the children under the care of Paul, as well as her parents, sister, and brother, and made sure to write whenever possible and even, on one or two occasions, inviting her family to visit her tiny Berlin apartment. But Paul, despite being both good-natured and a committed bohemian, had nonetheless begun to resent his wife for her stabs at self-fulfillment.

"Often," he wrote her earlier that year, "I even had the feeling that you were longing for hardships, because they gave you a reason to pursue and give in to your secret yearning for theater and acting instead of staying with the children. You were sitting, night by night, adoring old mimes and young opera buffos."

And yet, having a similar, creative temperament, Paul realized just how strong was his young wife's yearning for the stage. "It would be foolish to make accusations," he signed off, "being an artist myself. One cannot become an artist, one is an artist." Liselotte believed in such sentiments wholeheartedly. She had argued the very same thing two years before, tearfully claiming that since she was cursed to have been born an artist, she now had little choice but to follow her bitter fate. And still, she couldn't ignore the fact that, for all the talk of destiny and calling, her future was to be determined by forces much more elusive, namely the love of the masses and the adoration of the critics.

She finally spotted a vendor lazily opening up shop. She bought a copy of the tabloid and tore through it to find these words from one Hans Siemsen: "A blond, north German girl," the review began, "she will bring something very rare into cabaret: her own touch. She is what one might call 'harsh.' 'A girlie with hope for tomorrow, but a girlie—with pride,' she sings, and it suits her wonderfully."

Wilke stopped reading. She didn't cry, didn't laugh, didn't move. Her own touch. And that mention of the song, one of her favorites, a hymn to proud womanhood. Sure, she was called "harsh," but that, as everybody had been telling her for the past two years, was part of her charm. She was nothing like the playful and purring starlets that came one day and vanished the next. She was, or so she imagined, more in the tradition of the great female performers, a leaner and more angular Sarah Bernhardt. Harsh, she hoped, made for a longer, sturdier career. As the city awoke from its sleep, she marched home, vindicated.

But Weimar being its treacherous self, what she hoped would be her rising years turned out to be yet another arid stretch. She got a few more good reviews, won the admiration of a few more colleagues, secured a few more performances in small and airless subterranean clubs, but also watched with frustration, almost as if peering into someone else's life, as one catastrophe followed another.

Once, for example, the prestigious Deutsche Kunstlertheater dismissed her from its ranks after she failed to show up for an evening performance; as it turned out, Wilke, exhausted from her afternoon engagement, had sought to gather strength before having to jump on stage and repeat her routine once again a few hours later. She went to the movies and fell asleep in the dark, cool cinema, missing the show and losing a job.

Angry with the theatrical establishment, she sought employment with Ufa, the renowned film studio. Established in 1917 as a state-run producer of wartime propaganda, the studio was soon privatized and, plucking the most formidable talents at its disposal, helped birth the golden age of German cinema. It was on Ufa's lots that F. W. Murnau and Fritz Lang experimented with narrative and form, there that Robert Wiene directed *The Cabinet of Dr. Caligari*—still considered the pinnacle of cinematic expressionism—and there, only a year before Wilke entered its gates, where a young Marlene Dietrich performed in her first speaking role as the seductive and ruinous Lola Lola in *The Blue Angel*. With more than six hundred films produced in Germany each year through the 1920s and 1930s, and with, according to some estimations, more than one million tickets sold each day, Ufa was a major force in a booming industry. In 1927, however, Alfred Hugenberg, a rich and radically right-wing industrialist and politician, took over the studio and transformed it from a hothouse of artistic innovation to a factory for light entertainment. Instead of Wiene's tortured landscapes or Lang's distopian spectacles, Hugenberg favored Arnold Fanck's Bergfilm, or mountain movies, a genre devoted to bombastic glorifications of mountain-climbing and skiing. It was in one of Fanck's films, in fact, that Leni Riefenstahl made her major acting debut: more than anyone, Riefenstahl represented the prototype of the nascent Aryan heroine, without which no Bergfilm could ever be complete. Ufa also produced, at the behest of its new owner, a slew of anti-Semitic dramas, helping Hugenberg strike a relationship with Adolf Hitler and eventually securing him a seat in Hitler's cabinet. Finally, Hugenberg's Ufa churned out a series of weightless musical comedies, reflecting its patron's belief that cinema was a medium suited only for political indoctrination or mindless entertainment.

It was for a role in one of these comedies that Wilke tried out, hoping to become the next Dietrich and gain instantaneous fame and fortune. She let her hair grow and dyed it a more shocking shade of blond. Shortly thereafter, she got a part. Again, though, her good fortune ran aground. The film's director, unhappy with a certain scene, exploded and cursed at an aging extra. Wilke, coming to the man's defense, soon found herself shouting at the director. Just a few days into her new career as a film star, she was promptly fired.

Even more troubling, perhaps, were the developments in her personal life: realizing that his wife had chosen the stage over their home, Paul Wilke plunged himself into a succession of furious flirtations and it was not long before he had impregnated a teenaged girl. On March 23, 1932, on Liselotte's twenty-seventh birthday, he wrote to her and asked for a divorce.

She said yes, having long ago realized that her marriage could never live up to its youthful passions. Born Elizabeth Carlotta Helena Eulalia Bunterberg, she became known as Liselotte Wilke when she married. Desiring a new beginning, she thought a new name was in order. Many years before a kind Bremerhaven wine-seller, delighted at the sight of the young girl strolling down the boulevard and singing sweetly to herself, nicknamed her La La. Thinking back on those girlhood days, she also remembered fondly the Andersens, a branch of her family she had always liked. Resolved not to give up, she rechristened herself Lale Andersen and once again tried her luck in cabaret.

Her steely determination aside, Andersen must have considered on some level that her historical moment might be fleeting, and that the cabaret scene, if not dead already, was slowly being choked by a dearth of new talent, an increasingly disinterested public, and an overall feeling that what Germans often called *Kleinkunst*—meaning "small arts" and referring to lighthearted entertainment that had no place in serious theaters—had already exhausted its creative potential. As early as 1926, Kurt Robitschek, one of the cabaret world's most prominent directors, declared that the once-glorious, subversive, and refreshing tradition had died out: "[Today] there are only dance palaces where mediocre Kleinkunst is served between charleston and cheese, soup and foxtrot."

For artists like Andersen, such pronouncements were more than mere theoretical exchanges. Anyone trying to make a living by entertaining others in the Berlin of 1932 would have been acutely aware of a palpable change taking place in the city's cultural life; perhaps more than in most art forms, it was in cabaret that this change was most clearly reflected.

In the popular imagination, German cabaret has come, in the past five decades, to be portrayed in bold brushstrokes as a bawdy and brilliant scene where social mores were constantly tested, sexual boundaries dissolved, and where humor and anxiety were blended into an irresistibly intoxicating concoction. As is the case with every worthwhile myth, this perception of German cabaret, too, possesses slivers of truth but is nonetheless overshadowed by a more complex, and far more fascinating, reality.

Despite being so strongly associated with the years of the Weimar Republic, German cabaret began in the last years of the nineteenth century, when the country was still pressed under the censorious thumb of Kaiser Wilhelm II. In those not-so-distant days, a robust economy and a burgeoning, affluent middle class birthed a society that, while still living under the strictures of a monarchy, began to acquire a particular taste for acquisition. In his memoir of childhood in turn-of-the-century Berlin, the brilliant critic Walter Benjamin sketches a city sustained by a strong passion for commodities: "In those early years," he wrote, "I came to know the 'city' only as the theater of 'shopping.' . . . A chain of impenetrable mountains, nay, caverns of commodities—that was 'the city.' "

It did not take long for artistically inclined entrepreneurs to realize that if Berlin, in Benjamin's memorable phrase, was a "theater of shopping," then its theater, too, should engage not just the high-minded sensibilities of the educated aristocracy or the base lust for entertainment of the masses, but also offer a new breed of amusement, one that would possess the respectable veneer of legitimate theater while serving up content that was not quite so intellectually demanding. This idea, to be sure, had practical, as well as cultural, underpinnings. Cabaret's founding fathers were well aware that, unlike theaters, their institutions could turn a profit by offering not only a show but also food, drink, and tobacco. Less than a decade into its existence, the heady mixture of light entertainment and alcohol had already guaranteed the new art form a reputation as an oasis where the more open-minded members of the bourgeoisie could purchase a few hours of safe, toothless transgression.

One critic described the typical cabaret in 1910:

A great deal of champagne is consumed and a great number of cigarettes. On the stage stands a black grand piano, at which genuinely lovely music is occasionally produced. Occasionally. But usually just reheated popular tunes. A *conferencier* tries to emit clever words of introduction between each "number," a *chanteuse* twitters a little song, which, because the author's name is mentioned, is considered "literature." An elegant gentleman comic tells some jokes and acts out verses of a *couplet* in a charming way: a daring remark, a juicy punchline—people smile, they laugh, they applaud, they sip a bit of champagne, they flirt with the lady at their table or at another table, and the "real" ladies are delighted that they can sit in the midst of such a "stunningly interesting" milieu for a few hours.

As could be expected, the original vision of the cabaret scene's founders, that balance between high- and lowbrow, was soon replaced by an increasing demand for curiosities and mindless fun. Men such as Ernst von Wolzogen, the founder of Berlin's first cabaret, watched with horror as the tasteful mélange of music, drama, and comedy he had once offered fell out of favor, and the cabaret stages were instead populated by somnambulists, hypnotists, acrobats, child prodigies, and people who could imitate the voices of animals, all of whom were gazed upon with wonder by audiences puffing on cigars and feasting on overpriced, mediocre food. German cabaret, the anarchist poet Erich Mühsam wrote shortly before the beginning of the First World War, was "artless, without poetry, castrated."

And yet, the postwar years and the hyperinflation plaguing the republic breathed new life into the ossified art form. By early 1923, the money was literally no longer worth the paper on which it was printed and a culture of uninhibited spending soon blossomed: If money was losing value every day, went the common logic, one might as well spend it and enjoy oneself while it was still possible. That same year, there were thirty-eight different cabarets operating in Berlin, most of which went to great lengths to provide their desperate patrons the illusion of opulence, by means of both lush interior decorations and ever-raunchier programs, with female nudity now considered de rigueur.

A few artists, refusing to succumb to commercialism's dictates, pushed for what they called "literary cabaret," a more civic-minded and politically conscious breed of entertainment. Trude Hesterberg, for example, a striking beauty and a star of early Ufa productions, went further than anyone in her Wilde Buhne, or Wild Stage, cabaret, which was devoted almost entirely to educating its patrons and exposing them to sophisticated literature, atonal music, and other forms of artistic experimentation. The majority of institutions, however, took a decidedly less enlightened path and were content to serve their tuxedo-clad clientele little save for witty smut. The popular songs from the era are almost singularly obsessed with excretions, reproductive organs, and every conceivable combination thereof. The most popular genre of the 1920s consisted of *Dirnenlieder*, or whore songs, in which young women, bathed in red lighting and wearing clownishly applied makeup, would saunter onto the stage and pronounce "Ich bin eine Dirne" (I am a whore). What followed was an account of the whore's exploits, covered in a thin film of sentimentality and moral outrage, but always focused on the most lurid of sexual details.

Their emphasis on licentiousness gave cabarets a newfound popularity, which continued to grow even in the second half of the 1920s. By the time Lale Andersen came to Berlin in 1929, dreaming, like many young actresses of that period, to become well known for fairly high-minded popular entertainment, she was disappointed to discover that what the Moloch of cabaret needed were young maidens willing to bare their breasts, pretend to be prostitutes, or belt out frivolous or sentimental ditties. The audience, she realized only too well, wanted not to think but to be thrilled; writing in 1926, the respectable composer and critic Hans Heinz Stuckenschmidt put forth a disparaging picture of cabarets and their patrons: "Ostentation, color, nudity, the newest jokes, exciting music, tempo, clowning, tension, fashion, blasphemy, pathetic intoxication, something for the heart, smut, irony—these are its [cabaret's] props. That's what today's man wants, who, worn down and tired, no longer has the energy to solve problems in the evening."

This was a particularly grim discovery for Andersen. For her, art had always been her refuge from the drudgery of daily life. Growing up in a small apartment, raised by parents who adhered to stringent Protestant values and advocated hard work and discipline above self-discovery and imagination, she had always looked to literature, drama, and music as her salvation. On her thirteenth birthday, when most girls her age would have asked for dresses, she asked her parents for works by Schiller and Shakespeare. And while most of her peers spent their days strolling up and down the city's leafy throughways dressed in their finest clothes and doing their best to attract the attention of the opposite sex, Lale preferred to read and daydream. By the time she turned fourteen, she asked for an accordion, the instrument favored by local musicians who crooned about the sea and the lives of sailors. She taught herself to play and soon mastered most of the repertoire she heard around her. By no means introverted, she nonetheless preferred to spend her days in an imaginary world where all was beautiful, meaningful, and gallant rather than resign herself to a life that was bound to turn her, just like her mother before her, into a joyless *hausfrau* and a dutiful parent.

It is not difficult to imagine, then, how great her thrill must have been when, as a young woman of seventeen, she chanced to go on a boulevard stroll one day and came across the handsome face of Paul Wilke. She had always yearned for the company of artists but had never before met one, to say nothing of one who seemed so keenly attracted to her. Wilke introduced his future bride to his friends, like him carefree and jocular, and Andersen's head was soon clouded by cigarette smoke and impassioned talk of art. Wilke was nothing like her father, the perpetually absent and often-exacting pilot-boat captain, and she happily married Paul.

But children could not be accommodated in this artistic dream. Andersen was soon pregnant, soon pregnant again, soon confined to her home, and then locked into the mundane obligations of motherhood. Wilke moved them to Bremen, a larger port city not that far away, where he was finding success as an artist. Participating in traveling shows, and in demand by the local art crowd, Wilke was thriving, spending more and more nights away from home, flirtatious and happy as always.

Andersen was despondent, despite her love for her children. Having tasted a little of the bohemian life, she craved art not so much as an Eden of aesthetic pleasure but rather as a putative springboard to fame and fortune. Her husband's life intrigued her, a life of parties and plaudits. She, too, wanted to be adored and admired, to be surrounded by people who complimented her on her talent, taste, and striking good looks. After all, she thought, what were all those hours of reading and playing accordion good for if not as preparation for her future career? If even a wine-seller in a small, seaside town was moved by her singing to nickname her La La, wouldn't audiences in Berlin be similarly impressed?

And yet a chance to make it was hard to come by. Spending every free evening in local theaters, attending performances indiscriminately, making the acquaintance of every artist who passed through town, she still had to return home to breastfeeding, changing diapers, and cooking meals. Worst of all, as 1929 rolled in, she was pregnant again, about to become a mother for the third time. She was suffocating.

In October 1929, six weeks after she gave birth to a boy they named Michael, Andersen decided she could no longer live a life of domesticity. She informed Wilke she was leaving, at least temporarily, and moving to Berlin. There was little he could say to his wife: He had, after all, courted her by accentuating his artistic nature, a nature, he boasted, that was given only to creativity and inspiration and not to the doldrums that others call life. Now, when she herself was invoking the same beliefs, when it was she who was speaking of freedom and creativity and passion, there was little he could do but give her his blessing, particularly given the fact that he continued to lead a romantic life outside of marriage. Andersen informed her family that she was leaving, and asked a sister, Thekla, and a brother, Helmut, to watch her children. She packed a small suitcase and boarded a train to Berlin, where she knew not a soul.

It was of little wonder, then, that in 1932, faced once more with the need to start from scratch, Andersen was dismayed but not without hope. She had spent nearly three years eking out a living as an actress and a singer, and could certainly continue to do so. Besides, she had had, late in 1931, a string of moderate successes, both in the cabaret scene in Zurich and in Munich as well as in Berlin, where she played a small part in *Mahagonny*, an opera by Bertolt Brecht and Kurt Weill mocking American culture and criticizing the excesses of capitalism. She had also begun to make a few acquaintances, and discovered a knack for attaching herself to men who she hoped would promote her career.

It is, of course, perfectly plausible to look at such connections with a jaundiced eye, accusing Andersen of opportunism; in the precarious circles in which she moved, however, naked ambition and true passion were often indistinguishable.

The first of these men was Willi Schaeffers, a popular actor and impresario of the time. While the two, as far as is known, were never romantically involved, the plain-looking Schaeffers nonetheless took to the tall, attractive blonde and arranged gig after gig for her. With bitter irony, though, she noticed that most of these engagements required her to show up at smoky caverns wearing a sailor's outfit and sing the very same songs she had practiced as a young girl. For Andersen, who had sacrificed all to escape the small hometown, being typecast as a singer of provincial North Sea songs was somewhat of an insult, especially as they also required her to suppress her femininity in favor of a more androgynous appearance. But sea songs she sang, mainly with Schaeffers's cabaret troupe, the Ping Pong, and both audiences and critics adored them. In September of 1932, another newspaper review was published, praising Andersen for the way she performed "with an artist's taste mariners' songs, which include seriousness and tragedy but also find expression in the vivid life of homeless seamen, those who only have something to win, never to lose."

Slowly, she noticed, she was being asked only to sing. She had always thought she was a decent actress, but even she couldn't deny that it was her voice, more than anything else, that fascinated people. In a scene filled with mellifluous voices—her friend, Ilse Trautschold, had a velvety voice that made her the star of the Ping Pong—Andersen's voice stood out. It was, critic after critic told her, harsh. Not only that, but she had a peculiar demeanor onstage, one that more than one observer described as "primitive" and which evoked the arm-flailing totality of theatrical eras past. But more than anything, it was her diction that made people stop to listen: she did not so much sing as simply pronounce the words while keeping the music's beat, rolling syllable after syllable off her tongue and, unlike so many other entertainers, never showing off her voice at the expense of the lyrics.

All of the above made her a natural candidate for the Kabarett der Komiker. Established in 1924, the KadeKo, as it was known, quickly emerged as the flagship of the cabaret movement. Seating 950 patrons, it allowed its audience the luxury of sitting in an opulent theater while still being able to enjoy a drink, a smoke, and a quick conversation here and there. Rather than retain, as virtually all similar institutions did at the time, a fixed troupe of entertainers, the KadeKo offered Berlin's up-and-comers short-term contracts, keeping them onstage for as long as popular demand so desired. Similarly, instead of a fixed set, the KadeKo offered a two-part program, starting with traditional cabaret, featuring songs and novelty acts followed by a short play or operetta, sometimes by renowned authors such as Anton Chekhov or Heinrich Mann, the brother of the more famous Thomas Mann. The KadeKo, then, was largely perceived as having restored some of the literary and intellectual panache the cabaret scene had lost when it went the route of pure populist entertainment. Still, for all its supposed high-mindedness, the KadeKo was intolerant when it came to politics: "No matter what the viewpoint," exclaimed a 1926 program, "it's not interesting!"

Such an attitude did not work in Andersen's favor. Throughout 1931 and 1932, Schaeffers arranged for her to appear at the KadeKo several times, and she was always well received. But as her career developed, and as she began to abandon her signature sailors' songs for new ones that better suited her vocal sensibilities—focusing, naturally, on songs with poignant lyrics she could thrust forward— the KadeKo became an uneasy fit. The lyrics of the songs she chose were written by many of Berlin's literary luminaries, the majority of whom were devout Marxists. And while her stark voice and cutting pronunciation made her an ideal vessel for a song by, say, Brecht, the bourgeois audiences dining at the KadeKo were not particularly keen on having biting social commentary tossed in with their steaks and flutes of champagne.

Andersen, then, sought a new artistic home, one bigger than the Ping Pong and more accepting than the KadeKo. Early in 1933, she traveled to Zurich, where she had performed several times in the past with itinerant cabaret troupes. The reasons for her departure were more than merely artistic: On January 30, 1933, Adolf Hitler was sworn in as Germany's chancellor in a short and simple ceremony. Less than a month later, the Reichstag building was set on fire, an act the Nazis blamed on the Communists. A day after the fire, on February 28, Hitler's cabinet issued the Reichstag Fire Decree, suspending all basic rights and putting an end to habeas corpus. A week later, new parliamentary elections were held, giving the Nazi party more than 43 percent of the seats.

For Andersen and her colleagues in the cabaret circuits, these were nightmarish months. For all their shunning of politics, the majority of Berlin's artists realized that their brand of sexually promiscuous, prickly, and uninhibited performances would not be well regarded by the new masters in the brown shirts who revered tradition, despised Marxism, and were obsessed with the characteristics of race and blood. In 1933, of course, most were still largely unaware of the scope of the looming calamity, and yet, with the Reichstag protruding as a charred omen in the center of Berlin, Andersen prudently left town for a while.

She might have returned home sooner if it weren't for Rolf Liebermann, a charming Jewish man who caught Andersen's eye. The nephew of celebrated impressionist painter Max Liebermann, Rolf was a more urbane version of Paul Wilke. Writing many years after the fact, Andersen reminisced that "[Liebermann's] body had the perfection of a Greek statue." He had shiny, wavy hair, a strong forehead, and wore fine suits. A composer, Liebermann used his celebrated last name—his uncle was an honorary citizen of Berlin and served, until a few months after Hitler's appointment as chancellor, as the president of the Prussian Academy of the Arts—to make the acquaintance of artists passing through Zurich. When not socializing, he spent most of his time and resources following the great conductor Arturo Toscanini around.

Enamored as she was with this free-spending bohemian, Andersen soon realized that, like Wilke, Liebermann, too, had much flair but little in the way of practicality or common sense. Decades later, writing in her autobiography, Andersen lamented the fact that she "got another one of those poor fantasists," and she spent much of her time with Liebermann worrying about finances.

Her worries were not in vain. While the next two years were a flurry of creativity and romance, with Liebermann composing and arranging her works and with performances in small cabarets freeing her up to sing the songs she was most passionate about—with words by Brecht, Erich Kästner, and Kurt Tucholsky—she was nonetheless sharply feeling the burdens of material existence. A few of the shows in which she starred went bankrupt, and more than once she was forced to flee the wrath of financiers, leaving behind debt and unfulfilled commitments. As much as she despised and dreaded life on the run, she was infatuated with Liebermann, who had a way of painting the whole miserable affair in lush colors, effortlessly tapping into her girlhood infatuation with the lofty ideal of the struggling artist. They moved from club to club, playing France and Germany, recording and composing and singing. Finally, in December 1935, their relationship came to a brusque end. Trying to reenter Switzerland after a concert abroad, Andersen was arrested by the border police, informed that she was considered by the Swiss government to be an "uncontrolled person" who led a "flawed and indecent life," and sent back to Germany. For a short while, she considered trying to sneak back into Zurich and live with Liebermann clandestinely. But the overwhelming debt, his ineptitude in all things financial, and her obligations to her children, whom she still saw occasionally, all advised against it.

Now thirty years old, her career a series of stops and starts, and her love life in shambles, she returned to Berlin. Little did she know that it would be another man, one with whom she shared a brief encounter in 1932, that would eventually catapult her to international superstardom.

III

Song of a Young Sentry

IN 1932, Norbert Schultze decided to spend an evening at the Groschenkeller, a fashionable cabaret in Berlin. While most twenty-one-year-olds would have felt hopelessly out of place in the nightly assemblage of famous, well-dressed patrons such as Brecht, Weill, and Hesterberg, Schultze, a composer and musician of some renown and even greater promise, was already one of the club's regulars. A pianist for Die Vier Nachrichter, or The Four Messengers, Schultze had recently helped to lead his group on a rare streak of no less than forty sold-out shows at the Groschenkeller and, as a result, had become almost a fixture of the club's rotation. So, when he paced down the three steps that led from the street to the crowded and cavernous space and opened the door, it was as if he were walking into a second home. He certainly looked the part of the at-ease insider: Plump and jovial, his was not the commonly handsome figure that decorated so many of these nightspots but rather one of those rotund and well-defined frames that makes a statement just by walking into a room, someone who, by being so clearly and nonchalantly at odds with the atmosphere, must certainly belong to the highest circle of chosen habitués. Schultze was lucky: in just a few short months, he had penetrated the fortified rings of Berlin's cultural elite, been crowned their dauphin, and given all the rights and privileges a young man could dream of.

Schultze, whose appetite for the nightlife was as sizable as his gut, took to evening after evening of drinking, playing music, and chatting up young women. Now, on an evening off, and after more than a month of hectic performances, he was finally a spectator. As Schultze and the rest of the crowd settled into place, Liselotte Wilke, a young blonde with short hair and a sailor's outfit, marched across the stage and prepared to sing. As Schultze watched her steady herself, he was struck by her slim figure and sure, controlled movements.

As soon as Wilke opened her mouth, though, Schultze felt a pang of quiet revulsion. For a serious student of music like himself, reared on Brünnhildes and Isoldes, Wagnerian women with tremulous voices, Wilke was a disaster. Her voice was harsh, her register much too high. Instead of singing, she spat out words. Although she sang traditional sailors' songs, she sounded, to the young composer, unforgivably modern. And yet, Schultze was mesmerized: no matter how offensive he found the young woman's voice, her looks sang to him a different song, sweet and seductive.

After Wilke was done with her set, Schultze approached her. She was even more striking up close. One would have expected Schultze to say something soothing to allay Wilke's jitters that, as he knew from his own experience, were an inescapable part of performing in front of a roomful of stars. He could have, perhaps, whispered sweet nothings to her, filling her ears with wit and encouragement. Instead, he blurted out the first thing that came to his mind: "You'll never make it!" Quickly, as an afterthought, he added that while she was a nice girl and all, her voice, alas, was simply too rough.

Hurt, Wilke nonetheless stayed silent. It was not the first time someone had told her that she couldn't sing, and even if it had been, she certainly would have thought twice before retaliating against the wunderkind of Berlin cabaret. With a smile, she made some coy remark, and soon the two were engaged in lively conversation, the tension between them having dissolved. As the evening eventually narrowed to a close, Wilke invited Schultze up to her apartment. He, naturally, was eager to accept her tempting offer.

Schultze could hardly believe his luck after leaving Wilke's building the next morning. Although she, for the record, never acknowledged any romantic connection with Schultze, the composer, in later life, returned to the theme of this evening in interview after interview, each time describing his passionate encounter with Wilke in more and more rapturous terms. For someone like Wilke, this brief romance would have been a dalliance like many others, but to Schultze it was a revelation. As Berlin woke, the portly young man floated down the grey cobblestone streets on his way back home, swept away with pleasant feelings of affection and gratitude. He had won it all, the sold-out shows, the well-known friends, and now the bed of a sultry singer. But this last one, the singer, meant something else to him, more than a mere fling, more than the spoils of fame. There was something about that woman, he thought, that transcended infatuation, something that went beyond lust, something that recalibrated his attention not on her but on himself. In appreciation of her charms, he returned home later that morning, and dashed off a few compositions in honor of his new acquaintance.

It was not long, however, before Schultze, like all of Germany's artists, saw that the cabaret scene that had once smiled on him was being violently transformed by the new masters of the land. To the Nazis, Berlin's freewheeling culture, dominated as it was by leftists, liberals, and Jews, represented an insidious threat to the pure Aryan culture they wished to see reborn in a Germany cleansed of non-Germans. To them, the playful criticism of the ruling classes that the cabaret shows engendered amounted to treason and the black musicians and American jazz that were celebrated in its rollicking halls were a cancerous tumor rotting the German soul. Nude dancing girls were thought to express the sexual perversions unleashed by the Jewish psychoanalyst Sigmund Freud and the atonal music beloved by the avant-garde crowd was an assault on proper German melodies and the glories of Wagner. It all had to go.

Tellingly, Joseph Goebbels, who would later become the Nazis' propaganda minister and the ultimate arbiter of culture during the Third Reich, visited the Kabarett der Komiker in January of 1930 to see Karl Valentin, a comedian from Munich. It is not hard to imagine the humorless Nazi sitting amid a mixed, fashionable crowd that reveled in cynical observations spiked with ironic barbs. The short and deformed future czar of culture must have cringed in his chair anytime he heard some beautiful, bright young thing casually mixing vulgar slang from across the Atlantic with the German language that Goebbels and his cohorts considered noble and sacred. He was disgusted by the spectacle and left the performance keenly aware of the threat posed to Aryan culture by the uncensored stage. Although Valentin was not a Jew, Goebbels returned home that night and wrote in his diary that the performance was "a totally Jewish affair. In part insufferable, in part weak, but also in part not without wit. Naturally it was all asphalt," the latter being the Nazi term used to denote anything cosmopolitan, international, non-German, and therefore worthless.

On March 23, 1933, the Enabling Act, which allowed Hitler to govern and pass measures without the parliament's consent, was passed in the Kroll Opera House, a space once favored by avant-garde performers in Berlin. The Weimar Republic was officially dead, and, for the stars of the cabaret, politics had gone from being the familiar topic of breezy jokes onstage to a deadly business. While many of them took their cues from the KadeKo's motto, shunning politics in all of its forms, all soon discovered that political affiliation was now the only yardstick by which they were measured. The new political reality revealed itself in a fiery blaze. In May of that year, as the trees lining Berlin's Unter den Linden boulevard were beginning to sprout new leaves, a massive book-burning rally was held steps away on the Opernplatz. There, in the shadow of Berlin University's neoclassical buildings, opposite the ornate State Opera and capped at the far corner by the verdigris dome of St. Hedwig's Cathedral, a well-organized horde of brown-shirted Nazi party members worked themselves into a quasi-religious frenzy as they tossed 20,000 books ransacked from the university's library into a raging bonfire. The volumes, which included works by Sigmund Freud, Karl Marx, and Erich Maria Remarque, were deemed by the Nazi authorities to be degenerate writings and were accompanied to oblivion by ritual incantations chanted by the fascist crowd. Erich Kästner, the cabaret darling, witnessed the macabre procession and shuddered as he saw his own works hurled into the leaping flames. "Against decadence and moral decay!" the thugs screamed as they tossed book after book onto the pyre. "For discipline and decency in the family and state!"

And yet, as shocking as the burning must have been to Berlin's intellectual and artistic elite, Goebbels and his lieutenants realized that it would take more than a spectacle to overpower a city in which, just five months earlier, the Communists outpolled the

Nazis and, together with other leftist parties, garnered 54 percent of the vote. In order to debilitate the opposition, Hermann Göring, the Nazi interior minister of Prussia, appointed loyal party members to positions in the police force and instructed them to battle it out with liberals in the streets. Before long, a chain of detention centers and concentration camps, including the notorious Columbiahaus prison, were being built around the city to contain Berlin's undesirable elements.

Cabaret, with its cosmopolitan connotations, was among the first targets of the newly empowered Nazis and their network of prisons. Hans Otto, a performer in the leftist German Workers' Theater League, was accused of subversion and swiftly killed in 1933 at the Columbiahaus, while Erich Mühsam, the anarchist poet and pub performer, was murdered in 1934 at the Oranienburg concentration camp because of his affiliation with the Communists.

Some artists, more sensitive to the shifting tides than others, managed to position themselves in line with the new sentiments early on. Werner Finck, a star of the Berlin theater, was quick to stage anti-Semitic parodies of Yiddish plays during the late twenties and, in October of 1929, founded a troupe he called the Catacombs. The reference was clear: "2,000 years ago the Catacombs were the refuge of the first Christians," Finck explained. "Today they are the refuge of the last ones." He would, he promised, stand up to Jews and Jewish influence on the stage, and his career flourished for a while under the Nazis.

In September of 1933, Goebbels, comfortably ensconced as the Nazi propaganda minister, established the Reich Culture Chamber, an umbrella organization that controlled what was to become the new culture of a resurgent Germany. Subordinate chambers were established for film, theater, music, press, writing, visual arts, and radio. Acceptance by one of the specialized chambers was a necessary prerequisite for the success of any artist or writer, with Jews and other non-Aryans strictly forbidden from joining. To ensure ideological purity, most of the Culture Chamber's work during its first two years was devoted to divining the racial loyalties and identities of Germany's creative elite, a task made difficult by the theater world's tangled warren of altered names and murky connections.

Trude Hesterberg, for example, the doyenne of serious, political cabaret, was, unsurprisingly, one of the artists who ran afoul of the Nazi cultural officials early on. Although she had been a member of the Nazi party since January 1933, her theatrical activities and associations brought her under the microscope of Hans Hinkel, who in his dual roles as the secretary-general of the Fighting League for German Culture and the commissioner for theater in the Prussian Ministry of Art, Science, and Education exercised an iron grip over the Reich's artists.

Hesterberg's first encounter with the zealous bureaucrat came late in 1933, when she was careless enough to perform in one of Oscar Straus's traveling operettas. A few shows in Dresden went by without a hitch, but in Stuttgart the troupe ran afoul of the Nazi cultural machine, which denounced the entire show as "decadent and immoral" on the basis that its music and lyrics were written by a Jew.

Hesterberg, who could sense the great calamity coming her way, preemptively wrote Hinkel a groveling letter. She was, she pleaded with him, a "Berliner, German, Christian." A few days after performing it on stage, she denounced Oscar Straus's work as "unhealthy from a racial standpoint." She expressed her earnest hope that her association with Straus and his music would not be interpreted as national disloyalty. A lecherous man who was always happy to have attractive supplicants, Hinkel indulged Hesterberg, telling her that for the time being she was free to continue performing as she wished.

But the newfound emphasis on ideological loyalty unleashed a dark wave of self-interest; ambitious artists eager to make a name for themselves understood that, rather than toil on the stage, they could take significantly shorter paths to fame by currying favor with the grim clerks of the Culture Chamber. Soon after Hinkel pardoned her, a strange letter appeared on the Nazi official's desk. It was written by Charlotte Jungman, a woman who claimed to be Hesterberg's maid. Confirming the maxim that no one is a hero to his valet, Jungman stated that Hesterberg, whose home she cleaned and whose laundry she washed, could not be considered reliable "from the standpoint of a National Socialist state." Signing off, Jungman requested an audience with Hinkel to reveal, she wrote, lurid details that she simply could not bring herself to put down on paper. Hinkel, presiding over a system devoted entirely to the collection and manipulation of such tidbits, agreed immediately. A few days later, Jungman showed up, telling Hinkel tale after salacious tale of Hesterberg's misconduct.

The gossip was all Hinkel required to launch a fresh campaign against the singer. He wrote Hesterberg a letter and, based on Jungman's accounts, accused her of fraternizing with Heinrich Mann, the writer who fled into exile after his citizenship had been revoked by the Nazis on account of his Communist sympathies. Hesterberg, Hinkel wrote, was "always glad to be seen in public with Herr Mann during his Marxist period" and was also happy to perform in Parisian shows that supported reconciliation between the nations. There was, Hinkel concluded, "no guarantee that [Hesterberg] stands on the grounds of the National Socialist worldview." Her career, therefore, could not be allowed to continue.

Outraged, Hesterberg sent Hinkel an angry response. She denied ever performing in peaceful shows in Paris and reminded him that she had undertaken "cultural propaganda in Sweden and Scandinavia" during the First World War. Furthermore, she wrote, she had recently defended Germany in Czechoslovakia and added that not only did she believe in the National Socialist worldview but had been "a supporting member of an SS unit since January, that is, before the national upheaval."

Convinced that Hesterberg was duly subdued, Hinkel gave the singer permission to perform once again. And yet, having suffered a long and tortuous year of political intrigue, Hesterberg, like so many of her other colleagues, was nothing but a shadow of her former artistic self. Her next show, titled "The Muses' Swing," reflected that fact well; it was held at the Pavilion Mascotte, a turn-of-the-century hall far removed, both geographically and spiritually, from the glamour and sophistication of her more modern, international haunts along the Kurfürstendamm. The show's producers, eager to display their unequivocal ideological purity, stated in the program notes that they were proud to welcome audiences "once more into a popular cabaret which contains nothing foreign. Thus you will hear only numbers that are anchored in our nature and whose music is derived from folk songs. For the peoples' voice is honest, it is genuine and free." Featuring such hyperventilating tributes to Germany's imperial past as "1905 in the Mascotte" and "The Kaiser's Waltz," the show folded after only two performances.

More than merely monitoring political sympathies, however, the Culture Chamber also sought to reshape the aesthetics of German art and entertainment, guaranteeing that each symphony, each painting, each poem, reflected the traditional values of the Fatherland. They were to glorify war, celebrate the peasantry, and encourage patriotism. Modernism in all of its forms, from abstract painting to atonality, was deemed to be "degenerate," and was therefore banned. Thus, the proud Aryan music of Bach, Wagner, and other Germans like them was widely performed and celebrated, while German-Jewish composers such as Gustav Mahler and Felix Mendelssohn were suppressed and branded as "culturally Bolshevik." Also, Jewish or not, any composer who experimented with the revolutionary twelve-tone system of Berg, Schoenberg, and Webern or any other similar modern musical elements was deemed degenerate as well, representing, to the Nazis, a dangerous internationalism.

It was in this paranoid, provincial, and xenophobic environment that Norbert Schultze's star began to rise. And it was an environment that left him baffled: no hater of Jews, no ardent anti-Communist, no rabid fan of Hitler or single-minded nationalist, he nonetheless found himself closely aligned with the Nazis on one front—the front that mattered most to him—music.

Schultze, too, found the modernists repugnant and idolized, as did the bureaucrats of the Culture Chamber, the might and grandeur of Wagner. Raised to admire and revere traditional German music, he was not unhappy to see the new masters of the land reinforce his own musical sensibilities. They were, after all, the tastes he developed as a child.

Born in 1911 to affluent middle-class parents in the Prussian city of Braunschweig, Schultze enjoyed, by all accounts, a remarkably uncomplicated upbringing. His early childhood was one of happy contentedness in a home that was both harmonious and well kept.

His family had a natural taste for music and would gather every night to listen to his grandparents play the piano together. The young boy was captivated by the selections from the symphonies of Mozart and Haydn that filled the family home each evening and, at an early age, developed a special liking for Schubert's marches. That, perhaps, was because the military was second only to music in the Schultze family's esteem: with Norbert's father and grandfather having both served their kaiser—the former in the army during the First World War and the latter as a surgeon sent on official business to Tokyo—the young Norbert came to understand at an early age that war was some magical realm of the adult world, filled with secrets, deep meaning, and adventure. Ever the duty-bound son of Prussia, one of Schultze's first youthful compositions was titled "Maikäfer, flieg! Dein Vater muss in Krieg!" (Ladybug, Fly! Your Father Must Go to War!)

While his father was away on the battlefields, however, Schultze's grandparents ensured that their precocious grandson took his piano lessons seriously. By the age of thirteen, his imperial childhood now having faded into a Weimar adolescence, Schultze had already composed a song based on verses by the romantic poet Ludwig Uhland and was proficient on the violin. He then studied at the music conservatory in Cologne, where he studied harmony and instrumentation with Philipp Jarnach—considered, at the time, one of the most important contemporary composers—and conducting with Hermann Abendroth, the man who, in 1934, would replace the Jewish Bruno Walter at the helm of the Leipzig Gewandhaus Orchestra. His was, in short, among the most superb classical trainings a serious student of music could ever wish for.

And yet, Schultze was never able to claim the position of a serious composer. That realm, it seemed, was carefully guarded by an entrenched class of luminaries, the first among them being Richard Strauss. The famed composer and conductor, with the apathetic look and the deadened eyes, had dismissed Schultze as a craftsman of popular tunes, and, together with a few other serious-minded peers, deemed him artistically unworthy and studiously ignored the young man at every turn.

Schultze was hurt, but not for long. While still in school in Cologne, he was convinced by a group of fellow students to join the Vier Nachrichter cabaret group as their piano player. Schultze's dreams of the famed Wagner festival at Bayreuth and the grand opera houses of Europe were soon overpowered by visions of other, more earthly pleasures, the kind that easily befell a young student and star of the cabaret. He shed his last name—Schultze, he thought, was insufferably Prussian—and introduced himself as Frank Norbert, a name he considered swank and sophisticated.

Luckily for Schultze and his colleagues, 1932 marked the solemn centennial of Goethe's death, and the Vier Nachrichter had the perfect tribute, a lighthearted revue titled "Goethe Was Wrong Here." Looking to add a feminine touch to the stage, the four young men auditioned a few female performers; one of them in particular, a petite actress named Vera Spohr, attracted Schultze. Over the course of a long German tour, with multiple performances in virtually every large city, Schultze and Spohr became close. As 1932 drew to a close, they married.

Their wedding had a maturing effect on Schultze. As a husband and provider, he realized, he would no longer be able to hop from town to town and bar to bar, befriending fellow artists and bedding young women. The married life, he found, was a more sedentary existence, a life spent in one place as a happy family, a life much like the one he had in his youth. As 1933 dawned, Schultze and his new bride left Berlin behind and moved to Heidelberg, where he settled into a respectable job directing operas at the City Theater. Yet it was there, nestled in Germany's picturesque south, in a fairy-tale town of cobblestone streets, that Schultze caught his first whiff of Nazi paranoia.

An investigation was launched by some minor Nazi official into exactly what type of family name Schultze was hiding behind his "Frank Norbert" façade. Schultze was easily able to provide ample documentation that proved his pure Aryan lineage, parrying the official inquisition without much effort, and his troupe, which had no Jewish performers, soon regained official sanction. Maintaining the healthy aversion to politics that he had developed early on in his career, Schultze felt that this unpleasantness was just a phase, some sort of silly teething of the young regime, and that all would be fine in the end.

He was soon convinced otherwise. In 1933, he moved his family to Darmstadt, where he accepted a better job as a musical director of a larger, more prestigious company. There, in a city that was among the first in Germany to boycott Jewish businesses and whose main square had been recently rechristened the Adolf-Hitler-Platz, Schultze made the unhappy acquaintance of his fellow musician Carl Friedrich. Schultze would later write that Friedrich, a conductor with whom he was forced to work, carried the swastika "not only in his buttonhole but also in his head." A fervent true believer, Friedrich harassed his orchestra with tirades and lectures about the Nazi ideology, the dangers of the Jews, and the righteousness of the cause. The apolitical Schultze, looking to get on with the music, did not take well to the constant hectoring and was soon considered by the members of Friedrich's camp to be a disloyal German on account of his less-than-enthusiastic responses to the conductor's harangues.

Although Schultze's salary of 300 marks a year was triple what he had been making in Heidelberg, and although he and Vera had just welcomed their first son, Roderich, into their lives, the constant agitation and annoyance of working in such a politicized environment convinced Schultze to try his luck elsewhere. And so, in pursuit of a peaceful life, he bid Darmstadt farewell and set out for Munich.

The heart of Bavarian culture, Munich, the city where so many of Wagner's operas had premiered, should have naturally extended a hearty welcome to Schultze, an ardent admirer of traditional German music. Yet soon after he arrived in the city, he was turned down by every production he approached for work. It did not take too long to learn the reason behind his shunning: by opposing Friedrich, Schultze had been deemed "unsuitable for Nazi theater ideology" by the Culture Chamber and had been spied on during his time in Darmstadt. For the first time in his brilliant career, Schultze found himself with few options and even less money. Staying in Munich was out of the question: home to the historic Beer Hall Putsch, the conservative city was bursting with sympathy for the Nazi cause. The only refuge would be familiar Berlin.

Schultze returned to the capital in 1934, a time of great upheaval. On June 30, Hitler, wishing to consolidate the various competing arms of the Nazi terror machine under his reign and fearing the growing political independence of his paramilitary Stormtroopers, ordered the assassination of their rabble-rousing leaders in a series of killings that would come to be known as the Night of the Long Knives. Over the course of that gruesome evening, loyal Nazis who had once paraded the party's banner with pride and dedicated their lives to the cleansing of the Aryan nation were set upon by their comrades-in-arms and brutally murdered. Although it had little effect on the lives of ordinary Germans, most nonetheless watched with terror as the Nazi dictatorship revealed yet another hollow cavity in its violent soul.

Against this backdrop, Schultze tried to keep a low profile and focus on his work. Reunited with the Vier Nachrichter group, he and his friends won an engagement at the Berlin Theater with a show they called *Die Nervensäge* (The Pain in the Neck), another lighthearted musical comedy. Still popular, the foursome sold out most of its shows, and Schultze earned some much-needed cash. Back on his feet and on a bit of a tear, Schultze decided in 1935 to leave the group for good and make a name for himself as a solo artist. As it turned out, he exited the cabaret stage at the perfect time.

At that depressing moment in German history, theaters and concert halls that had previously won the acceptance of the Nazi officials were being eyed with newfound suspicion. Even Werner

Finck, the performer whose anti-Semitic Catacombs act seemed to follow the Nazi lead, quickly found himself on the wrong side of the authorities. A jokester by nature, Finck had, in the proud tradition of cabaret, been aiming what he thought were harmless jabs at the ruling elite while he accommodatingly bent his scripts and opinions to suit its prejudices. But the Culture Chamber had little patience for his gags. They viewed with disapproval one skit in particular, in which a man enters a tailor's atelier to be fitted for a new suit. The man, eager at first to get measured by the doting tailor, soon becomes anxious and is overcome by the sneaking sense that he is, in fact, being sized up not for a suit but for a military uniform, sending him running out of the shop in sheer terror. Summoned for interrogation by Hinkel's men, Finck claimed to be mocking the cowardly attitudes of those Germans who didn't embrace National Socialism. Nevertheless, he was accused of alluding to Hitler's push to overturn the Versailles Treaty provision that banned universal German conscription, a topic that was strictly off-limits for discussion or satire.

In another scene, one of Finck's actors portrayed a man sitting in a typical Berlin café. Seduced by a woman who invites him to sit with her, the flattered Casanova begins to get up and make his way over to her table when he suddenly realizes, to his shame and dismay, that he has been tricked by a prostitute. He recoils in disgust, but before he can regain his balance is approached by yet another woman, this one a volunteer collecting money for the Winterhilfswerk, a Nazi organization widely suspected of doing little more than financing the lavish lifestyles of top party officials. The pious charity worker asks the man if he would like to make a donation to help his nation, and he, in an aside, cracks that he'd probably be better off with the prostitute.

To the authorities, even such harmless bits transgressed the boundaries of acceptable speech. The same ominous assessment was cast on the popular Tingel-Tangel cabaret. At the Tingel-Tangel, a group of actors were pretending to play cards, coyly mispronouncing the word for ace, *As*, with the word for carcass, *Aas*. For the overly sensitive undercover representatives of the Culture Chamber sitting in the audience, the pun was nothing if not a direct assault on the nation's leaders. Soon, six performers from the Catacombs and the Tingel-Tangel were arrested and taken to the Columbiahaus prison, detained for several weeks and interrogated repeatedly by the Gestapo. Newspaper reports of the arrests carried the official line, stating that the shows had displayed "signs of pure Bolshevism," and railed against the show's patrons, which, they wrote, consisted "mainly of Jews and other state-negating elements."

No longer part of this highly scrutinized scene, Schultze had taken up a position at the AEG-Telefunken record company as a coordinator of milquetoast productions. To supplement his income, he began writing tunes for radio commercials on a freelance basis, the most successful of which was a well-received military march for a furniture store. To be sure, the soundproofed rooms and modern studio equipment he found at Telefunken weren't as inspiring as the baroque concert halls of his dreams, but Schultze was truly grateful for the steady income and, no less important, the relative cover his regular job provided from the Culture Chamber's eyes.

And yet, putting his talent to use selling merchandise left Schultze wanting more. In his free time, when he wasn't working on toothpaste commercials, Schultze began to sketch out an opera based on the German children's story "Schwarzer Peter" (Black Peter). With Telefunken's studios at his disposal, Schultze spent more and more time working on the project, and the more he toiled, the more his ideas began to crystallize. Every free moment he had now went into writing, rewriting, and arranging his opera, the one composition, he hoped, that would catapult him back into fame and fortune. In need of a good librettist, Schultze turned to Walter Lieck. Together, the two men diligently cobbled together a workable opera. In it, Schwarzer Peter—a children's game akin to Old Maid—served as the backdrop to the story of a fairytale king living in an innocent and enchanted time. With its naïve, childlike plot and a serious score that borrowed heavily from the classical German tradition—Wagner in particular—*Schwarzer Peter* proved to be an easy sell for Schultze; in 1936, it premiered at the Hamburg State Opera in a performance accurately titled "An Amusing Opera for Young and Old."

It was a huge success. In times of uncertainty and political repression, nothing pleased both patrons and critics alike more than the opportunity to enjoy an uncomplicated and delightful bit of light music. Soon, *Schwarzer Peter* was the talk of the Reich, performed in opera houses throughout Germany.

Schultze, recognizing his big break, returned to composing full-time. In a short time, he won a solid reputation for nonpolitical works that charmed their listeners. He wrote another opera, *Kaspar*, and a cantata based on Vivaldi's *Four Seasons* that he called *Sunshine and Rain*. He wrote viola concertos and soundtracks for movies. He was affluent once again and hoped to finally enjoy quiet, prosperous years as a renowned songsmith.

Reality, however, rudely intervened once again. On December 8, 1937, Goebbels, still unsettled by the Catacombs and Tingel-Tangel affairs, banned any mention of politics or the army, whether positive or negative, from the stages of the Third Reich. The edict, he wrote in his diary, came as "a real deliverance to me." Germany's theaters were now but faded reflections of their former, glittering selves. The Plaza, for example, once considered alongside the Scala and the Wintergarten to be one of Berlin's premier vaudeville halls, was taken over by Goebbels in 1938 and transformed into a peoples' venue for hackneyed show tunes and pointless acrobatics, evenings of mindless entertainment that were devoid of any sense of plot or meaning. It marked the final realization of Goebbels's vision of public theater, one that he had developed over the course of many lonely, luckless nights at the Kabarett der Komiker and other fashionable cosmopolitan venues years earlier. And although Schultze's compositions were not political in nature, he still suffered from the slow suffocation of Germany's theaters and struggled to find venues for his work.

One night in 1938, Schultze, who by then had witnessed the deportation and suppression of a large number of artists with whom he had worked during the formative years of his career, returned, as he had many times since, to the Groschenkeller. While the building itself was familiar to him, inside the atmosphere had drastically changed. No longer a comfortable spot to hear interesting music and watch pretty performers, the Groschenkeller had become a pub and a hangout for those of Hitler's thugs who had survived the Long Knives. Schultze, who paid the swaggering Nazis that had overrun the club no mind, went solely for the company of the musicians who could still legally perform in Germany. At once spotted by the singer Jan Behrens, Schultze was approached by the baritone and asked to write some chanteys for Behrens to sing on the radio. He had in mind, he said, some verses by a writer he had come across, and he handed Schultze a slim volume of poems. It was Hans Leip's *Die kleine Hafenorgel*.

Schultze flipped through the book and glanced at the titles of the various poems. One of them, "Song of a Young Sentry," caught his eye and, after a quick reading, seemed to suggest an organic melody. He thanked Behrens for the book and promised him a few compositions.

When Behrens heard the simple songs Schultze came up with a few days later, though, the serious singer couldn't help but feel disappointed. These were momentous times, after all, and Behrens had wanted to use his powerful voice to express something of their essence. He felt that Schultze's compositions were nowhere near as manly or vigorous as he had hoped they would be. "They're for little girls!" he said.

Schultze was taken aback by the criticism. His songs, he felt, did justice to Leip's stirring words. Unlike his days at Telefunken, where each ditty could take hours to compose, the tunes for Leip's poems seemed to leap, ready-made, from his imagination. "Song of a Young Sentry" in particular had taken him no longer than five minutes to compose, the music simply flowing from his fingertips as he sat at his piano and read Leip's sad and sentimental words. Determined not to let the compositions go to waste, he began to search for another singer to bring them to life.

Sending the sheet music for his composition to several of his old colleagues, he decided, almost as an afterthought, to dispatch a copy to Lale Andersen as well. He had vaguely followed her career in the six years that passed since their passionate encounter, and while he detested her voice, he nonetheless thought that she, with her peculiar diction, might be a suitable interpreter for these lighthearted pieces with such strong lyrics. He wrote Andersen a nice note, saying he thought her voice would be perfect for his versions of either Leip's "Wenn du kein Mädel weisst" (If You Do Not Know a Girl), or "Drei rote Rosen" (Three Red Roses).

Andersen responded and said she would be thrilled to work with Schultze. She also liked his suggestions but was intrigued by one he hadn't mentioned: "Song of a Young Sentry." She was already singing a version of the song, composed by her friend Rudolf Zink, and was quite happy with it. Whereas Schultze's composition was sentimental and romantic, Zink's tune was a more elegiac affair, unfolding like a sorrowful waltz. Ever the competitive student, Schultze was intrigued to learn that another composer had tried his hand at the same text and suggested to Andersen a friendly wager: at her next show, he proposed, she would sing both versions, letting the audience's reaction determine which was the better song. She agreed, and the applause she received after she performed the two versions left little room for doubt. Her listeners, largely apathetic to Zink's tune, were swept away by Schultze's.

His senses ever attuned to potential commercial success, Schultze suggested that he and Andersen record the song and try to get it played on the radio. It had been a while, he thought, since he'd seen audiences react this favorably to a composition, any composition, and he wanted to capture some of the evening's momentum. A record deal, he reasoned, should prove easy enough to get, particularly for someone as accomplished as himself.

And yet, in the following weeks, more than thirty music companies rejected Schultze and Andersen's pitch. Much like Behrens, they replied that the song was the wrong tune at the wrong time, with a different sensibility than the military-minded pomp or the airy show tunes sanctioned by the Culture Chamber. It was, claimed one executive after another, too sentimental, too melancholy, and too sweet to succeed in 1938 Germany. With faith in his little tune, though, Schultze refused to let it fade into oblivion. If a military feel is what the market wants, he thought, a military feel is what it will get. Going back to his desk, he took out the sheet music to "Song of a Young Sentry" and added a martial element right at the beginning of the song. As the son and grandson of Prussian military men, he knew from the earliest days of his youth the bugle call that ordered the Prussian armies to their evening curfews, the *Zapfenstreich*, and it was with that same call that he decided to begin "Song of a Young Sentry."

The bugle call was all that the executives at the Electrola record company needed to sign off on the project; at that time, recording anything that evoked, however remotely, a military air was thought to sell records. Electrola signed Schultze and Andersen to a deal and, in the fall of 1938, over the course of a few hours, with a studio orchestra, "Song of a Young Sentry" was recorded.

It sold just under seven hundred copies and was largely ignored by both the critics and the public. Bugle call or not, it wasn't masculine enough for a nation slowly and steadily marching toward war. And while Lale Andersen's voice, harsh and high-pitched, might have intrigued the sophisticated aesthetes of Berlin's cabarets, it was a far cry from the popular tastes of mainland Germany, especially as the lyrics she was singing dealt with the parting and sorrow of war as opposed to its glory and honor.

With record sales so abysmally low, Schultze and Andersen prayed for salvation from the radio, hoping that repeated broadcasts might spark an interest in their tune. But history, as is often its habit, intervened, displaying an impeccable sense of timing and a healthy dose of irony: "Song of a Young Sentry" was aired for the very first time on the night of November 9, 1938, a night that would forever be remembered for things far grimmer than the doleful song of a young sentry.

IV

"Bombs! Bombs! Bombs!"

EVEN in the midst of the steady, spiraling descent into madness that was the Nazi state, the events of Kristallnacht stand out. Nothing radically new, of course, happened on the evening of November 9, 1938: concentration camps and mass arrests, synagogue burnings and vandalism, anti-Semitic outbursts and random acts of violence, had all been an inseparable part of life in Germany for at least half a decade prior to that night. What was new, and terrifying, was the scope of the convulsions: 7,000 Jewish shops were ransacked, 30,000 Jews were shipped to concentration camps, 1,574 synagogues were plundered, 267 of them set on fire, and at least three dozen Jews were murdered that night.

Observing with horror, foreign correspondents based in Berlin all noted that the events of the two-day-long, organized bloodletting were an extraordinary surge of psychosis. "Mob law ruled in Berlin throughout the afternoon and evening and hordes of hooligans indulged in an orgy of destruction," wrote the *Daily Telegraph's* Hugh Carleton Greene. "I have seen several anti-Jewish outbreaks in Germany during the last five years, but never anything as nauseating as this. Racial hatred and hysteria seemed to have taken complete hold of otherwise decent people. I saw fashionably dressed women clapping their hands and screaming with glee, while respectable middle-class mothers held up their babies to see the 'fun.' " A day after the attacks, the *Times* of London struck a similar tone:"No foreign propagandist bent upon blackening Germany before the world," stated an editorial, "could outdo the tale of burnings and beatings, of blackguardly assaults on defenseless and innocent people, which disgraced that country yesterday."

The shock extended even to high-ranking officials of the Reich themselves. Even at the time of the beatings and lootings, Germany was still taking pains to portray itself as a distinguished member of the family of nations, and a campaign of brutality directed against its own citizens—a campaign clearly too efficient and comprehensive to be, as the Nazi official explanation meekly claimed at the time, the result of spontaneous outbursts of Aryan wrath following the assassination of a junior German diplomat by a young Jewish student in Paris—was diplomatically detrimental. No less senior a figure than Heinrich Himmler blamed the entire event on the folly of one man, Joseph Goebbels:"I suppose that it is Goebbels' megalomania and stupidity," Himmler wrote shortly after the pogrom, "which are responsible for starting this operation now, in a particularly difficult diplomatic situation."

Himmler's assessment, most historians now acknowledge, was accurate. In late 1938, Goebbels's standing in the pinnacle of Nazi officialdom was as precarious as ever. More than anything, he needed a cataclysmic event, one whose magnitude would restructure the intricate machinations of Hitler's inner circle and allow Goebbels to once again secure his imperiled spot as Hitler's confidant.

Despite emerging, in popular imagination, as the quintessential Nazi, a demon second only to Hitler himself in his capacity for evil, Goebbels's relationship with the movement he so doggedly served was never an easy one. He was born to a family of modest means, and a severe case of osteomyelitis, a bacterial inflammation of bone marrow, left one of his legs shorter than the other. He spent most of his childhood encased in a metal frame and wore a special shoe on his limp leg. At five feet five inches, with slightly protruding eyes and a high forehead, he was as far as anyone could be from the very ideal of the Aryan man he himself, in his role as propaganda minister, helped create.

Nevertheless, Goebbels persevered. Disqualified for military service because of his crooked frame, and thus denied his chance to fight in the First World War, he turned instead to the life of the mind, eventually pursuing his doctorate at the renowned university in Heidelberg. Little about Goebbels the graduate student suggested the monstrosities that were to follow. The subject of his thesis was the eighteenth-century German novelist Wilhelm von Schütz, an early champion of the emancipation of German Jewry. Guiding Goebbels in his intellectual pursuit were Friedrich Gundolf and Max Freiherr von Waldberg, two of the country's most eminent literary scholars at the time, both Jewish.

While a precocious student, life outside the academy was significantly more difficult for the young Goebbels. Eager to join the ranks of the German intellectual elite, he began churning out novels, plays, and copious amounts of tepid Romantic poetry. Very little of what he wrote was ever published, but one piece stands above all, a semiautobiographical novel, *Michael*. In it, the protagonist—who, Joachim Fest, the renowned historian of the Third Reich, noted, has a name that connotes an otherworldly, cherubic enlightenment—yearns, like its author, for a military life. "To be a soldier!" Michael cries. "To stand sentinel! One ought always to be a soldier."

Unable to live up to his physical ideals and failing at gaining any prominence as an artist, Goebbels became increasingly frustrated. Having abandoned his literary aspirations, he now wrote mainly in his diaries and made his living as a bank clerk. But the sting of defeat never left him. Loathing both his own frailty and the cultivated elite that rejected him, he drifted, quite naturally, toward the vehement, virulent, and anti-intellectual spirit of the Nazis. Fest wrote of Goebbels:

> This was the source of his hatred of the intellect, which was a form of self-hatred, his longing to degrade himself, to submerge himself in the ranks of the masses, which ran curiously parallel with his ambition and his tormenting need to distinguish himself. He was incessantly tortured by the fear of being regarded as a "bourgeois intellectual." . . . It always seemed as if he were offering blind devotion [to Nazism] to make up for his lack of all those characteristics of the racial elite which nature had denied him.

Goebbels joined the Nazi party in late 1923. Then twenty-seven years old, he quickly realized that the party was standing at a major ideological crossroads. Hitler having just been imprisoned after the notorious Beer Hall Putsch, aspiring Nazis fought one another over the right to define the movement. And while many distinct factions arose to claim prominence in Hitler's absence, the main struggle for the premier spot was waged between two camps, each emphasizing a different component of the National Socialistic creed. For Rudolf Hess and Julius Streicher, Nazism's priorities lay first and foremost in restoring Germany to its past national glories, a feat that could never be possible without ridding the Fatherland of the Jewish cancer eating away at its heart. Gregor Strasser, on the other hand, a young and capable Nazi organizer in northern Germany, thought the socialist element held the key to Nazi domination: as Germany was struggling under the yoke of inflation and poverty, he argued, it would be irresponsible, not to mention politically unwise, not to give precedence to aiding those in need.

Goebbels sided squarely with Strasser. An educated, reasonable man, he realized the socioeconomic potential of Strasser's designs. In 1925, he wrote in a party newspaper of which he was the editor, that "with us in the west, there can be no doubt. First socialist redemption, then comes national liberation like a whirlwind." Later that year, he penned an open letter to Communists and socialists, urging them to join forces with the Nazis and fight against the true enemies of the German people, the exploitative capitalists. "You and I," he wrote, "are fighting one another although we are not really enemies." Goebbels's strategy appeared to work, at least in the short term; as historian Richard F. Hamilton noted in his seminal study *Who Voted for Hitler?* Goebbels's entreaty motivated more than a few of Germany's leading Communists to release a string of anti-Semitic statements in an attempt to signal solidarity with the Nazis.

Goebbels soon realized he had bet on the wrong horse. In February 1926, released from prison and having just finished penning *Mein Kampf,* Hitler summoned sixty Nazi leaders to a meeting in Bamberg, a Bavarian town that was part of the Nazi fiefdom controlled by Streicher, the publisher of the vociferously anti-Semitic newspaper *Der Stürmer.* The choice of location was far from random. In a two-hour speech, Hitler gave his minions a clear idea of where he stood in the bipartisan struggle of socialists versus nationalists: the former, he stated, were in the wrong, as the real enemies of the German people were not the capitalists but the Jews and the Communists.

Devastated, Goebbels suffered a crisis of faith. Not only was his own stature as a rapidly rising star under Strasser now reduced to nothing, but the ideology he had come to believe had the potential to redeem Germany appeared to be hijacked by irrational zealots. "I no longer fully believe in Hitler," Goebbels wrote immediately after the meeting in 1926. "That's the terrible thing: my inner support has been taken away."

Hitler, however, was too shrewd to let a man as capable as Goebbels fall victim to political infighting. Recognizing that what Goebbels sought most desperately was recognition, Hitler invited him to Munich in April, two months after the Bamberg meeting, and sent his personal chauffeur to meet the limping Goebbels at the train station. When Goebbels arrived, Hitler spent the first few minutes of their long audience scolding him for supporting Strasser and socialism. Then, however, he complimented him on his intelligence and skills as an organizer, and offered to forget all of Goebbels's past lapses of judgment in return for his unquestioning loyalty thenceforth. Again, Goebbels's diary provides a telling window into his soul.

"I love him," Goebbels wrote of Hitler the day after their meeting. "Such a sparkling mind can be my leader. I bow to the greater one, the political genius."

From that moment on, Goebbels strove to prove himself to his new master. Appointed as gauleiter, or regional party director, of Berlin in the fall of 1926, Goebbels quickly set up the newspaper *Der Angriff* (The Attack), and set out to wage war against the very same leftists he had, just the year before, tried to coax into a political partnership. His battles took shape on two fronts: Convinced that the course of history would be determined in the streets, Goebbels orchestrated a symphony of violence, unleashing the Nazi Stormtroopers, clad in brown shirts, on anyone from Communists to Jews to intellectuals. Bernhard Weiss, Berlin's deputy chief of police, a Jew, and a decorated hero of the First World War, was a favorite target whom Goebbels hoped to goad into reacting. In 1927, Weiss, fed up with Goebbels's constant Jew-baiting and the Brownshirts' unruliness, did just that, pleading with the city's Social Democratic government to outlaw the Nazis. An eight-month ban ensued, and Goebbels, delighted, could now legitimately claim the mantle of the persecuted underdog.

But street fighting and political brinksmanship were only the blunt instruments in Goebbels's arsenal. Fists and clubs, he realized, were effective against one's committed foes, but to win the sympathies of the vast, disinterested masses, subtler strategies were essential. In 1930, after he blindly sided with Hitler against Gregor Strasser and his brother, Otto, who once again sought to direct the party leftward, Goebbels was rewarded with the editorship of the *Völkischer Beobachter* (People's Observer), the Nazis' national newspaper, a position that put him in charge of the party's entire propaganda apparatus. An election was coming up, and Goebbels wasted little time. In addition to writing compelling copy for his paper, he pioneered, as is now well known, the use of both radio and cinema in political campaigning, and unfurled a steady stream of theatrics to ignite the imaginations of Germany's youth. Torch parades and brass bands, radio addresses and cinematic productions were all used to bombard the Reich's young citizens with dramatic, emotional messages. German youth responded accordingly: infatuated with the Nazis' high profile and flashy orchestrations they voted for Hitler's party en masse, giving the Nazis their first serious showing in a national election.

This, as he often admitted to his diary, was the aspect of Goebbels's job that most appealed to him. The very publishers and intellectuals who rejected his efforts a decade before had received him, as the Nazis rose to power in 1933, as the final arbiter of cultural life in the Republic. On May 10 of that year, just a few months after the Nazis' assumption of power, Goebbels, newly installed as the Reich's minister of popular enlightenment and propaganda, orchestrated the massive burning of the 20,000 "objectionable" books at the Opernplatz, the very one Erich Kästner witnessed with such unease. More than a mere political move, it is hard not to interpret Goebbels's glee at the book burning as the ultimate revenge of a scorned writer.

But burning and banning, Goebbels understood, were not in themselves sufficient. He also realized that seeking solace in consistency was ill advised. Much, he knew, depended not on any steadfast ideological criteria but on Hitler's own likes and dislikes, a capricious taste that, for example, scorned American jazz music as modernist, vulgar, and decadent while it adored the adventures of Mickey Mouse, a particular penchant that was met with subdued grudges of disapproval by the party's chauvinistic ideologues. And so, navigating the uncharted waters of taste making, Goebbels resorted to simple formulas, infusing a healthy dose of frenzied political propaganda into endless servings of mindless entertainment. This approach served another of his passions: despite having married Magda Quandt in 1931, Goebbels had always been a tireless womanizer—a passion, some historians have argued, that had its origins in a desperate drive to make up for his puny, twisted frame. Now, as the overseer of the Reich's cultural life, he possessed both clout and access to the country's most gorgeous women. Spending much of his time in Ufa's studios in Babelsberg, near Berlin, he became known among the film industry's disgruntled artists as "Bock von Babelsberg," or the horny goat from Babelsberg, often spending exorbitant amounts of time on some studio lot or another, luring one young actress or another into his nearby villa on Lake Wannsee.

It was one such actress, however, that nearly cost him all of the power he had so carefully cultivated, driving him, in the fall of 1938, to instigate the organized brutality that was Kristallnacht. Her name was Lida Baarova, and she was a Czech-born beauty who, like most objects of Goebbels's infatuation, embodied the

Aryan ideal he was so ardently promoting. She had blond hair and brown eyes whose expression shifted between the secretive and the playful. She had a sharp, angular nose and neatly arched eyebrows. Most alluringly, she had a blasé attitude that charmed a man as rigid and repressed as Goebbels. In the early 1930s, with Marlene Dietrich's star on the rise, such seductive virtues were more than enough to get any young actress popular in Germany a warm welcome in Hollywood, and Baarova's invitation to Southern California was not late in coming. She refused it, however, preferring to stay in Germany, where she embarked on a passionate affair with fellow actor Gustav Fröhlich, the star of Fritz Lang's extraordinary *Metropolis*. She was deeply committed to Fröhlich when, in 1935, she met the new propaganda minister.

The two men in her life could not be more dissimilar. Whereas Goebbels was short and limping, Fröhlich was tall and strapping, a movie star not only in Germany but also in Hollywood, where he spent long stretches in the early 1930s. Whereas Goebbels's features were sunken and ashen, Fröhlich radiated, on-screen and off-, the fleshy glow of well-being and health. And while Goebbels was cold and calculating, a master of cynicism and wry comments, Fröhlich was outgoing to a fault, a perpetually smiling chap quick with a handshake or a slap on the back, moving about with the undisturbed ease of one who had never known rejection or ridicule.

For a young woman in her prime, the choice between the two lovers would seem obvious; and yet, Baarova, freshly engaged to Fröhlich, found herself more and more attracted to the small man in the black uniform with the sleek black hair who lived, as it happened, a few blocks away from the new house she and her fiancé had bought. Morning walks with this strange man who had entrée to the highest offices of power gave way to afternoon meetings with him, often in studios and under professional pretense, and, by late 1936, to clandestine nocturnal entanglements. While Fröhlich was the more attractive man, Goebbels was ever the manipulator, constantly telling his beloved that only an unfortunate twist of fate kept her from gaining as much fame as Dietrich, an unpleasantness that he, in his capacity as minister, had every intention of correcting. In the Nazi cosmology, access to the party machine meant everything and was therefore closely guarded. Eager to impress Baarova, Goebbels doled out invitations to parties and audiences with the titans of the regime, including Hitler himself. It may never be known whether it was her ambition or a sincere attraction to Goebbels's influence and intelligence that swayed Baarova, but she left Fröhlich and devoted herself to the minister.

Goebbels was overjoyed. After a string of rejections by actresses—most notably, by some accounts, Leni Riefenstahl—he finally found a woman who complemented the way in which he liked to see himself. Unlike the stern, intelligent, independent, and mildly attractive Magda, Liduška, as he now called her, was radiant and subservient, dazzled by might and more than willing to silently hang on Goebbels's arm. She did so, in fact, in the summer of 1938 as she accompanied Goebbels to the festival in Bayreuth celebrating the life and music of Hitler's favorite composer, Richard Wagner.

The festival carried a special meaning for Hitler. Not only did the music move him, but Winifred Wagner, the wife of the composer's son Siegfried and the head of the Wagner clan in the 1930s and 1940s, was a close friend and supporter; it was on stationery that Winifred had sent Hitler while he was imprisoned for his role in the Beer Hall Putsch that the Nazi leader wrote *Mein Kampf*. Sitting in the Festspielhaus—the enormous nineteenth-century theater that Wagner himself had designed, with its invisible orchestra pit to enhance, or so the composer claimed, the audience's absolute immersion in the drama onstage—Hitler was therefore greatly dismayed and unsettled to hear sounds that decidedly did not belong to Wagner's *Tristan and Isolde* coming from somewhere nearby. They were Magda Goebbels's muffled sobs, and soon the scorned woman caused a great commotion as she stormed out of her seat and left the theater.

Later that evening, the minister's wife walked up to Winifred Wagner's house, where Hitler was spending the night. She clasped both his hands and apologized profusely to the dictator for disrupting the performance. It was just, she said, that she couldn't control herself, given her husband's blatant infidelity. To sit there, she told him, surrounded by her friends, well aware that all present knew that the cheery blonde seated next to her husband was more than an acquaintance, was more than a proud German woman could bear. Besides, she continued, ever the tactician, the festival was attended by members of the international press. How, she asked Hitler, might Germany look to the world when its own propaganda minister—with his Aryan wife and five blond children—runs around with a foreign mistress?

The true meaning of her insinuations was not lost on Hitler. The chief focus of Nazi foreign policy was the annexation of the Sudetenland, a swath of western Czechoslovakia inhabited mainly by ethnic Germans. With a campaign of terror, pressure, and propaganda designed to browbeat the international community into accepting Germany's annexation of Czech territory, Baarova's nationality was particularly embarrassing. Hitler promised Magda that the problem would be solved and wished her a good night.

The next morning, Goebbels was summoned to Winifred Wagner's house for a brief and harsh audience with Hitler. The Führer's orders were two: Goebbels, he said, must return immediately to Berlin, and just as swiftly cut off all contacts with his mistress. Surprisingly, Goebbels offered some resistance: He truly loved Baarova, he told Hitler, and was willing to give up everything for her. He offered his resignation, and requested, with as much dignity as he could muster, that Hitler consider appointing him as Germany's ambassador to Japan, so that he and Baarova could live far away from the power plays of Berlin. Magda, Goebbels reassured Hitler, would fare just fine. Both men knew that Magda, scorned and hurt, indulged in a series of ill-advised activities, including an affair with a young man named Hanke, one of her husband's leading lieutenants. In fact, thrilled by Goebbels's potential departure, Hanke had already penned a mawkish letter to Hitler, begging him to bless a union between him and Magda in case of a future divorce. Now, Goebbels, too, suggested that Hanke might be a better mate for Magda than himself.

Hitler, however, refused. The affair, he repeated tersely, was to end.

Despondent, Goebbels obeyed, sinking into a severe depression that deepened considerably in October, when he learned that the Gestapo had ordered Baarova to leave Germany without delay and to never return. Adding to his personal chagrin was a sense of professional malaise. He had made his political fortune doggedly hunting down enemies, and now, with the Nazis safely in power and the dictatorship firmly in place, there seemed to be no enemies left to persecute. In need of both a personal and professional rebirth, Goebbels turned to the one source that could, in the Germany of 1938, always be counted upon: the Jews.

Learning of the assassination in Paris of a German official, Ernst von Roth, by Herschel Grynszpan, a young Jewish student, Goebbels realized he had a golden opportunity to launch a massive onslaught against the Jews. His timing, too, couldn't have been better: the news reached him as he was dining with Hitler and other key Nazis. Learning of the events, Hitler, angry and sullen, had left the room without giving his usual speech. Goebbels wasted no time in delivering an address of his own: taking the podium, Goebbels announced to the Nazi elite that "the Führer has decided that such demonstrations should not be prepared or organized by the party, but insofar as they erupt spontaneously, they are not to be hampered."

There was no question in anyone's mind that Goebbels's words were a strict order to unleash chaos. A few hours after the dinner, at 1:20 A.M., SS official Reinhard Heydrich sent a telegram to his subordinates titled MEASURES AGAINST JEWS TONIGHT. It left little room for doubt regarding the extent of the regime's involvement in orchestrating the attacks: THE CHIEFS OF THE STATE POLICE, the telegram stated, OR THEIR DEPUTIES, MUST IMMEDIATELY UPON RECEIPT OF THIS TELEGRAM CONTACT, BY TELEPHONE, THE POLITICAL LEADERS IN THEIR AREAS ... WHO HAVE JURISDICTION IN THEIR DISTRICTS AND ARRANGE A JOINT MEETING WITH THE INSPECTOR OR COMMANDER OF THE ORDER POLICE TO DISCUSS THE ARRANGEMENTS FOR THE DEMONSTRATIONS.

Despite the responding criticism, Goebbels was pleased. Kristallnacht once again stirred up the sensation of imminent crisis, the stormy sea in which he swam best. For Lale Andersen and Norbert Schultze, however, the pogroms couldn't have arrived at a more unfortunate time. Their tune, "Song of a Young Sentry," was soft and gentle at a time when the country's culture czar pushed for violent and triumphant military music. The lyrics spoke of young lovers separated by war; the Nazis, preparing for battle on a massive scale, wanted words that praised the nation, the leader, and the martial spirit. After its initial airing on Kristallnacht—when few would have even heard the song— "Song of a Young Sentry" failed to win any acclaim.

The song was a commercial failure for Schultze, and another misstep in Andersen's fizzling career. Despite occasionally crossing paths several times, in the early months of 1939, neither artist spoke of their botched collaboration. They had, to be sure, greater things to be worried about: Goebbels's ever-tightening grip on all forms of entertainment, dwindling venues that were still dedicated to serious music, and, above all, an inevitable war.

Despite having promised, at the height of the Sudetenland crisis, that the swath of Czechoslovakia represented Germany's last territorial claim in Europe, Hitler was clearly and deliberately preparing for further annexation. While the Versailles Treaty, forced on a defeated Germany in the wake of the First World War, clearly forbade Hitler "to maintain or construct any fortification either on the Left bank of the Rhine or on the Right bank to the west of a line drawn fifty kilometers to the East of the Rhine," he began, as early as 1936, to rearm the Rhineland, building up his banned army, navy, and air force. In March of 1939, Germany invaded the rest of Czechoslovakia. Soon the hope for "peace in our time" expressed by Arthur Neville Chamberlain—the British prime minister who led the effort to appease Hitler in 1938 by capitulating to his territorial demands over the Sudetenland— was quashed. Immediately after the invasion of Czechoslovakia, the British offered to protect Poland, clearly the next target of the German army, from Nazi aggression. Britain's pledge was followed on May 19, 1939, by Poland and France signing a mutual agreement guaranteeing to defend one another against Germany's rebuilt forces. On September 1, 1939, as Hitler invaded Poland, France and Britain declared war.

Most German citizens felt the war little or not at all at this time, as it wasn't until the summer of 1940 that British bombers began striking Berlin and other German cities. Andersen and Schultze, however, were affected almost immediately. Still recovering from her failed romance in Zurich with the dashing Rolf Liebermann, Andersen spent the second half of the 1930s scrambling to reinvent herself. As soon as she returned from her Swiss adventure, in

1935, she didn't fail to notice that the artists who were her friends
and whose songs filled her records and concerts were now being
banned, their works burned, and they themselves often opting for
self-imposed exile. Furthermore, in a society obsessed with a rig-
idly traditional interpretation of family values, she was considered
an inept parent. The ideal, every German was taught, was Goebbels: Reel after reel, photo after photo showed Joseph and Magda
smiling, relaxed, hugging their five blond children. A mother
who had abandoned her children to pursue a career as a cabaret
entertainer was at risk of becoming a pariah, and several of Lale's
acquaintances suggested that she make a point of being seen, and
photographed, with her children. She was only happy to do so,
vacationing in the North Sea island of Langeoog, not far from
Bremerhaven, and spent time with her family.

However, there was another matter, more difficult to smooth
over or overcome: not only was Liebermann Jewish, but he was a
scion of a prominent Jewish family that Goebbels and his minions
took particular pleasure in hounding. In addition, Lale had not
only been his lover but, still enamored, continued to correspond
with him, even though she knew that the Gestapo was very likely
to intercept their communications. In an effort to mask her relationship with Liebermann, Andersen made a public showing of
her next companion: his name was Karl Friedrich Pasche, nicknamed Fritz, and known to his friends as Paschi. He was a pianist
that she met shortly after her return to Berlin. His genial nature
and gentle features made him a pleasant-enough presence in her
life. Though no record of great passion exists, photographs taken
in the summer of 1939 show Pasche, Andersen, and her three
children, all fair-haired, in their bathing suits, smiling on the
Langeoog shore. It was precisely such images that Andersen
needed to show to the world, and they were made readily available to her fans. Radiant and happy, surrounded by a loving fam-

ily, she looked, in the picture, every bit as much the archetype of Aryan motherhood as Magda Goebbels.

But even with her reinvention as a mother, it was herself as a singer that Lale Andersen most needed to reinvent. Until her return from Switzerland, she was still the songstress of the sea— the willowy blonde with the short bob who dressed up in a sailor's outfit and spread herself suggestively over a grand piano. It was an act that worked extremely well in cabarets, but now the cabarets were no more. Now was the time of radio, of Nazi rallies, of Goebbels's ingenious slogan *"Kraft durch Freude"* (Strength Through Joy). Andersen grew her hair long, parting it in the middle and letting her tresses fall in waves down her back. Well aware of the Aryan obsession with racial origins, she capitulated to a rumor she had heard early on in her career. A drunk patron in a dingy Berlin bar bellowed to his friend that the pretty woman singing songs about the sea on stage was a well-known Danish entertainer, and the assumption that Andersen hailed from Scandinavia stood.

Without ever confirming the rumors directly, she made no effort to correct her erroneous biography in the press and even took it one step further. She replaced her androgynous sailor suits with a white dress hemmed with blue embroidery, a well-recognized Norwegian costume. Andersen wore her new clothes all the time, and, by early 1940, most of the articles written about her claimed that she grew up in Oslo and spent only small portions of her childhood in Bremerhaven. As a seductive German woman with short hair and men's clothes, Andersen was suspicious and depraved. As a sensual, long-haired diva of Scandinavian origin, she somehow evoked the spirit of the Vikings, a tribute to the Aryan race and therefore perfectly appropriate.

Lale's musical repertoire also did much to strengthen her new identity as a true Aryan. A concert program from early 1940 is exemplary: gone are the Kästners, Brechts, and Weills, replaced with "At Night on the High Seas," billed as a Norwegian folk-song; "Lyckan," a Swedish folk tune; and "Sorte Rudolf," a Danish sailors' song. The selection of songs had to be preapproved by the authorities. The performance was at a Nazi benefit for the army, and the program was emblazoned at the top with the words "*Kraft durch Freude.*"

Andersen's rebirth paid off handsomely. Following the concert in 1940, she was commissioned to go on tour to entertain the German soldiers abroad. After overwhelming Poland in just over a month, the Nazis had invaded Denmark and Norway in April 1940, and then subdued Luxembourg, Belgium, the Netherlands, and France. The massive German forces, spread over the Continent, were in need of distraction. Goebbels's office, cooperating with the army, was only too happy to enlist the Reich's artists, and, for the most part, the artists were only too happy to oblige. It is not hard to understand why: The German economy was now entirely devoted to the war effort. Food was scarce and luxuries disappeared altogether for all but the most privileged few. The artists dispatched to entertain the soldiers, however, stayed in luxurious hotels with comfortable sheets and thick towels where they were served far more sumptuous dishes than the rudimentary meals now so common back home. Andersen's photo album from the period reflects this well: rather than grim accounts of the war or photos of military encampments, she and Pasche collected colorful postcards and brochures of the grand hotels in which they stayed. It was, ironically, the most rewarding stretch of Lale Andersen's life to date.

Norbert Schultze, on the other hand, was feeling far less content. He was twenty-eight years old when the Wehrmacht marched into Poland, and, like most other German males of healthy mind and body, lived under constant fear of being called into military duty. And, in early September of 1939, he was. It was a terrible blow for him. Sure, his "Song of a Young Sentry" was a dismal failure, but he still had a hit with *Schwarzer Peter* and he was still sought after as a popular composer. Now, however, a letter in a small brown envelope instructed him to abandon his art, abandon his hopes, abandon his career, and go fight. And in the infantry, no less, the men most likely to find themselves in the most hellish battlefields. For a few days, he sulked around the house, unable to work, and anxiously awaited the call to come that would take him from his home.

But the war to the east ended by early October, and Schultze was temporarily spared from enlistment. In the meantime, he was instructed to compose the music for a film commissioned by Hermann Göring's Ministry of Aviation. Entitled *Feuertaufe*, or *Baptism by Fire*, it was a classic Nazi affair, complete with planes descending ominously from the sky and filled with plenty of fire, explosions, and religious symbolism. After his travails in Darmstadt and Munich, working for the Nazis—Göring, no less—was a tall order for Schultze. He had watched the events of Kristallnacht with horror, and saw the impending war as nothing but an omen declaring that the same kind of brutal madness that cloaked Germany was soon to descend upon the entire continent, if not the world. Besides, his true passions always lay with the sweeter, more innocent tunes—as the "Song of a Young Sentry" affair demonstrated all too well, he hadn't the knack for bombastic military stuff. And yet, a job was a job, especially if it could spare him a long and deadly assignment on the front lines. Drawing on his boyhood affection for all things military and his penchant for German Romanticism, Schultze began work on a grandiose, operatic, and superbly horrifying soundtrack.

But his imminent enlistment still hung above him like a sword. Every day, he would report to work in a ministry office in Berlin, not knowing whether or not that same evening would be his last as a civilian. It clouded his mind. Sensing that their composer was preoccupied by his worries, the executive at Tobis, the company producing the film for the ministry, decided to intervene. Appealing to high officials close to Göring, they asked that Schultze's name be added to the "Führer's List," a small and exclusive roster of men deemed to be "in a reserved occupation," and therefore too valuable to serve as ordinary soldiers.

A few days later, the officials reported back: Schultze, they said, was already on the list. The letter calling him to duty was a mistake. Through the grapevine, Schultze later heard that he owed his place on the precious registry to one Dr. Scherler, a lieutenant of Goebbels's who had attended the premiere of *Schwarzer Peter* and walked away impressed by the young composer's style and musical taste. Although he had never met Scherler in his life, and although he imagined him to be just another zealot and artless Nazi bureaucrat, Schultze now felt gratitude toward the man who had saved him from the threat of death and privation. In return, all he had to do was compose music for the Propaganda Ministry, a price that, considering the circumstances, struck him as nearly negligible.

With renewed vigor, he immersed himself in his work, relishing the opportunity to work with ample resources at his disposal, so different from the impoverished days of cabaret. More than anything, he realized, the soundtrack would fail or succeed depending on one song. Entitled "Bomben auf Engelland" (Bombs over England), it had these stirring lyrics: "Kamerad! Kamerad! Alle Mädels müssen warten!" (Comrade! Comrade! All the girls must wait!). The tune, Schultze thought, needed to be equally as compelling, equally as manly and robust. It was the centerpiece of the whole production, and he spent most of his time trying out various tunes, none to his liking.

To be sure, the lyrics were far from an ephemeral entreaty. In July 1940, Hilter launched Operation Sea Lion, an all-out assault

on Britain that was slated to end triumphantly with the Wehrmacht encircling London and conquering all of England up to
the 52nd Parallel, thereby ensuring the surrender of the rest of the
country. The major obstacle to that plan, however, was the Royal
Air Force, which was to be dealt with in a suboperation called
Operation Eagle. The directives of Eagle were simple: paralyze the
RAF to prevent it from offering up much resistance as the German fleet crossed the English Channel. Soon though, the Luftwaffe generals recalibrated the objectives of Operation Eagle even
more terrifyingly. Instead of merely attacking RAF bases, they
argued, the German air force could hasten the fall of England by
pummeling its cities with repeated rounds of strategic bombings
on civilian targets.

Thus began the famous Battle of Britain. On July 10, 1940,
squadrons of German bombers, massed in clouds of Heinkel He-
111s and Messerschmitt Bf-110s, descended onto Britain. The
German swarm, numbering one hundred planes in all, executed
massive nocturnal attacks against targets in Kent and York. The
following days brought more of the same. The RAF, in turn, sent
its Spitfires to engage the Nazi planes.

Germany's rulers, however, and Göring first and foremost,
envisioned the campaign as the crown jewel of a summer already
rich with stellar military achievements. If Britain fell, it was clear,
little else would stand in the way of the Nazi domination of western Europe. "Bomben auf Engelland," therefore, was to be a rous-
ing hymn to a great victory.

Toying with different tunes, Schultze grew increasingly frustrated. It occurred to him again and again that his nickname, Little
Mozart, the same moniker that once gave him so much pride and
pleasure, was now a liability, for what he needed was not sweet
melodies but the fierce, rugged notes of war, bars that drove not
pleasure but resolve into the hearts of young men. And while

"Song of a Young Sentry" came to him in a furious burst of inspiration, "Bomben auf Engelland" was refusing to be born. A few weeks into the composing process, Schultze received an invitation that increased his anxiety tenfold. He was expected, it read, to be present the next morning at No. 10 Inselstrasse, on the shores of Lake Wannsee—the residence of Joseph and Magda Goebbels.

Schultze was not a bit surprised. While the lyrics for "Bomben auf Engelland" were credited to an anonymous soldier who, overjoyed by the thrill of battle, scribbled down words of inspiration, no one at the Ministry of Aviation had any difficulty recognizing the real author. The words were classic Goebbels: "We feel bold luck in the refuges and the heights of the eagle!" went the opening lines. "We climb to the gate of the sun, we leave the earth!" This was followed by the repetitious command to "drive hard at the enemy" with "Bombs! Bombs! Bombs!"

The following morning, Schultze, filled with trepidation, made the journey to Goebbels's home. Located on Schwanenwerder, or Swan's Isle, a bucolic patch on the shores of Lake Wannsee just outside of Berlin, the house was the epicenter of a dense web of Nazi residences and institutions now crowding the neighborhood formerly populated by wealthy Jewish industrialists. Among Goebbels's neighbors were the architect Albert Speer, who had bought his house on the cheap from a Jewish family forced to flee Germany; Theo Morell, Hitler's personal physician; and the Reichsbräuteschule, or Reich Bride School, a finishing school training the finest Aryan maidens to become model wives and mothers in the service of the Fatherland.

Goebbels himself, by far the neighborhood's most prominent resident, cherished his house. He, too, bought it for a pittance, paying only 270,000 marks, far below the property's value. Moving in, he wrote elatedly in his diary: "I have my own house. On the lake, and thoroughly happy. A refuge. I can relax and regain strength."

The house at 10 Inselstrasse was indeed conducive to relaxation. A two-story, fifteen-room mansion, it allowed the Goebbels clan—Joseph, Magda, her grown-up son from a previous marriage and five (later six) small children—to live in great comfort. Although boxy in shape and with little external flourishes except for two protruding verandas on the ground floor, the house's internal design displayed both Goebbels's background as an educated, cultivated man and his stature as a demigod in the Nazi universe. As Schultze marched into the minister's study, he saw him standing underneath an enormous oil painting, leaning against an endless row of elegant bookshelves heavy with leatherbound volumes. Beside him stood a wooden globe as tall as Goebbels himself, an ornament that left little room to wonder about the man's aspirations. In the middle of the room stood an enormous black grand piano.

After a brief introduction in which Goebbels was charming, taking genuine interest in Schultze and his musical background, the minister asked the composer to sit at the piano. He delivered a short speech about the importance of "Bomben auf Engelland," never admitting authorship of the song's lyrics but praising its words as an authentic and passionate manifestation of the German fighting spirit, a spirit that now, in a time of war, was ever so important. Then he asked Schultze to play.

Doing his best to calm himself under such trying circumstances, Schultze put his fingers on the keyboard and began playing, offering Goebbels what he hoped was a sufficiently masculine version of the song. As polite and accommodating as he had been while greeting Schultze, Goebbels was now growing impatient and rude. Waiting to hear no more than a bar or two, he waved his hands and stopped Schultze from playing further, ordering him to tighten up the tune. Schultze took a few moments to think, and played a few bars in a major key. Goebbels screamed at him. Schultze waited a few more moments, tried again, and was once more interrupted by Goebbels, who was now breathlessly pacing about the room.Then, as Goebbels stood perched behind Schultze while the young composer tried to work out the piece's climax, Goebbels rushed in and slammed on the piano's keys to emphasize what he felt should be the strongest points. Schultze, of course, said nothing.

This bizarre duet lasted slightly over an hour and resulted in a melody that was every bit as stirring as Goebbels had hoped. Olympian in nature, hypnotically repetitive, with a soaring brass section that appealed to the feet, the ear, and the heart all at the same time, it was a masterpiece of musical propaganda. But it was Goebbels himself who added the finishing touch just as he was walking Schultze to the door. The minister, having by then regained his composure, let a smile creep across his face as he suggested that, just as the song begins, after the brief introduction that recalled a classic military march, Schultze should insert recordings of actual Heinkel bombers. Unable to refuse what he thought was a crude touch—especially as he himself had deployed a similar strategy when recording "Song of a Young Sentry"—Schultze nevertheless complied, and the song soon began with the low, menacing growl of an airplane. Goebbels was right on the mark; the rumble of aviation greatly excited many young male listeners, and "Bomben auf Engelland" became a huge hit that propelled the film to success.

Impressed with Schultze's achievement, all branches of the armed forces contacted him soon after the release of *Feuertaufe*, requesting that he compose soundtracks for their movies as well. Schultze was honored; Nazis or not, this, after all, was work not for the party but for his beloved military, and, at that, work that kept him out of combat and in the relatively small circle of people who could still, even as the war was flaring up, lead a life of luxury in Berlin. As the war progressed, Norbert Schultze gave musical expression to the seemingly unstoppable advance of the German military machine.

There was, however, one more issue that needed his immediate attention. Years before, when his name change was called into question, Schultze had learned firsthand the Nazi obsession with displays of loyalty, and yet he, the burgeoning military composer, the man no longer called Little Mozart but Bomber Schultze, was not a member of the party. In the fall of 1940, eager to ensure that his spot on the Führer's List would not be revoked, Norbert Schultze walked into the party's headquarters, paid his dues, and became a card-carrying Nazi.

V

Radio Belgrade

THE FIRST few months of the Second World War provided some needed relief for Lale Andersen and Norbert Schultze. Having lost touch after "Song of a Young Sentry" fizzled in the face of the coming war, the two artists nonetheless benefited from the very same military machine that had indirectly undermined the success of their song. By early in the summer of 1940, after both Norway and Denmark had been subdued by Germany in triumphs so routine and uneventful that the English-speaking world referred to the conflict as the "Phony War," the Nazi propaganda machine focused on portraying its acts of war as benign and natural, escapades serving not some German thirst for domination but rather something that answered the unspoken yearnings of the countries conquered for redemption by the defenders of the imperiled Aryan way of life.

No one could perpetuate this fiction better than Lale Andersen. Still largely and erroneously regarded as Scandinavian, she was shipped out, in the spring of 1940, on a tour of Germany's newly acquired military bases in Denmark and Norway. There, newspapers, controlled by puppet governments eager to portray themselves as grateful subjects of the liberating Aryan warriors, printed ads promoting Andersen's concerts, which featured small and cheerful Danish and Norwegian flags. The gesture couldn't have been clearer: Andersen, the ads suggested, was a daughter of Scandinavia who saw it as her patriotic duty to entertain and welcome the German troops, singing in German and representing, in person, the stuff of Nazi propaganda.

All of these ideological and political underpinnings, however, were largely lost on Andersen herself. At war as in peace, she measured success and failure strictly according to the fluctuations of her own renown and saw the summer of 1940 as a rare stretch of fame and fortune after years of hardship and relative obscurity. Furthermore, it seemed like an opportune time for her to rescue her static career as the entertainment industry, like all others, was gearing up for Germany's war effort and looking to enlist qualified personnel.

The situation was made especially acute by the recent defection of Marlene Dietrich, by far the brightest star in Germany's celebrity constellation, to the United States. Dietrich had moved to Hollywood in the early 1930s, and refused, in 1937, an official Nazi entreaty to return to Germany. In 1939, she became an American citizen, and with her newfound legal status allowed herself an ever-greater degree of freedom to express her contempt for her homeland's new masters. With Dietrich not only missing in action but now a virtual enemy combatant as well, the diligent men of the Culture Chamber felt the need for a replacement. They sought someone equally as glamorous and captivating as Dietrich, but who would take orders and serve, not embarrass, Germany.

None of their candidates suited their needs more than Zarah Leander. A less threatening beauty than Dietrich, this young act-

Gardefüsi-
lier Hans Leip im Jahre
1915, ehe er in den Osten
ausrückte.

Hans Leip in uniform, 1915.

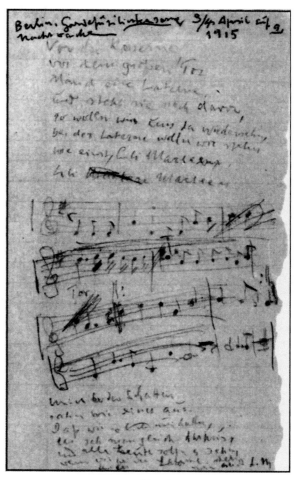

Hans Leip's original handwritten version of
"Song of a Young Sentry," dated 1915. Leip composed his
own music to accompany the poem, a tune much slower and
sadder than the one made famous by
Norbert Schultze.

Betty (Lili)

Sketches by Hans Leip of the
homely Lili and the seductive
Marlene, the two romantic
interests the poet welded in
his mind to create his
famous heroine.

Marleen

RIGHT. *Lale Andersen: "A blond, north German girl, she will bring something very rare into cabaret: her own touch," wrote a critic early in her career.*

BELOW. *Lale Andersen and her mentor, Willi Schaeffers, performing sailor songs on an appropriately themed stage in Berlin, 1932.*

ABOVE. *A young and studious Norbert Schultze, soon to be known as "Little Mozart," poring over his compositions.*

LEFT. *An early album cover of "Lili Marlene." The illustration aptly portrays the charming young woman who captured the hearts of so many soldiers in song.*

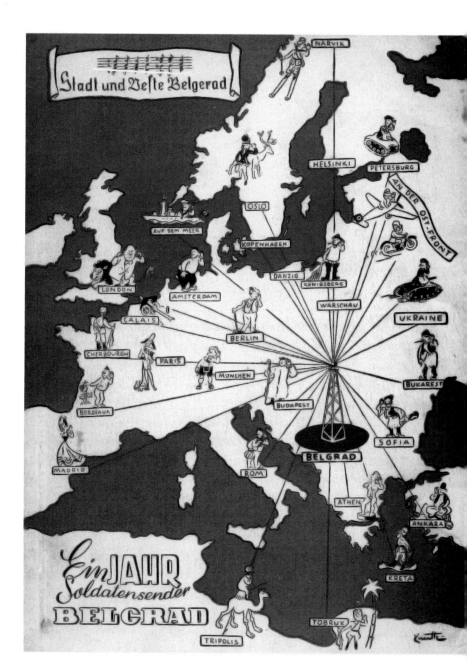

ABOVE. *"Soldiers can die, but an evening without 'Lili Marlene' is unthinkable":* German soldiers listening to Radio Belgrade.

LEFT. *Berlin, 1942: "All I want to do is get out of this country." As Lale's fame grew, so did the scrutiny of the Nazi machine.*

OPPOSITE. *A German map portraying the vast geographic and cultural range of Karl-Heinz Reintgen's Radio Belgrade.*

RIGHT. *"Lili Marlene," an American B-24 Liberator bomber, participated in the D-Day offensive and flew missions over Germany. It was lost on December 28, 1944.*

BELOW. *Lale Andersen with English veterans of the Eighth Army, 1950: With the war over, the Allied soldiers, too, were finally free to meet the woman whose voice had come to mean so much to them as they fought in the deserts of Africa and the hills of Italy.*

ress first caught the eye of the Nazi officials in 1936, when she was spotted by Culture Chamber officials in the film *Axel an der Himmelstür*, a parody of America and Hollywood. Incredibly, despite her relative lack of experience and despite her being a Swedish national who had never, unlike the majority of her German colleagues, taken the trouble of pledging allegiance to the Nazi ideology and its champions, she was offered a three-picture deal by the Ufa film studio. Even more remarkable, though, was the fact that rather than seize the opportunity, Leander sent strict terms to Ufa: She demanded, and received, 200,000 Reichsmarks, with 53 percent of the money transferred in Swedish kronor to an account she held in Stockholm. Goebbels seethed when he was informed of Leander's hard bargaining, and testily called her "an enemy of Germany." And yet, he knew that he had no choice: Ufa had created a star in Marlene Dietrich and now needed to drown her out with someone who could beat Dietrich at her own lust-ridden, enigmatic, and irresistible game. Leander, despite her greed, was just too perfect for Goebbels to reject.

The rise of the Swedish actress bode well for Lale Andersen. While Leander looked nothing like Andersen—who had more in common with Dietrich's chiseled, angular features than with Leander's soft, smooth, round face—their biographies had many parallels. Like Andersen, Leander, too, was a frustrated mother and housewife who had dreamed of fame, eventually leaving her family to pursue her career. Both women joined a traveling cabaret troupe and toured Germany, and, like Andersen, Leander was a quintessential outsider with Nordic airs. And as Leander assumed the throne of German arts and entertainment through the fortunate defection of Dietrich to Los Angeles, couldn't Andersen hope that a similar shift could well be in store for her—she who could be every bit as pouting and mysterious and gorgeous as Leander was? And what better way, in this time of effortless, fashionable war, to achieve such fame than through a strong military fan base? Andersen could enjoy the potential rewards of being the soldiers' sweetheart, a career trajectory that would carry her voice from crowded barracks to the German airwaves and to great acclaim.

Norbert Schultze, meanwhile, was enjoying life in the increasingly comfortable company of those few civilians deemed by the Nazis as vital to the war effort and thus spared from conscription. Ensconced in a luxurious Berlin apartment and handsomely paid for his efforts, Schultze churned out compositions for his new patrons. A list of his works from this period reads like the chronology of the German army's advance. After composing the anthem to the Nazi attack on Britain, he wrote "Panzers Rolling in the Desert," conceived as the soundtrack to the German dash across Africa, and, later in 1941, wrote the score for "Das Russlandlied," which was the hymn, written by Goebbels, that accompanied the German army as it invaded the Soviet Union. The fact that Schultze was asked to compose "The Russian Song" only served to prove his chosen position inside the Nazi machine. The composer, given the lyrics in complete confidence, was let in on the secret, in advance of even some in the army's brass, that Germany was planning to invade the Soviet Union, which at that time had signed a nonaggression pact with the Nazis. Expressing his overall loyalty to Germany's new leaders, Schultze also composed a handful of songs in praise of the Reich's leaders and their ideology, including the infamous "Führer befiehl, wir folgen dir" (Leader, Lead Us and We Will Follow), a musical tribute whose slogan came to represent the omnipotence of Hitler and the sway he held over the hypnotized masses.

With the war progressing smoothly and Berlin's young men sent to the barracks in order to learn the art and science of making war, Schultze thrived. Though a married man and a father, he nonetheless enjoyed the new urban equilibrium, one in which any mildly attractive man, particularly one who had access to the Nazi Party and a healthy bank account, could do very well with the capital's lonely ladies. A gregarious and vivacious man, he followed his days of working on the Reich's marching music with evenings spent in bars and cafés, wooing young women with bottles of champagne and the allure of his celebrity. It was a strange and unexpected opportunity to relive his youthful years, when he was the star of the cabaret scene and could easily seduce any number of adoring girls. His latest ascent into fame and fortune was, needless to say, quite ironic. It was the Nazis, after all, who had put an end to his rise in the mid-1930s when they barred him from Munich's stages, gutted the cabarets, and rewarded artists not on the basis of merit but of loyalty. After years of disappointment and pedestrian jobs, he was once again a star. It was a force greater than any matrimonial vow or filial piety could contain, and soon he and Vera were divorced.

While Schultze celebrated his freedom and fortune in Berlin and Andersen entertained soldiers throughout Nazi-occupied Europe, Karl-Heinz Reintgen, a young lieutenant in the German Army, was himself marching in his own way to the beat of the new Nazi order. In prewar Germany, Reintgen was one of the millions destined for a contented, if uneventful, life. He was average in height and build, with kind eyes and thinning hair. A natural tinkerer, he was, since childhood, enamored with radios. Born in 1916, Reintgen came of age as radio sets were entering the living rooms of Germany's homes, and from a young age he found himself enraptured by the large wooden boxes and their glowing glass dials. As a child, he would take his family's radio apart and put it back together again; as an adult, he found employment in a medium-sized commercial radio station.

By the time Reintgen had begun working in radio, it had already been established as an integral part of the Reich's society.

Goebbels zealously nurtured the new medium. While German radio stations were broadcasting for only a little more than thirteen hours a day in 1932, by 1938, when Reintgen was first promoted to a managerial position at his station in north Germany, those same stations, under the strict orders of the Culture Chamber, were disseminating tunes and information for twenty hours every day.

Reintgen, then, was entering the right industry at exactly the right moment, his own passions harmoniously aligned with those of the regime. Furthermore, he was thrilled to discover that German radio, even under the Nazis, was far from a stifling affair. Ever the shrewd analyst of the human psyche, Goebbels realized that a broadcast lambasting its listeners with political pomp was likely to fall on disinterested ears. Instead, to keep it compelling, he instructed the radio men to pursue a heady mix of entertainment, sentimentality, and carefully concealed morsels of ideology. He expressed his views lucidly in March of 1933, addressing a host of radio stations which, anxious to curry favor with the newly installed government, dedicated their frequencies to nothing but military march music and pro-Nazi programming:

> On no account present political opinion unadorned and exposed to all and sundry. On no account imagine that the best way of serving the National Government is by having marches blaring out night after night. . . . There must be opinion, but opinion need not mean tedium. The imagination must employ all methods of making the new opinion sound modern, up-to-date and interesting to the broad masses.

The idea, as one observer put it at the time, was that the more music broadcast on the radio, the more open the listener becomes to the messages weaved in between the songs. In 1938, therefore, more than 60 percent of all commercial broadcasts in Germany consisted of dance music and light tunes, 2.5 percent of folk music and marches, 8 percent of serious, classical works, and the rest, less than 30 percent, to political speeches.

Such a breakdown suited Reintgen perfectly. Coming to work each morning, he could function less like a clerk serving some overarching ideology and more as a professional broadcaster. He realized, of course, that one could not work in radio unless one belonged to the Culture Chamber, which he himself had joined at a young age. He also knew that certain types of music—first and foremost jazz, which the Nazis considered an evil genre spawned by an unholy alliance between the negroes of Harlem and the Jews of Tin Pan Alley—could never find its way onto the airwaves. But all of those technicalities struck him merely as the price of doing business, no different than other demands and limitations set on professional men in other industries in other parts of the world, as part and parcel of the imperfections of modern life.

Neither Reintgen nor most of his contemporaries could discern the ominous current bubbling underneath the foundations of German radio in those years, subject, as it was, to Goebbels's ultimate plan to numb minds with kitsch and piffles before he filled them with hateful propaganda. He was striving for a certain kind of song that would tug at the heartstrings just so. Ever the intellectual, he took pains to define this musical prototype precisely, settling on the phrase "the romanticism of steel."

"Gone," he wrote as early as 1933,

was the nerveless flaccidity which surrendered before life's seriousness, which denied it or fled from it; and forward strode the heroic view of life which today resounds from the marching step of brown-shirted columns, which attends the peasant as he draws his ploughshare through the earthen clod, which has given back the worker a meaning and a higher purpose in his struggle for existence, which saves the unemployed man from despair and which imbues the magnificent achievement of German recovery with an almost soldierly rhythm. It is a kind of romanticism of steel that has made German life worth living once again: a romanticism that does not hide from the harshness of existence, nor seek to escape from it into the blue yonder; a romanticism which has the mettle to face ruthless problems and look them firmly and unflinchingly in the eye.

The "romanticism of steel," therefore, was no simple construct, uncomplicated enough to appeal to society's least sophisticated members and at the same time complex enough to appear weightier than mere mindless entertainment. It was a paragon of middle-brow culture, a genre that caressingly gave the uncultivated a sense of intellectual self-worth and understanding. Listening to any song in the "romanticism of steel" tradition, a farmer or a worker was spared the feeling of bafflement that, to untrained ears, inevitably accompanied an atonal composition or a difficult symphony. But rather than present their compositions as mere airy entertainment, the "romanticism of steel" composers draped their songs with cloaks of pathos and grandeur, suggesting to the listeners that before them stood a work of great value and nuance, complete and very, very deep. With minds thus complimented and quieted, the road was paved for the advance of propaganda's more insidious armored columns.

Reintgen, unaware of Goebbel's master plan, happily played one song in the "romanticism of steel" tradition after another, particularly reveling in the work of Zarah Leander, who by the late 1930s had established herself as the chief purveyor of this uniquely fascist brand of Top-40 pop. He genuinely enjoyed

Leander's songs, finding them touching and heartfelt. He was twenty-three, had a job he loved, and a life that seemed to hold in store little but comfort, music, and joy.

The war changed all that, as it did for all young German men. A few weeks after the invasion of Poland, Reintgen was called into service and before long found himself, given his education and skill, enrolled in an officer's course. Although he had for the time being remained in Germany and although his military training was neither physically demanding nor emotionally taxing, Reintgen was overcome with a sense of paralyzing dread. All around him in the barracks swirled tales of injury, death, and suffering, stories that deeply affected the naïve mind of the radio station manager with the unassuming childhood. He was made uncomfortable by the political situation, and his innate patriotism was prickled by the unsettling chauvinism of the Nazis, their belligerence, and their zeal. And yet, he was a soldier and had no choice; he had to serve. He did, though, resolve to try to negotiate for himself a position that would keep him away from the front lines.

He soon thought of a plan. As a director of a radio station, he had seen how Goebbels and his Culture Chamber smiled upon the medium, how strongly they believed in its capacity to communicate to the masses. Wouldn't the same, he asked himself, be especially true in wartime? And wouldn't the armed forces, therefore, relish in having an experienced broadcaster at their service? With an assertiveness uncharacteristic to his mild nature, he began to pursue his commanding officers, insisting that the proper place for him was not in a foxhole with a rifle but in a studio with records, broadcasting reassuring sentiments and popular songs to soothe the nerves of the brave men at the front. Soon enough, and with the intervention of a Culture Chamber acquaintance, his plea was sent up the army's hierarchy. It was answered. Reintgen was ordered to report to one Colonel Kratzer at the army's Supreme Command in order to begin work on a network of newly established radio stations the army had set up in each of their conquered theaters.

Reintgen now spent his days waiting to meet with the busy Kratzer, and, instead of seething about his interrupted youth, consoled himself with the notion that a stint in the army might actually prove beneficial to his career, giving him the sort of professional experience and gravity that is rare for men his age. He was also looking forward to his first assignment, imagining himself in a terra-cotta building in some sandy, tropical oasis, broadcasting uninterruptedly to gruff and grateful listeners, free of the workaday drudgeries of city or bureaucratic life. These fantasies kept his spirits up, but with each day that passed, he grew a little more unsettled, a little more anxious.

In April 1941, Colonel Kratzer finally called. He summoned Reintgen to his office and, in his characteristically hysteric manner told the young man that the time had come to deploy. "You're a radio broadcaster!" he shouted at Reintgen, his high-pitched tone making the words sound almost like an accusation. Reintgen confirmed that he was indeed just that, and Kratzer ordered him to fly to Zagreb immediately. The German army, he said, had just invaded Yugoslavia, and, in setting up a puppet government there, would need a radio station to keep the populace in check and the troops entertained and informed.

"Don't wait!" Kratzer shouted at Reintgen. "Go now!"

Hastily, Reintgen arranged for a seat on a small military plane headed for Zagreb and was in Yugoslavia the following day. He arrived at the local army barracks, was shown to his room, showered, and was set to leave for the radio station when a soldier knocked on his door and delivered a telegram. Its hyperventilating tone left little room for doubt as to the identity of its author.

LIEUTENANT REINTGEN! it read, YOU ARE TO ASSUME COMMAND OF THE STATION IN BELGRADE IMMEDIATELY! No further explanation was given.

Not yet unpacked, Reintgen summoned a driver, boarded another plane, and was in Belgrade by nightfall. What he saw there gave him little comfort; the next morning, a soldier drove him to the radio station, or at least what was left of it. The site of much resistance, Belgrade was thoroughly bombed by the invading Germans, who did not spare the small, one-story building that housed the local radio studios. Reintgen stood amid the rubble, looking around. There were wooden beams with splinters jutting out like teeth from an open mouth. There were chunks of concrete hanging in the air by thin threads of metal. There were bits of wall, charred by fire and pockmarked by bullets. And there was a transmitter, lying underneath a mangled metal desk.

Reintgen examined his new office. The building, he knew, mattered not at all. For a radio station to function the sole necessity was a working transmitter. He kneeled down and pulled the large white metal box, weighing nearly eighty pounds, from the debris. A few of its plastic knobs were misshapen by the heat, and one or two of the gauges were broken, but overall the thing appeared to be intact. Reintgen started kicking at the wreckage and soon discovered the transmitter's companion piece, another bulky box that provided the transmitter its power. He took both devices back to his barracks, plugged them into a power source and prayed for the best. Slowly, the gauges and dials began to tremble and the battered machines began to emit their familiar electrical purr. Reintgen was happy; he had in front of him his very own radio station.

Finding a new building was not a big problem. As a lieutenant in the occupying army, he had the authority to confiscate whatever edifice struck him as suitable, and a quick drive through Belgrade's devastated streets revealed just such a building. It was on an unassuming grey block near the fringes of town, populated by elongated concrete rectangles that housed the local government's lesser offices. Reintgen chose one such building, formerly home to Yugoslavia's Ministry of Agriculture, and installed himself in a second-story office there. Using a nearby transmission tower in a well-sited location that allowed him to broadcast to all of Europe and points beyond, Reintgen's Soldatensender Belgrad—Soldier's Radio Belgrade—went on the air in April 1941.

But even with a roof over his head and the proper equipment at his disposal, Reintgen soon learned that running a military radio station was a challenge greater than any he had previously encountered in his professional life. He and his staff of five had to fill twenty-one hours of news and entertainment programming each day with only fifty-four records. Reintgen played his few albums in an endless rotation, and strained his mind looking for a quick solution to the dearth of broadcast materials that plagued his new station. Finally, he decided that help could only come from without. He summoned one of his subordinates, Kistenmacher, a young man he trusted completely, to his office and sent him out on perhaps one of the easiest raids of the war: Kistenmacher was to travel to Vienna for a few days, and there, in the city of music, obtain all the records he could possibly get his hands on. Any kind of record, Reintgen added, would do, as long as the young soldier returned with enough music to fill all those hours of airtime.

But trustworthy as Reintgen thought his young protégé to be, Kistenmacher must have found the charms of a short leave in Vienna too precious to spoil with trifles like the army and orders. Whatever he did with his short leave is lost to history, but his activities did not include searching for records. Only with a few hours to go before he had to board the plane back to Belgrade did the young soldier finally attend to the mission at hand. Heading to Vienna's State Radio offices, he charmed his way into the dusty basement cellar where all of the excess records were kept. Official radio stations of the Nazi state had no shortage of albums they could no longer use, and the young soldier, finding a box filled with politically suspect records and other assorted flops, quickly snatched up as many of the discarded albums as he could carry. Most were fluff, but one he found with the vaguely martial title "Song of a Young Sentry" seemed like it would fit Reintgen's bill. Kistenmacher added it to his thickening pile and quickly made his way back to Belgrade. Telling Reintgen nothing of his extracurricular activities in Vienna, the soldier explained that records were very hard to come by, and that the few he was able to collect were a testament to his skill and resourcefulness.

Reintgen sifted through the pile, his exasperation growing deeper and deeper as he thumbed one obscure record after another, wondering how on earth he was expected to entertain anyone with such a collection of unexciting music. Then, however, he caught a glimpse of "Song of a Young Sentry," and a smile crept onto his lips.

To a man working in a radio station, records come to inhabit a special place in the mind, a pristine realm occupied solely by names of composers, arrangers, and lyricists. Such was the case with Reintgen: upon seeing the record, it took him no more than a minute to reach into his vast musical database and locate the song. It was, he knew, a commercial failure. Reintgen recalled broadcasting it once or twice in 1938, when he was still the manager of a civilian radio station, and then burying it underneath a pile of records. He had never particularly cared for the song. Broadcasting hours of "romanticism of steel" songs, the "Song of a Young Sentry," Reintgen thought, had sentimentality but not fire. Therefore, it was no triumph in the Nazi mold, no work of uncomplicated terror and beauty, but rather just a sappy song, melancholy to a fault. He also vaguely remembered that the lyrics spoke of a young woman waiting for her lover, a soldier, to return from the war, and was unsure that such depressing words were what his listeners craved. Soldiers, after all, hate nothing more than to be reminded of the aborted lives they had left back home. He looked at the record once again, and the more he thought about it, the more he found it fundamentally mismatched for his purposes.

And yet, two realizations propelled Reintgen to remove the record from its sleeve and place it on the record player in his office. First, and quite obvious, was that he had in his possession a painfully small number of records, and removing any one of them from rotation was therefore ill advised. But it was another, more personal memory that prevailed. Back in 1938, one of his colleagues at the radio station where he worked adored "Song of a Young Sentry," commenting on its beauty each one of the handful of times that Reintgen put it on the air. Reintgen had kept in touch with the fellow, and knew that he was now, like everybody else, a soldier. Maybe, he thought, his friend was even within range of Radio Belgrade's humble transmitters? And maybe he's listening, and will be overjoyed when he hears the obscure song he loves so much playing on his field radio? Awash in reveries about life before the army beckoned, Reintgen put the needle in the record's groove and began to listen.

The first notes delighted him; what he heard was the unmistakable bugle call of the *Zapfenstreich*, the well-worn call to the evening's curfew. It was a recognizable military sound, and therefore useful for a soldier's station. He listened on.

The following notes were just as he had remembered them: sweet and simple, almost plaintive, like something a child might hum in a moment of distraction. Then came the voice: he didn't know who the singer was—the name on the sleeve, Lale Andersen, was not familiar to him—but he was struck by the harsh timbre, finding it slightly offensive. And then the words: hurried goodbyes, sorrowful departures, yearnings for better, more peaceful days. Reintgen cringed. Still, his dearth of alternatives and his fond memories proved stronger, and he placed the record in a small pile of those he intended to broadcast in the near future.

On August 18, 1941, four months after assuming his position as Radio Belgrade's commander, Reintgen decided it was finally time to bring "Song of a Young Sentry" into rotation. He had exhausted his other options and played some of his records so often that the quality of the sound was beginning to deteriorate. He gave the fresh tune to one of his soldiers, and later that afternoon the song aired for the first time on Radio Belgrade. It aired again later that day, and a few more times each day as the week progressed, the customary order of business for a radio station with so few resources.

Like most weeks in the life of Radio Belgrade, the week in which "Song of a Young Sentry" was first broadcast was a quiet one. Originally established to entertain and inform the German soldiers engaged in war in the Balkans, the station soon found its raison d'être somewhat hampered when, in June of 1941, the German army completed its conquest of Albania, Yugoslavia, mainland Greece, and the Greek islands. The war in the Balkans, it was clear even to the lowliest private, had but one goal: access to the Mediterranean, and from there to Egypt and the Middle Eastern oil fields. When the German invasion of the Soviet Union began in June of 1941, another goal became visible: just by looking at the movements of the army on the map, one could quickly realize that Hitler's plan called for a pincer move, with the forces in Africa not only seizing the oil fields, thereby robbing the British of invaluable assets, but also eventually moving up through Turkey to assault the Soviet empire in its eastern provinces, forcing it into a war on two fronts. Radio Belgrade, then, was, in the summer of 1941, broadcasting mainly for the crucial German forces in North Africa, those sunburnt men living in the desert with little time or presence of mind to bother a military radio station, as their counterparts in Europe sometimes did, with complaints, requests for songs, or even regards for loved ones back home.

Suddenly, however, all that began to change. A week or so after introducing "Song of a Young Sentry" into the rotation, Reintgen, who considered 1,000 letters from soldiers a week the absolute maximum his small station could handle, was now receiving 2,000, then 3,000, then 4,000 letters. All said more or less the same thing: the song, which the troops simply called "Lili Marlene," was their musical salvation in an otherwise bleak soldierly existence. People wrote to Radio Belgrade looking for Lili Marlene, their imaginary heroine, while some, unable to make out their darling's name on those distant radios, addressed their letters instead to someone known as Vili Marlene. But what was important to the troops locked in battle halfway around the world wasn't the song's precise name. It was what its words and melody meant to them during restless nights on foreign fields. One fighting man in North Africa wrote to the station to say that "soldiers can die, but an evening without 'Lili Marlene' is unthinkable."

A true broadcaster, Reintgen spent very little time pondering the reasons for the song's sudden popularity. Instead, he rearranged the station's playlist, making sure that "Lili Marlene" was broadcast at least once every hour, and sometimes as often as every other song. Letter after letter confirmed the merit of Reintgen's decision; from all over North Africa, German soldiers wrote in and confessed their love for the song in terms rarely employed by fighting men. They spoke of loneliness and fear, of yearnings and uncertainties, of a strong passion for the life they left at home.

Reintgen was overjoyed. The song, it seemed, had single-handedly turned his small station into a major and influential broadcaster. Although no surveys were taken at the time to try and ascertain the number of Radio Belgrade's listeners, the thousands of letters flocking in each week convinced Reintgen that his was the finest of the German army's pet radio stations, enjoying unprecedented popularity and a fiercely loyal listenership.

There was, however, one problem with Radio Belgrade's new devotion to "Lili Marlene": after a few weeks of playing the song nonstop, Reintgen began to realize that more than a mere springboard to success, "Lili Marlene" was gradually taking over the station, eclipsing all of its other broadcasts and becoming synonymous with its programming. Any novice broadcaster would have realized, as Reintgen did, that playing one immensely liked song several times an hour was bound to end in catastrophe, as listeners are eventually sure to have their fill of even the catchiest of tunes. Reintgen had had his fill already; every time he heard the *Zapfenstreich*, that Prussian bugle call that opened the song, he became annoyed, and he made a point of going to another room or simply tuning out every time the sweet melody came on the air. Finally, after two or three weeks of increasing animosity, he made the decision: no more "Lili Marlene"—not even occasionally. If Radio Belgrade was to regain its independence as a military radio station, it had to wean itself from this sappy song, no matter what the consequences. The listeners, he thought, would have no choice but to do the same.

A few nervous days passed without a word. Then, the deluge: whereas before Reintgen and his staff had received 3,000 to 4,000 letters each week requesting to hear more of "Lili Marlene," now the station was inundated with 8,000 letters angrily demanding that "Lili" be broadcast once more. Still, Reintgen persevered. A week later, 10,000 soldiers wrote to protest. Reintgen still refused. Soon, it was 12,500, and Reintgen could resist no more.

And yet, placing the song once again into heavy rotation was out of the question. Instead, Reintgen sought a creative solution. One dawned on him almost immediately: "Lili Marlene," he realized, was not so much a song as it was a musical ritual, a brief lyrical respite during which the soldiers could safely ponder loved ones left back home and romance unfettered by war. That being the case, he thought, why not play the song just once a day, three minutes before the 10 P.M. news broadcast, the day's last? It made perfect sense from a propaganda perspective as well: listeners eager to hear "Lili Marlene" would then stay tuned to the all-important news program. Besides, playing the song just once gave it an air of sanctity almost, as if it, of all songs, stood alone in the hearts and the minds of the soldiers.

The following day, Reintgen instructed his soldiers to broadcast yet another playlist free of "Lili Marlene." At 9 P.M., he took the microphone and inaugurated a new program, *We Greet Our Listeners*, in which he and others at the station read out messages from soldiers to their loved ones back home and vice versa. At three minutes before 10 P.M., he paused for a few moments, then said ceremoniously: "And now just for you, for everyone here and there, 'Lili Marlene.'"

It was the first airing of "Lili Marlene" in more than two weeks. A day or two later, Reintgen understood that his decision to allot the song the 9:57 P.M. spot was an appreciated one: The torrent of letters continued, with no sign of weakening. However, soldiers were now writing not only to express their affection for "Lili Marlene" but also to request that the song be dedicated to their wives and girlfriends at home.

The letters revealed three basic truths, each one more astounding than the other. First of all, Reintgen was shocked to sift through the mail and find postmarks coming from as far as Hamburg and Berlin. At night, with little interference from military radio equipment, his humble transmitter was capable of carrying the signal much farther than he had realized, reaching not only the soldiers stationed in North Africa but also their families in Germany itself.

Second, the song, he learned, had almost instantly acquired a special meaning not only for the uniformed men but also for their sweethearts. Maybe, he thought, it was the sentimental lyrics, or maybe the tune, or maybe the theme of a young woman waiting for her loved one to return from the war. Whatever it was about "Lili Marlene," the young women of Germany had come to see it as a link to their men, as if by listening to the song they were, for a few minutes, reunited with their loved ones.

Speaking many years later, one such young woman, Hildegard Klimkeit, explained her attachment to the song:

> The song was my only connection to my husband, and every night I had the feeling I wasn't alone listening to Lale, but my husband was listening too. I can't really describe the feeling, it's absurd, but it was like that, and I just felt close to him. And I thought that the enemies that lie in the trenches opposite the Germans hear the song as well, and those soldiers just lie in the trenches a few meters apart from one another, listening to Lale sing, and I was listening to Lale sing as well. It was a thought that never left me. . . .

Klimkeit's vision of the warring men on both sides lying in trenches and listening together to "Lili Marlene" was far from being a hopeful fantasy of reconciliation. The third realization that struck Reintgen—and this one hit the hardest—was that "Lili Marlene" was winning fans among the Allied Forces just as it was among the Wehrmacht's. More than a few letters came from British soldiers, all expressing their admiration for the song. One day, Reintgen opened a letter addressed simply to "The Sentry" that had somehow found its way to the station; inside was an American five-dollar bill, with the request to give a greeting to a British soldier. The writer was from the United States and had tuned in to Radio Belgrade's short-wave signal, which Reintgen now realized was reaching America's eastern seaboard.

Although the British soldiers had, except for the handful of German speakers, no way of understanding what the song was about, something about the melody, about the bugle call, about Lale Andersen's voice, transcended words and conveyed the song's meaning. The Allied troops, fighting the Nazis in the Egyptian desert, soon adopted Lili as their darling as well, seeing in her the epitome of every woman left behind at home to wait and worry.

Reintgen learned of this strange instance of cultural transcendence firsthand in the fall of 1941. Sitting in his office one day, the door burst open and in walked three German soldiers dragging a bedraggled-looking fellow. By the shreds of uniform that still clung to his bloodied body, Reintgen could tell that he was a pilot in the Royal Air Force, probably shot down somewhere over the Balkans. Why, he wondered, were the soldiers taking a prisoner of war to a radio station?

In English, the captive began to speak. Still tightly held by his guards, he told Reintgen that his wife listened to "We Greet Our Listeners" every night. She was nine months pregnant and due to give birth the following week. Could you please, the man pleaded with Reintgen, let her know on the air tonight, in English, that I have been taken prisoner and am alright?

Reintgen turned over the man's request in his mind. The men of the Culture Chamber, obsessing over all radio broadcasts both military and civilian, would not look kindly on a German radio station broadcasting greetings to an enemy's wife in the enemy's language. The Army brass, locked in a bloody battle with the British, was likely to frown upon such an act of mercy as well. But

Reintgen, a lifelong believer in the power of radio, a medium that was about bringing people together, felt that there was no way he could refuse the British soldier's request. He nodded his head, told the man he would do it, and watched as the prisoner was dragged back into the hallway. That night, Reintgen himself got behind the microphone, and, midway through the program, speaking in his heavily accented English, assured the pilot's wife that her husband was alive and well, and wished her a safe and successful childbirth.

As he expected, it sparked the fury of many higher-ups, and Reintgen was forced to endure several days of angry, red-in-the-face phone calls and hysterical, accusatory telegrams. But he never regretted what he did that day, and was always happy to hear of the calm his broadcasts brought to the chaotic battlefields. He had heard from General Fritz Bayerlein, one of the highest-ranking men in Germany's Afrika Korps, that every night at three minutes to ten, as "Lili Marlene" came on the radio in the desert, the fighting men on both sides of the trenches would hold their fire and crane their necks to listen.

Werner Hoffmeister, a soldier in North Africa, recalled, forty years after first hearing "Lili Marlene," the effect of these nocturnal, musical cease-fires: "The front lines were very close to one another," he said. "In the evening, one could finally get out of the trenches, to stretch out. Then our radio, our connection to home, went into action. And the highlight of every night was the show by Radio Belgrade. And when we sat around in a circle during the evening, everybody listening quietly, there suddenly came from the other side, about eighty meters away, a noise somewhere and we could hear a voice: 'Comrades, louder, please!' It was the English, and the song had succeeded with them too. This way we had a real cease-fire, because during those times not a single shot fell and even right afterwards it was quiet."

Reintgen was thrilled. He was a patriotic German, sure, but gained a greater reward knowing that his station was no longer a mere instrument of Nazi terror and propaganda. Through the services of "Lili Marlene," for three minutes each night, it was an oasis of calm in the midst of a world at war. For the fighting men, it was certainly a blessing; to their political masters, it had become a threat.

VI

"A Small Piece of Home"

BY THE FALL of 1941, Berlin was a depleted city. Hitler's invasions had steadily drained the capital of its manpower, and the German people struggled with constant shortages of even the most basic goods. The lack of nutritious food in Berlin was causing its residents' teeth to dissolve, according to a local dentist, "like sugar cubes in water." With its cabarets tamed long ago, the main draw of the Kurfürstendamm was now the revolting "razzle-dazzle" cocktail mixed from grenadine and whatever cheap alcohol could be sourced from the city's nearly empty stores, while on the world-famous Unter den Linden, the lack of customers and upkeep had transformed the once-prosperous and elegant sidewalks into a streetscape of shuttered businesses.

Howard K. Smith, an American journalist working in the city before the United States had declared war on Germany, frequented the formerly ornate cafés of the capital. He noted that at one of his old haunts "the service . . . is not what it used to be, mainly because there are only three waiters and all are over seventy. They had been retired but, when the young men were called up in June, they had to be called back to work ten hours a day, lumbago or no lumbago. . . . Café Schoen across the street has no troubles about maintaining front. A couple of British fire-bombs destroyed the upper floors of the building and scaffolding was set up all around it to repair it."

Near those crumbling buildings on the tired Unter den Linden, Rudolph Schnëider, then eighteen years old and kitted out in his newly issued army uniform, walked one evening in search of a comfortable, undamaged café. Hailing from a small farming village in rural Germany, Schneider lacked Smith's worldly-wise knowledge of the city's restaurants but was still eager to find a pleasant place to grab a coffee and spend a few hours with some interesting company.

Since Schneider knew he wouldn't be staying in town for very long, he was hoping to get the most out of his short time in the capital. Sent to Berlin after basic training in Dresden, he was merely in transit, awaiting his transfer to North Africa, where he would be serving as a driver for the personal battle group of Lieutenant-General Erwin Rommel. By then, Rommel's Afrika Korps had already shored up the collapsing Italian forces in Libya, repelled the advancing Allies, and were now, in a stunning reversal of fortune, looking to seize the British headquarters in Cairo. It was better to serve there in the African desert than in Russia, so the conventional wisdom went. As Schneider cradled his hot drink in his hands, surrounded by friendly faces in a cozy establishment not far from the heroic Brandenburg Gate, he could reassure himself that, whatever the future had in store, in a few weeks' time at least he wouldn't be freezing on some desolate eastern steppe.

Soon, an isolated melody in the endless stream of news and music that was broadcast over the café's tinny *Volksempfänger*, or people's receiver—an inexpensive radio that Goebbels encouraged all German households and establishments to own—caught the attention of the crowd. People stopped their conversations mid-sentence to listen to "Lili Marlene." It was here that Schneider, for the first time, heard the song—broadcast, as it was, without lyrics. But Schneider didn't lack for words very long, for soon all of his fellow patrons put down their drinks and collectively sang the lyrics that would come to mean so much to Schneider over the course of many nights in the lonely, expansive desert:

Underneath the lantern
By the barrack's gate
Darling, I remember
The way you used to wait . . .

The café crowd sang the memorized words with joy, something that, at that time, was enough to be considered a not-so-subtle act of subversion. It was no secret that Goebbels, who had obsessively controlled every aspect of German culture, despised "Lili Marlene." "A dance of death lingers between its bars," he wrote, and the propaganda minister so accustomed to stage-managing every Nazi invasion with a soundtrack full of appropriate pomp and suitable tunes was apoplectic at this sentimental love song that was lulling Germany's vaunted Aryan warriors to sleep each night on the battlefields. Although no less a pop music expert than Hitler himself had expressed his admiration for "Lili Marlene," Goebbels's mind was set almost from the start on suppressing it wherever he could. He ordered the destruction of Lale Andersen's original recording matrix and banned Hans Leip's tender words from German airwaves. In a nod to the song's popularity with the masses, though, and unwilling to cause a public upset, Goebbels decided that the tune, composed by Bomber Schultze, could stay:

thus "Lili Marlene," on civilian radio still existed, but only in its instrumental form.

Goebbels also tried, but failed, to silence "Lili Marlene" on the military's radio stations as well. He was stopped by a number of Hitler's generals, Rommel included, who recognized the special place the song had in the hearts of their soldiers. The military brass angrily resisted Goebbels's attempts to pry the fighting men from their beloved Lili, and, relying on the great German reverence for regulations and rules, pointed out to Goebbels that Radio Belgrade was an army station active on foreign soil and was, therefore, immune from civilian restrictions imposed in Germany proper. "Lili Marlene" may be hounded at home, they declared, but she would remain unmolested under their command in Yugoslavia.

Occasionally, Goebbels would lose patience with such niggling technicalities and send off testy démarches to Radio Belgrade's liaison officer demanding the station stop playing the song, but the officials in army broadcasting would invariably ignore, brush aside, or otherwise conveniently misplace the propaganda minister's requests. Paying no heed to petty infighting, however, and though they could not hear the complete version of "Lili Marlene" as it came across the small speaker of the *Volksempfänger* that evening, the customers of the small Berlin café were still nevertheless able to illustrate for Rudolph Schneider the compelling power of the song's sweet, sad poetry as he heard them sing its words, for that first time, over his cup of coffee.

By November 1941, Schneider's café days were coming to a close. After spending the previous few weeks exploring the capital, he was eventually off to North Africa. Schneider's arrival in the desert coincided with the inauguration of the Allies' Operation Crusader, a bold plan designed to roll the Afrika Korps out of the green oases of Cyrenaica in Libya and disrupt the planned

German and Italian advance toward British-held Egypt before it could even begin. Operation Crusader relied heavily on the newly formed English Eighth Army, a melting pot of a unit that counted among its ranks soldiers from all corners of the English-speaking world, from Australia, India, South Africa, and elsewhere. This mélange of fighting men pieced together from across the globe, which would later go down in history as one of the most illustrious units of the war, was to have its first go at combat as a single force in pursuit of Operation Crusader's objectives.

For the first two days of the battle, it appeared that the Allies held all of the cards. As the Eighth Army's tanks slipped across the Wire—a sinewy, rusting line of Italian metal fencing that marked the border between Allied Egypt and Axis Libya—the commanders of the Afrika Korps seemed to be unsure as to what was barreling toward them. Rommel and his deputies knew of enemy reconnaissance along the front lines, but, so the story went, it was only when they managed to catch a BBC evening news broadcast from London announcing the launch of a massive campaign in the desert involving 75,000 Allied soldiers that they began to grasp the magnitude of the situation facing them.

Although the Axis forces had been initially hoodwinked by the hodgepodge Eighth Army, once Rommel and his deputies realized what they were up against, they were able to orchestrate a spirited defense and soon ordered their panzers into a counterattack. In time, the Afrika Korps regained the initiative and successfully forced the Eighth Army back over the Wire. Major Robert Crisp, a South African tank officer who was among the Eighth Army soldiers retreating during the reversal, coped with the confusion and disarray of the days' events by clinging to whatever snippets of gentler times and relief he could find amid the rapidly changing situation. Even after the sun had set, he and his exhausted comrades were forced to slog on in their drive toward safer, more secure shelter as they guided their reliable American-made Stuart tanks across the empty desert:

> Deluges of sand and dust kicked up by tracks flooded into turrets, splashing on the inert, shapeless forms of gunner and operator already in a realm of unconsciousness that could never be called sleep, showering on the tank commander, trying by reassuring chatter over the inter-com to keep his driver awake. ... Most of us allayed the weariness and the discomfort of those night marches by tuning into the BBC or that Middle European station which, night after night, played "Lili Marlene" for the benefit of the Afrika Korps and the tear-jerking nostalgia of the Eighth Army. So the night and the snatched sleep and the unwilling dawn.

By the time dawn broke on November 24, 1941, it was clear that the Eighth Army's first great effort was a mess. After renewed fighting simmered down in early 1942, an ominous quiet settled across the North African front as the Axis forces prepared to continue their offensive. Meanwhile, the Allies scrambled to plan for Rommel's seemingly unstoppable drive toward Cairo, the Suez Canal, the oil fields of the Middle East, and the gates of the Soviet Union beyond.

From the Allies' point of view, things were looking grim. Most of Europe was now solidly under Nazi control, and while Hitler's hordes had not been able to snatch Moscow from the Soviet Union, they were busily preparing to collide with the Red Army at Stalingrad. Out in Asia, the British forces were in full retreat in Burma and had already surrendered Malaysia and Singapore to Japan. The United States, drawn unwittingly into the war by the surprise Japanese attack on Pearl Harbor, had yet to achieve a secure footing in the Pacific, and the outcome of the fight in that distant sea was far from certain. For the Allied soldiers stationed around the globe in the spring of 1942, thoughts of an eventual victory were hard to justify and worries were both common and legitimate.

In North Africa in particular, things were moving from bad to worse. The Afrika Korps had broken free from Gazala and had seized the important coastal city of Tobruk. The city, which had withstood an eight-month siege the year before, fell to Rommel after a one-day siege on June 21 and, in a single stroke, 33,000 Allied soldiers were taken prisoner. Winston Churchill, floored by the loss of Tobruk and worried about the effect the city's capture would have on the spirit of the Allied soldiers serving around the world, glumly wrote that "defeat is one thing, disgrace is another." Needless to say, Hitler was thrilled with the performance of his generals, and Rommel, as he listened to the evening news on his radio after the day's conquest, was surprised to hear that he had been promoted to the rank of field marshal for his efforts.

For the common soldiers, though, it was a broadcast of a different sort that soothed them in the nighttime. Exhausted from combat and marching, caked with sand and burnt by the sun, the soldiers of the Afrika Korps gathered to listen, as they did whenever they could, to Radio Belgrade and their haunting "Lili Marlene." The familiar song was a gateway through which they could return to the sweetness of their faraway homes and loosen the war's rigid grip on their minds, if even for a few minutes. A German soldier wrote in a letter:

> We lay a few kilometers in front of Tobruk. Each day we go out in our tanks. In the evenings we are tired and weary and we are laboring under thirst. We want once more to wash up, and have something to see besides sand, horizon and blue heaven. Then rings out on the radio a woman's voice and she

sings of the young sentry and his girl that waits for him under the lantern. We listen to the song not for the first time; we listen to it often. This song has a real value—we laugh as though the radio was a small piece of home. It is always the same. Each evening, take us, "Lili Marlene."

In a different corner of that same vast landscape, Harry Hudson and a group of his friends from the Eighth Army were tuned to Radio Belgrade just like their opponents farther west in the desert. Unlike the victorious Germans, though, Hudson and his platoon from the Royal Army Service Corps, far from enjoying the day's spoils, were instead beating a hasty retreat to a more defensible position in a state of controlled chaos, and, as night fell, waited alongside their thirty dust-caked Chevrolet trucks. The vehicles, parked in pairs along a line that stretched the length of thirty football fields, looked, from the starlit sky, like the exposed spine of some enormous, ancient beast. It was all part of a massive supply convoy that, during the day, would be racing toward the new English line, bringing fuel and arms to the displaced Allied fighting men fortifying their position on a defensive line anchored by the railway station of El Alamein near the Mediterranean coast and the impassable Qattara Depression thirty-five miles to the south.

Some of the heavily laden trucks had backs that were covered by canvas tarps; others, looking more rakish, had beds that were left open and exposed to the elements. A few even sported large, cumbersome radios that were powerful enough to pick up the faint signals beamed out of the European stations. Naturally, these were the more popular trucks in the desert, and it was around one of them that Hudson and his friends gathered while one of the men clamped jubilee clips to the truck's battery and used the vehicle's electricity to power up the radio.

Huddling together for warmth and covered with as many blankets, overcoats, and caps as they could find, the men ignored the stench of sweat and petrol, their fatigue, and the creeping cold. They waited in a darkness perforated by the amber tips of lit cigarettes and bathed in the ethereal green glow of the radio dial. They spoke of home, played cards, and waited until 9:57, when they could once again reunite with Lili Marlene.

For Hudson, the song's importance came not from its words, sung in a language he did not understand, but rather from the escape the melody brought him. Exhausted Allied soldiers throughout the desert in range of radios were humming along with Lale Andersen's lilting voice and, if they found themselves really needing lyrics to express their anxiety, fears, or fatigue, they simply invented their own to fit the easy tune. An unknown airman in the desert, trying his hand as a lyricist, expressed his frustration with the lackluster results of the English campaign in North Africa in one such version:

There is a bomber squadron, way up in the blue
They're off to bomb Benghazi, 'cos there's nothing else to do
They fly all day, they fly all night
The pale moonlight reveals their plight
They're going to bomb Benghazi, they're going to bomb BG

To be sure, while the men of the Eighth Army had entertainment options in the North African desert other than Radio Belgrade, there was something different—deeper—about "Lili Marlene." It was a folk song—Schultze even admitted as much— and, true to the type, had the universal appeal of all good provincial melodies. For men like Hudson, used to English landscapes freckled with silver birches and red-berried Rowan trees, life in the strange, sandy deserts of Egypt found its perfect companion in the equally foreign and faraway sound of "Lili Marlene."

Luckily for Hudson and the other Allied soldiers, if they weren't able to catch Radio Belgrade's evening signal, they could still try to hear "Lili Marlene" the next day on one of the many propaganda marathons that the American-born radio host Axis Sally broadcast their way from deep within Hitler's Reich. During her shows, Axis Sally—née Mildred Elizabeth Sisk of Portland, Maine—made wild claims of Churchill's incompetence and alluded to the sneaky Yanks who were no doubt sleeping with the soldiers' wives back in England. In between anti-Semitic outbursts, Axis Sally nevertheless occasionally serenaded the soldiers with "Lili Marlene" and, for that, briefly, her perfidy could be forgiven.

In London, however, "Lili Marlene" was bringing out emotions of a different sort. Concerned citizens from across the British Isles had been writing letters to the BBC demanding to know why their brave soldiers losing ground in the desert were listening to a Nazi tune and not something homegrown. Even the erstwhile broadcasting service's man in Cairo dispatched a bitter missive to his higher-ups, complaining that British soldiers were failing to tune in to his station. "Dissatisfaction with BBC programmes among the troops is practically universal and the number and bitterness of their complaints is a serious matter," he wrote. "Practically all our troops in the Middle East habitually listen to Axis radio in preference to the BBC. This is partly because such stations as Belgrade are better heard here than our own short waves. But men repeatedly tune in to the BBC then switch over to the Germans in disgust." The reason, he continued, was the British radio's insistence on constant commentary: "If they tune in to a BBC music programme they know they won't get more than a few minutes without someone starting talking or a chat programme taking over." His recommendation, therefore, was simple. "Cut the talk," he wrote bluntly. "Cut all the explanations and excuses. Give us straight music. . . ."

Although he did not mention "Lili Marlene" by name, it was clear to everyone that it was primarily the Allied attraction to that German tune that drove listeners away from the BBC and toward the seductive embrace of Radio Belgrade. It was a contentious issue, and one that was taken seriously by British officialdom. The question of "Lili Marlene" was raised at both the War and Home offices, which had earlier established the Dance Music Policy Committee to deal with just such an issue.

Morris Gilbert, a BBC executive, wrote in an internal memo that "one school of policy makers held that the song should be resolutely barred, on the score that it could not help but attract and seduce and enervate the war effort. Anything so warm, so simple, so appealing could not but arouse sympathy and kindred softer feelings towards its German creators."

If banning "Lili Marlene" was going to be the only way to undo the damage caused by the tune to sensitive English ears, Britain's leaders realized that the Allies would have to create a supersong of their own, one that captured something of Schultze's infectious, singsong melody and Andersen's sensuous intonations in order to forestall an open revolt from the soldiers in the field. Wouldn't it be easier, opposing voices suggested, to simply record an English version of "Lili Marlene," play it to the men often, and, over time, dilute the Nazi connotations of the song?

Fortunately for the Allied soldiers, this simpler and far less provocative course of action won out. Tommie Connor, a British songwriter who was responsible for such hits as "I Saw Mommy Kissing Santa Claus" and "It's My Mother's Birthday Today," translated Hans Leip's poem into English. He managed to retain the original lyrical structure and made sure that the new words fit Schultze's familiar tune. At the suggestion of none other than Winston Churchill, the young British sweetheart Anne Shelton, only fourteen at the time, was chosen to sing the reworked song.

By 1944, the BBC had a bona fide hit on its hands. By the end of that year, the Allied soldiers could at last listen to a de-Nazified "Lili Marlene" on their radios, unencumbered by either the noxious slander of Axis Sally or the strange gibberish of foreign-tongued Radio Belgrade. One of Connor's verses went as follows:

> *Orders came for sailing*
> *Somewhere over there*
> *All confined to barracks*
> *Was more than I could bear*
> *I knew you were waiting in the street*
> *I heard your feet, but could not meet*
> *My Lili of the lamplight*
> *My own Lili Marlene.*

Eventually, American and English stars such as Marlene Dietrich and Vera Lynn would go on to record their own versions of "Lili Marlene." Dietrich, of course, had the power and Hollywood pedigree to ensure that her interpretation would eventually surpass all the others in popularity.

Still, as the war raged in North Africa, Rudolph Schneider was by himself, cruising through the sands in an open-topped staff car across the desert. His happy days in Berlin's cafés now behind him, Schneider spent many long hours guiding his vehicle across the lonely landscape, leaving hundreds of miles worth of neat, shallow tracks in his wake. While he ferried messages from one senior officer to another, Schneider's days were filled with hurried driving assignments followed by hours spent parked under whatever shade he could find. It was a solitary existence, but as he guided his dusty car back to headquarters, surrounded by thousands of empty acres, he thought nothing of his isolation.

Running errands over hundreds of miles of desolate terrain, Rudolph Schneider listened to "Lili Marlene" on his staff car's radio. Unlike Hudson and his English friends, who for a long time could only appreciate the song's melody, Schneider had been aware of the song's lyrics and deeper truths for almost a year now. As the singer's hollow voice iterated verse after verse, he sank in his seat, the sweet words stifling his breath almost every time he heard them:

From my quiet existence
And from this earthly pale
Like a dream you free me
With your lips so hale

Schneider heard those words and imagined himself as the soldier and his long-lost sweetheart as Lili. He, too, longed for the reunion with his beloved. He thought often of her patient vigil at home and began to cry.

Here, he wasn't alone: At other times, when he did manage to find himself at headquarters with fellow soldiers at 9:57 P.M., they would lay their weary backs on the icy sand and listen, in silence, to the radio. Soon after "Lili Marlene" began to play, the sobbing would begin. The collective crying always amazed Schneider: Here were men who had heard the screams of comrades being burned alive in blazing tanks, who had seen friends crushed by these machines or slain by bullets, who had the taste of sand and blood constantly in their mouths, all without betraying a hint of emotion. But when the song came on, the men—young conscripts, husbands, grown men with children—wept. This happened often. Here, he thought, was the true power of "Lili Marlene."

Something else was weighing on Schneider's mind. At the German encampments, where meetings were held and orders were sent in advance of the confident Axis assault on the crumbling Eighth Army's Alamein line, the recent entry of the United States into the fight against Germany kept tugging at Schneider's thoughts. A farmer by training, Schneider recalled learning of America's vast agricultural sector, with its advanced wheat-threshers, mechanical combines, and plentiful beehives. How could Germany, more or less alone in the world, survive against forces backed by a country of such farming prowess?

While other soldiers of the Afrika Korps thought of the war in terms of dive-bombers and armored columns, it was only natural for Schneider to see it as some enormous contest of agricultural output. Schneider had always imagined a future for himself in farming and had attended a professional school to learn the staples of the trade. As a teenager enamored by the romantic allure of Africa, he became interested in tropical and subtropical agriculture. Inspired by the Englishmen who sought to bring the latest technologies to the farthest reaches of their empire, he sought to bring the soil of the continent to life. He contacted an elderly British woman, a remnant of the dying colonial project, and obtained a position as a farmhand on her East African estate. He had hoped that his girl back home, a farmer herself, would be tempted by his African plan and convinced to leave Germany and join him in his grand adventure.

The war, of course, derailed Schneider's fantasy. Like all young, able-bodied German men, Rudolph was soon drafted and sent out for service not on some whitewashed Victorian farm but rather to a cruel, devastating war. And so he found himself fighting in the Africa of his dreams, wondering if Germany had blundered into a war of its choosing, unaware of the strength of the Allies, pitted only against the clock.

VII

"Can the Wind Explain Why It Becomes a Storm?"

AT FIRST, the stratospheric popularity of "Lili Marlene" had little effect on Lale Andersen. Still traveling throughout Germany and entertaining soldiers in Hitler's ever-expanding empire, she hoped that a rush of enthusiasm from her admirers in the military might catapult her to stardom and yet was content, in the meantime, with a life that offered her little glory but no great hassles. She was well fed, she often told herself, and there was a roof over her head, a safe shelter for her children and a steady source of income to keep her family afloat. With Berlin, and much of the rest of Germany, suffering the wrath of British bombers, such rudimentary staples were far from guaranteed, and every week letters would arrive from friends back home, letters that grew more terse and more bleak as supplies began to run low and as familiar buildings were reduced to rubble. Sheltered from the devastation, spending her days in well-manicured army bases in relatively unscathed landscapes, she was slowly coming to terms with seeing her girlhood dreams of being a famous artist dissolve in a haze of comfort.

She was growing older, she realized, and her striking looks, that swirling sensuality that captivated men when she was in her twenties, were slowly hardening. They had been reshaped by the sun and the wind and the passing time into a mask of middle-aged respectability, perfectly pleasant to look at but in no way truly stirring. Thus, she traveled from base to base, singing the same repertoire and spending most of her free time trying her best not to think about the war.

Slowly, however, she began noticing a strange phenomenon. It started out small: one time, in a concert in Denmark, she plowed through her usual program, with "Lili Marlene" being the fifth or sixth song of the evening. When the song's first notes filled the tiny hall, the two or three hundred soldiers present started clapping. The same thing happened a few days later, and by the following week soldiers were approaching her after the show, calling her Lili and asking for her autograph. As 1941 drew to an end, and Lale left Denmark for a short tour of Italy, the true extent of the song's immense popularity struck her with great force. Before, she had walked around army bases undisturbed, free to spend her days as she pleased. She was now met by throngs of curious men, accompanied by whistles and cheers—to put it simply, adored. Hardly would she arrive at a new destination than a bag of fan mail would await her response, demanding her attention and tickling her ego. Most profound of all was her impromptu name change: No one called her Lale anymore, often not even the officers who introduced her before her concerts. To her uniformed fans, to the civilians who recognized her in the streets, to the world, she was Lili Marlene.

On the surface, being rechristened as Lili should have made little difference in Andersen's life. Her entire career, it seemed, was an unbroken chain of assumed identities, from the boyish sailor getup of her cabaret years to her more recent incarnation as a faux-

Scandinavian Viking maiden. But all of these were based on some real aspect of her personality, tied, however remotely, to who Andersen was as a real human being. As Lili, she felt fictional. The popular song had turned her into every soldier's sweetheart, omnipresent and invisible at the same time. She was a star, that much was true, but in the eyes of her audience she now noticed a different gleam: they weren't so much admiring her as thinking of their own girlfriends and wives left behind at home, lost in personal reveries and dreaming of the real-life darlings, the memory of whom her song so powerfully evoked. She herself was just a conduit. She, her song, were vessels for the men's crippling loneliness. She was no Dietrich, no grand persona admired for its own inimitable radiance. She was a stand-in, a cutout, a holding place, known not by her real name but as an imaginary girl in a sad, sentimental song.

And yet, here she was, famous, and for a while that was the sole matter on which her thoughts rested. Having pondered stardom since an early age, when it finally crawled on her doorstep, she greeted it with a natural ease. At a press conference in Rome, surrounded by tens of journalists and dozens of photographers, her cheekbones gleaming in the incandescent fury of flash bulbs and her face framed by microphones, she treated her sudden fame as if it were a mere meteorological matter, as inexplicable, transcendent, and unpredictable as the elements. "Can the wind," she smiled mysteriously at her admirers, "explain why it becomes a storm?"

Such answers made her popularity grow even further. There was no better temperament for the tumultuous war years than Andersen's easygoing way, a soothing persona that, despite being so closely associated with the war's quintessential song, seemed impervious to the real ravages and violence that came with combat. In pictures from these days, late 1941 or early 1942, Andersen is seldom captured without an ornate hat, a luxurious coat, often draped in fur, and a smart, well-cut dress. The same papers that had, just a few months earlier, given her modest attention or none at all and had referred to her as Danish were now celebrating her, on their front pages, as the Reich's newest star. Reviewing a concert in Strasbourg in February 1942, a local paper described Andersen in fairy-tale terms: "She steps into the room in bewitching dresses," reads the article, "developing an infinite beauty in her motion, and sings songs with a disarming and dignified loveliness. . . . But it was not only her singing that was captivating, it was above all her charm and her internal beauty." The German papers were not alone in their praise. In Denmark, the press did its best to remind the population of Andersen's supposed local origins. In Italy, the papers each struggled to find grander superlatives with which to describe her. One of them, *La Stampa*, outdid all the others when it invited Andersen to visit its Turin newsroom. The next day, the paper printed a photo of Andersen reading a copy of the newspaper on its front page, with a typically hyperbolic caption: "We are proud to be the first Italian daily to bring to the acquaintance of the reading public the legendary vicissitude of the girl with the lantern, the fortunate artistic career of Lale Andersen." While *La Stampa* was hardly the first outlet to report on Andersen and her success, its coverage prompted an even greater hunger for the voice of "Lili Marlene." One popular northern Italian paper captured this frenzied spirit when it published, in March of 1942, an article about her that took up most of its front page, entitled simply "With You, Lili Marlene." The first paragraph, however, made it clear that it was Andersen, not the song's heroine, who was the article's true focus, promising its readers an incredible story of a young singer's rise from an "ill-fated debut to celebrity."

Returning to Germany late in 1941, Andersen was determined to enjoy the spoils of her success to the fullest. Having spent her

entire adult life wandering, from one apartment to the next, shuf-
fling from this country to that, her first step was to purchase an
apartment, a permanent address, she hoped, in which to see out
the remainder of the war in relative safety and comfort. Now that
she was in demand, with concert halls across Europe extending
invitations for gala performances, she was, for the first time ever,
in a position to allow herself the luxury of which she had only
dreamed. She remembered her first years in Berlin, remembered
running up and down the Kurfürstendamm, that magnificent avenue with its gilded storefronts and elegant cafés, where dashing
men and wealthy women spent hours of idle pleasure. Back then,
she was lucky if anyone asked her to perform at any of the avenue's clubs. Now, however, she was in a position to afford an apartment there. It mattered to her not at all that the Kurfürstendamm
was hardly the glamorous address it had once been; that its patrons
and merchants, a large part of whom were Jewish, were long gone;
that its cabarets and clubs were oppressed to the point of annihilation by the Nazi Culture Chamber. To Andersen, the Kurfürstendamm was still where one lived after hitting it big, and it was on
the second floor of number 92 Kurfürstendamm that she bought
a small flat. In January 24, 1942, she jotted triumphantly in her
diary: "I shine with all my heart and body. My goal for years, that
of standing in front of an audience that gives away its evening just
to listen to my little songs, has been fulfilled. Partly through con-
sistent hard work, party because of you, 'Lili Marlene.'"

The first four months of 1942 consisted largely of a dizzying
stream of sold-out performances across Germany. As had been the
case at every stage of her career, Andersen's change of status was
followed by a new wardrobe. The woman who had once dressed
in androgynous sailors' uniforms, and then put on simple peasant
dresses, was now being draped in heavenly evening gowns. In
March 1942, she was headlining a series of concerts at the Scala,
Berlin's most prestigious venue in those years, together with inter-

national stars that included the sleek-haired Bianco, the King of Tango. She took the stage in a long-sleeved white dress with a flowing, richly ornamented train. Her narrow waist was highlighted by the elegant gown's slender contours.

Glamorous acts like Andersen's, however, couldn't be fully accommodated by Germany's limited popular music scene. After years of dogged assaults by the Culture Chamber, there was little left of German stage culture to amuse the Reich's show-going public save for a smattering of amusement halls where curiosity acts, crass comedians, and singers all delivered innocuous, government-approved lines. Andersen found that she had outgrown that stultifying, two-bit environment and soon sought out bigger opportunities in the movies. The cinema, after all, was Goebbels's favorite medium and richly supported by the Nazi apparatus. In April 1942, ten years after her earlier film career had died with a whimper when she, an unknown hopeful, yelled at a director for abusing an elderly extra, Andersen returned to the Ufa lot and this time entered the studio gates a major star. She sang a song in the movie *G.P.U.*, a standard work of propaganda besmirching the Russians. Complete with scene after scene of sweaty Soviet agents torturing young, innocent, and perfectly coiffed German maidens, the film became a hit largely due to Andersen's participation.

But fame and fortune in Nazi Germany could never remain apolitical for long. The humorless bureaucrats who ran the Culture Chamber watched Andersen's star rise with trepidation. The blond chanteuse, they realized, possessed a real threat to their tightly controlled propaganda machinery, a threat rendered all the more powerful by its inadvertent nature. It was this threat that Goebbels had in mind in the fall of 1941 when he ordered the original recording of "Lili Marlene" destroyed and prohibited German civilian radio stations from broadcasting the song in anything but its instrumental form. After all, what was the point of mandating ownership of a government-issued radio receiver if the most popular song on the airwaves was some sentimental tune that did not possess the savage virility of a good military march? What good was propaganda if all people cared about was the story of a young woman waiting underneath the lamplight for her beau to return home from the war?

Lale Andersen, though, the singer of "Lili Marlene," posed a further challenge to Goebbels. The song, a recording, could be controlled, but its singer, ever so popular, was a different matter altogether. A former bohemian intellectual, the lover of celebrated and influential Jews, sophisticated and cosmopolitan, Andersen was very far from the Nazi ideal of the dutiful woman faithful only to Führer and Fatherland. Even though she had not displayed any subversive tendencies and cared more about gowns and pearls than politics, Goebbels's cultural cosmos could not withstand the presence of a bright star less than entirely faithful to the party. Andersen, it was decided, had to be brought into the fold and made to avow her unequivocal loyalty to Nazi dogma.

Quite naturally, this job of ideological hand-wringing fell into the eager lap of Hans Hinkel. There was precious little the Culture Chamber boss enjoyed as much as he did these campaigns of intimidation, especially when the target was an attractive young woman likely to resort to her sexual charms in order to spare herself the high official's wrath. Just as he had tormented Trude Hesterberg in 1933, feeding off the malicious gossip of the famous actress's maid, Hinkel, a plain-looking man with a bulbous face and a receding hairline, saw humiliation as the sharpest arrow in his quiver. Silencing an enemy, this failed journalist realized early on in his career as a Nazi cultural chieftain, was seldom enough, as disgruntled foes were all the more likely to seek revenge. The most effective way, therefore, was a complete annihilation of the subject's self-respect. When one loses one's dignity, he realized, the blow dealt is far harsher than even the most draconian of external measures.

A naturally prurient man, Hinkel was particularly obsessed with all matters sexual and made sure that his harassments had more than a whiff of the pornographic about them. In 1940, for example, Hinkel targeted popular movie star Joachim Gottschalk—often referred to as the German Clark Gable—for the unforgivable sin of being married to a Jewish woman, theater actress Meta Wolff. It would have been quite enough for a high-ranking official such as Hinkel to write curt letters forbidding theater and film directors from working with Gottschalk; that, indeed, was the way such affairs were ordinarily handled, with brief edicts effectively ending the career of whomever was deemed unpalatable to the regime. But Hinkel had his own touch. Gottschalk, he wrote in his letters, has become enslaved by his Jewish whore, entranced by her omnivorous sexuality. It was a classic Nazi stereotype, that of the Jewish woman as seductress. Hinkel relished using it, portraying Wolff as a promiscuous manipulator and her husband as an emasculated male. Mercilessly persecuted by the regime, unable to work, and threatened with deportation to a concentration camp, the couple and their young boy committed suicide in November 1941.

But whereas Gottschalk was a man, and could therefore only be insulted and demeaned, young women could be subdued in other, far more debasing ways. Forcing a woman into intercourse was not only a matter of pleasure for Hinkel, it was also policy. A woman who agreed to sleep with him against her will, he learned early on in his career, was often disarmed of her pride and her will to resist. Such demonic insights made Hinkel a ruthlessly effective censor, and his rise up the ranks was meteoric.

Installed at the head of the Culture Chamber, he had lost little time in asserting his position. Although he and his fellow Nazis professed to revile the Kurfürstendamm, turning the avenue into a symbol of the corrupt, nihilistic, and wayward Weimar Republic, it was precisely there that Hinkel had chosen to place his headquarters. A few blocks away from Lale Andersen's new apartment, it occupied the entire second floor of a stately neoclassical building. As was de rigueur with the Nazi elite, he, too, decorated his office with an enormous wooden desk, a couple of chairs, and not much more, using the vast, empty space as a means of intimidation.

Seated in his office one afternoon, Hinkel devised an elegant solution to the problem of Lale Andersen, a conundrum that had been preoccupying Goebbels for months. Censoring the singer, Hinkel thought, would only increase her cachet. Even in tightly controlled Nazi Germany, there was still plenty of room for unscripted, spontaneous eruptions of popular sentiments. He had learned that lesson the hard way with Gottschalk: when the actor and his family took their own lives, Hinkel himself instructed the media to remain silent on the matter. Still, rumors spread at great speed. Within a day of Gottschalk's funeral, throngs of ordinary Germans across the nation created impromptu memorials for their fallen idol. Continuing to ban Andersen's voice from the German airwaves, Hinkel feared, would have a similar effect, increasing her popularity even further and fashioning her as a folk heroine. The solution, therefore, was to embrace Andersen tightly, to surround her with the party's best and most loyal, to secure her faithfulness to the Culture Chamber and the ideas it represented. To do that, Hinkel understood, Andersen would have to be confined to an enclosed environment that he himself could supervise. Andersen, he decided, would go on tour.

Andersen's tour, beginning early in April 1942, displayed all of Hinkel's masterstrokes. It was organized under the auspices of a new organization, the Berlin Artists' Tour, designed to give participants the false feeling that they were invited by an independent association instead of controlled by the Culture Chamber. Again and again, Hinkel insisted that all official letters sent in the matter mark that the tour was open only to "elite artists," an exclusive and prestigious club outside of the Chamber's propaganda performers. And elite artists they were: alongside Andersen, Hinkel invited a handful of Germany's most adored entertainers, including such stars of stage and screen as Marika Rökk, Grethe Weiser, Franz Grothe, and Emmi Leisner. Individually, of course, each of these artists enjoyed all the perks of popularity, wielding much power and enjoying great influence. When put together, Hinkel hoped, they would cancel each other out. Separated from their friends and followers, trapped in a bus for many weeks, surrounded by other famous people, they would have little or no opportunity to nurture any dissidence. As a final touch, Hinkel secured a spacious and luxurious bus; his trapped songbirds would have a gilded cage.

And yet, receiving the invitation to go on tour, Andersen was thrilled. She suspected little of Hinkel's ulterior motives. She was well aware, of course, that German radio was forbidden from broadcasting her voice singing her signature song, but attributed it all to some sort of largely harmless wartime paranoia. And a tour would likely take her back to her beloved military bases, where she could sing for soldiers, the audience she most enjoyed. It wasn't just that she was a German patriot, nor only that she was supporting her country in a time of war, but rather that she had always found something about soldiers—a certain eagerness, cheerful gratitude, and warm candor—that made her cherish each performance in front of uniformed men. These, to her, were the true Germans, the young men who clapped uproariously as she took the stage, who choked up as soon as they heard the bugle call that started off her famous song, who came up to her after the concert and awkwardly told her about a sweetheart left back home, a sweetheart that was almost close enough to kiss whenever "Lili Marlene" played on the radio. These were the true Germans, not the mirthless, ruthless, dull party officials brimming with self-importance who filled Berlin. And these were the men to whom she was always happy to return.

Finally, there was a more pressing matter: hunger. Faced with massive, labor-intensive, war-related industries, millions of war prisoners, hundreds of thousands of German nationals incorporated from the occupied countries, and continuous British bombings, Germany soon found itself with a chronically empty stomach. The elements colluded in this shortage: inclement weather was responsible for a major potato shortage. Always efficient, Nazi officials calculated that by peeling a potato one wastes up to 15 percent of the foodstuff—30 percent if the peeling is done by a machine—and banned the peeling of potatoes altogether by late 1941. In February 1942, a new edict ordered Berlin's restaurants to remain closed except for a few hours a day, a few days a week, and, best of all, to shut down whenever possible. In March, with the situation deteriorating, a new food-rationing system was introduced. Bread allowances, the government announced on March 19, will be reduced from 5 pounds a week to 4 pounds and 6 ounces; fats from 9.5 to 7.5 ounces; and meat from 14 ounces to 10.5 ounces. By April, even that meager allowance was tough to come by, particularly in a densely populated urban center like Berlin. A tour, Andersen thought, would surely entail decent meals, as army bases were traditionally considerably better stocked than even the most bountiful civilian stores. Happily, then, she showed up at the pickup spot on the appointed day and got on the bus.

The tour's main direction was east, to the so-called German protectorates in Poland and Czechoslovakia. The first few days were pleasant. Most of her friends having fled Germany after the rise of the Nazis, and she too busy touring to cultivate any new acquaintances, Andersen was thrilled to have the leisure and opportunity to meet new, like-minded people. She especially befriended Grethe Weiser and Emmi Leisner, and delighted in their conversation. Their companionship was all-the-more welcome given the fact that Hinkel's tour, as they soon found out, was intended not for the ordinary grunts, Andersen's beloved audience, but for the SS, the Nazi party's elite unit. Chosen solely on the basis of fanatical adherence to the party's principles, and entrusted with the most murderous of duties, the SS men, Andersen soon discovered, were a chilling bunch; they were cold and conceited, many of them awkward youths who would have been sentenced to a life of quiet, impotent rage had the Nazis' new world order not entrusted them with great power. They therefore perceived of themselves, to a large extent, as being exempt of displaying civility, which caused the artists on the bus great anxiety.

But artists, Andersen knew full well, seldom have the privilege of choosing their audiences. She was resigned to continue to sing in front of abrasive SS officers night after night. What bothered her more and more as the days passed and the bus made its way east, was Hinkel. Having decided to personally oversee his elite artists' tour, he was present at every turn, on the bus and during the performances, in the dressing rooms and in the hotel lobbies. He was loud and patronizing, flashing his menacing grin like a weapon. Andersen found him impossible, but realized that it would be most unwise for her to offend the chief arbiter of culture, no matter how beastly he might behave. She smiled, played dumb, pretended to be oblivious to his sly remarks. She did her best to be the innocent-looking blonde, happy just to sing and dance. She avoided him skillfully, like a nimble boxer dodging her opponent.

All that ended abruptly. As April drew to a close, Hinkel informed the artists that the following day they would enjoy a special visit to the Warsaw Ghetto. In an area constituting barely 5 percent of a city of more than a million people, the Nazis crammed nearly half a million Jews, transferred from across Poland. By the time Andersen and her colleagues were slated to visit, average food rations in the ghetto were limited to 253 calories a day. The artists, Hinkel said happily, would visit the ghetto's hospital and see firsthand how efficient and compassionate was the regime's policy concerning the Jews.

But Andersen knew the Warsaw Ghetto to be an example of anything but compassion. She was still in touch with several of her Swiss-Jewish friends, who informed her of some of the terrors the Nazis visited upon Jews across Europe. Also, she was well traveled and quick to befriend people she met. She had heard, often from military men resentful of the senselessness of the Nazis' obsession with obliterating the Jews, rumors of great cruelty. Finally, in Warsaw, her own eyes convinced her. As the bus inched along the ghetto's fence, Andersen was overcome by a paralyzing sense of shock. Looking at the skeletal figures, seeing the bloodless faces, their eyes sinking in their sockets, she couldn't move. She couldn't move even when Hinkel ordered everyone off the bus. She stayed seated. Grethe Weiser and Emmi Leisner remained seated as well. Hinkel screamed. The women wouldn't move—couldn't move. Threats were hurled, to no avail. Finally, Hinkel led the few compliant artists on a tour of the ghetto, leaving the three trembling women behind. They didn't speak to each other, not a word. There was nothing to say. They knew that their actions would have consequences, and that they would have to pay very dearly for their impudence. But they were not deterred. Punishment was not a cure for their paralysis. A few hours later, the others, led by a silent but furious Hinkel, returned to the bus, and the group drove off to a nearby hotel to spend the night. Lale Andersen went to bed expecting the worst.

She didn't have to wait for long. A few hours after she had fallen asleep, she was awakened by one of Hinkel's henchmen pounding on her door. Dressed only in her nightgown, she let him in. Hinkel, the man said, expected her to report immediately to his room, where she would have to give an explanation for her actions earlier that day.

Panicked, Andersen tore through her suitcase looking for an appealing outfit, ran her fingers through her hair, checked herself in the mirror. She was in real danger, and her best bet, she thought, would be to resort, as much as possible, to that same old strategy that had gotten her through the tour thus far, to put on the same carefree façade and hope to charm the Nazi official into submission. She left her room and walked over to Hinkel's, trying her best to keep a steady pace and a clear mind.

Hinkel was still dressed. She was surprised to find no anger in his voice, only a trace of that same expression of bemused menace that seemed to be permanently fixed on his face. He asked her in. He was as polite as someone like him was capable of being. He told her to take a seat. Then he put on some music and asked her to dance.

Andersen realized right away what was going on. She wasn't the only one playing a game. Hinkel, too, was masquerading as something he was not. But she also knew that very soon all pretenses would come to an end, that a confrontation was inevitable, and that she would have to make a decision that would affect her for a very long time. Any moment, she thought as she danced, trying to keep Hinkel as far away from her as she could, any moment now the man will make his move.

Slowly, Hinkel's hand snaked down the length of Andersen's shirt, finally resting on her lower back. With all the grace she could muster, Andersen gently guided his hand back to her hips, doing her best to make it seem as if her rebuttal was nothing more than an elegant dancing move. Down traveled the hand again, this time allowed just a little shorter grope before being guided, a bit less gently, back to its place. And so it went, the terrible pas de deux: Hinkel's hands were moving faster, his grip getting stronger, his breathing heavier. He was no longer even pretending to dance, just swaying in his place and groping Andersen. She, too, was no longer dancing, but squirming, doing her best to stay out of Hinkel's reach, flailing her arms in an effort to fend off his hands. His movements more and more violent, hers more and more desperate. Finally, he clutched her to his chest with one hand, and grabbed her breasts with the other. Andersen had to make a choice. Compliance would rescue her from trouble, but at an unwelcome price. Resistance would surely mean severe repercussions. Hinkel pressed against her. With her free hand, Andersen slapped him in the face as hard as she could. Shocked, Hinkel let go of her at once. She immediately ran back to her room, locked the door, and sobbed through a sleepless night.

As the next day dawned, Andersen needed no instructions. She washed up and packed her bags, knowing her participation in the tour was over. A few hours later, after having said hurried goodbyes to her colleagues on the bus while doing her best to avoid Hinkel's steely gaze, she was on the train to Berlin.

Back again in her apartment, she sunk into a bitter, black depression. This was her life, she thought, every minor lift always followed by a major fall. It was the way it had always been: if she was getting famous with her sailors' songs one day, the Nazis would clamp down on cabarets the next; if she was making some headway in Switzerland, she was bound to be deported; and if she was finally an international superstar, she was nonetheless still doomed to be dealt a blow, a blow that would probably mean the end of her career. With Hinkel as her nemesis, she assumed that she had little chance of ever performing again in Germany and even slimmer odds of being played on the radio. What would she do, she wondered anxiously, with no foreseeable source of income, especially now that Michael, her thirteen-year-old son, was living with her in Berlin? For the first time in a long and tumultuous career, she felt bereft of hope.

And yet, something had to be done. Friedrich Pasche, Andersen's loyal pianist and close friend, came up with an idea. Any attempt to resume performances in Germany, he agreed, was likely to incur the Nazis' wrath. The only solution, then, was to seek engagements outside of Germany, particularly in Italy, a fellow, independent member of the Axis and therefore free of the German occupation. Her suitcases barely unpacked after the bus tour, Andersen packed in a rush and boarded a train to Italy.

Despite being fairly free to run its own affairs, Mussolini's state was nevertheless very much locked into Germany's orbit, and therefore acutely aware of even the most minute shifts in the Nazis' mood. Lale Andersen, according to the gossip spreading through the intricate web of officialdom that stretched across fascist Europe, was ideologically tainted—persona non grata. Her reception in Italy could not have been more different than the one she received during her previous visit, just a few months before. Then a sought-after star, courted by the press and cheered by excited fans, she was now met with cautious cordiality, indulgent but no longer enthusiastic. Even those theater owners, producers, and journalists who had not been informed of Andersen's rumored downfall were likely to wonder, she knew, why a star of her caliber, having just toured Italy, would return a few months later, cutting short what was supposed to be a triumphant return to her homeland. They were also likely to have heard about Hinkel's tour, and realize that she was no longer attached to the Nazi's

chosen group of elite artists. She did her best to secure performances and tried as hard as she could to stir the attention of the
press. Enough concerts were booked to keep her busy, and enough
tickets sold to generate a modest income. But every day of the
tour was a stinging reminder that she had fallen from grace and
would probably never rise to such heights again.

A few months later, the Italian tour was over. She had exhausted
all of its possible venues. Andersen was back on the Kurfürstendamm, hungry, confused, and unemployed. She had remained in
Germany throughout the war, stayed there even when so many of
her friends had fled to Switzerland, England, or the United States.
Germany was her homeland: it was where her children and her
family lived; it was where she felt most at home even as the Nazis
ravaged so many institutions and traditions she held dear. Now,
however, for the first time, she began to seriously contemplate an
escape. She could leave the kids in the care of Pasche and her
siblings back in Bremerhaven. She'd go on another tour and quietly slip into Switzerland, not to return for as long as Goebbels
and Hinkel and their ilk were in power. Gradually, and in utter
defiance of the intricate rules of safety required of anyone wishing
to live peacefully under the Nazis' zealous gaze, she increased her
correspondence with her friends in Switzerland, particularly with
Rolf Liebermann, her former lover, and another friend, the dramaturge Kurt Hirschfeld. She was well aware that any letter sent
abroad was likely to be carefully scrutinized by the Gestapo, even
more so when the recipients lived in neutral Switzerland and had
obviously Jewish surnames, and particularly when the author was
a famous singer who had recently rebuffed the head of the Culture Chamber. And yet, she didn't care.

"I hope all of this will finish one day and we can see each other
again," she wrote to Liebermann. "All I want to do is get out of
this country." And to Hirschfeld, a portly man, she wrote "Hirschie,

you have probably gotten so fat that next time I see you, I won't be able to hug you with my arms. I'll have to use my legs!"

The letters, of course, were intercepted by the Gestapo, and found their way to Hinkel's desk. In the eyes of the Nazi official, a German citizen could write no worse words. Not only did Andersen express her wish to flee the Fatherland, but her letter to Hirschfeld, to Hinkel's deviant mind, was of an erotic nature—the friendly hug clearly a veiled reference to intercourse. This was, Hinkel thought, a shameful example of *Rassenschande*, a favorite Nazi catchphrase meaning "race shame" and referring to Aryans who compromised the purity of their race by becoming amorous with lesser creatures, Jews in particular. The singer, Hinkel decided, had to be dealt with forcefully. He began drafting a document on the matter.

VIII

"We're the D-Day Dodgers"

WHILE HINKEL was devising his plots, the war in North Africa continued to progress. With Tobruk under Axis control and the scattered Allied armies scurrying for cover, Hitler's confidence in his desert campaign had reached a dangerous apex. Feeling himself just a few bold strokes away from the trade waters of the Suez Canal and the oil-rich fields of Iraq, Hitler, sure in his might, wanted Rommel to continue his westward dash and deliver a knockout blow to the Eighth Army at the Alamein line. Some members of the German brass, concerned that the soldiers were running low on supplies, advised the Führer against such an aggressive posture and wanted him to postpone the offensive until the important staging point of Malta in the Mediterranean Sea was secured. It would be better, they suggested, for the Axis armies relentlessly burning fuel in the desert to first build up a decent stock of munitions and take some time to rest their exhausted bodies and their equipment. Brushing aside such practical and unheroic considerations, a resolute Hitler sent a note to Mussolini explaining his rationale for pushing on to Egypt immediately and framed his thinking in the epic terms in which he viewed the entire war:

> Destiny has offered us a chance which will never occur twice in the same theater....The English Eighth Army has been practically destroyed. In Tobruk the port installations are almost intact. You now possess, Duce, an auxiliary base whose significance is all the greater because the English themselves have built from there an entire railway leading almost into Egypt. ...The goddess of Battles visits warriors only once. He who does not grasp her at such a moment never reaches her again.

The dutiful Rommel issued an order to his men: "All units reassemble and prepare for further advance." Thus into the breach rolled the Afrika Korps, and, by June 24, 1942, Rommel was again at the helm of the Axis armies rumbling toward the enemy. Brushing aside the light Allied resistance along the Egyptian frontier, Rommel's forces surged toward the Alamein line. Yet, as the Afrika Korps pressed on, it gradually began to outpace its crucial support elements. By the time Rommel's men had reached the main Allied positions, the Axis supply problem, already persistent, had become acute. The Afrika Korps soon found itself parched and exhausted by the unyielding advance, harried by the Royal Air Force raining bombs from above, and suddenly too far from any friendly depots for convenient restocking. By the first week of July, Rommel could count in his tired columns only a few hundred infantrymen, just thirty-six working tanks, and, in some units, no more than two rounds of ammunition per gun. He ordered his men to stand down on July 4 as they awaited reinforcement.

The Allies, sensing the shift, opened a counterattack. Although Rommel was able to contain this reversal for the time being, he knew that his men could not hold out for long in their present state. With the opposing armies locked in each other's sights, Rommel acknowledged a few weeks later his great summer campaign ended in a "dangerous lull."

While Rommel brooded over his situation and patiently waited for resupply, the Allied forces arrayed against him were being built up. As the Alamein position was only forty miles away from British-held Alexandria, men and matériel were being quickly and easily expedited from the friendly city to points all along the defensive line. Allied convoys steamed in from the Suez Canal and the Red Sea with supplies and soldiers, and arrangements were made for the delivery of President Roosevelt's promised gifts of the latest Sherman tanks and self-propelled guns, sixty-five Liberator bombers, and fresh soldiers trained for desert battle in the sandy wastes of sunny California.

By August, the skies began to darken as the tide of supplies shifted the military balance on the ground. Allied bombers were pounding Axis targets all across the North African coast, hitting ships on the open seas, and pummeling the vital transit hub of Malta. The Libyan ports were struck as well, with Tobruk suffering an especially severe beating on the eighth. For the Afrika Korps all the way out in distant Egypt, Benghazi and the battered Axis rear were far, far away. The delusional Hitler, adamant that Rommel give up no ground to the enemy, refused to allow anything resembling a retreat to a more favorable position. The men of the anemic Afrika Korps, thus shackled to untenable ground, were forced to endure a month of grinding attrition against an English Eighth Army whose strength was only growing and whose new leader, Bernard Law Montgomery, brought a ruthless strategic sensibility to bear on a situation that was looking worse and worse for Rommel every day.

The two commanders who faced each other across the searing

desert sands were a study in polar opposites. Whereas Rommel, the proud son of Germany, planned his operations on the fly and moved his units with the effortless nonchalance of an English gentleman, Montgomery, a London native, considered each feint carefully and advanced with the consumptive precision one normally associates with German engineers.

The two men differed in more than just strategic style, though. Rommel, who looked every bit the stern and distant leader with his erect posture, chest full of medals and intimidating sun goggles, was a commander universally beloved by common soldiers. Among other things, Rommel understood the hold that "Lili Marlene" had on his men and, even though he was well aware that the entire Nazi party apparatus was dead set against the sentimental song, raised no objections on behalf of propriety and pride when he heard Rudolph Schneider and the other young drivers in his personal escort listening to it on their wireless sets.

Sitting silently in the backseat of his staff car, then, his gaze fixed on some distant point, the great Rommel would indulge his enlisted men and allow them their brief, nightly communion with "Lili Marlene" while they made their way together through the desert sands. He never deigned to sing along, to be sure, and the men never quite caught him tapping his fingers or shedding a tear as he contemplated Hans Leip's words. Yet he nevertheless appreciated their power, the compelling melody, and the harsh sensitivity of Lale Andersen's delivery. Rommel knew that for his men, and for the men strewn all across the North African front, this song, this "Lili Marlene," was supporting them, keeping them from collapsing, and reminding the soldiers of all nations that they were, on some level deep beneath their khaki clothes, still human, still alone, and still longing to reunite with those they had no choice but to leave behind. So, on behalf of them, for three minutes in the evening, Rommel allowed the radios surrounding him to tune into more pleasant, emotional fare than the orders, reports, and dispositions that normally flowed through the metal speakers of his personal battle group during the day.

Over time, the Eighth Army soldiers in North Africa came to respect Rommel, not only for his tactical and strategic sense but for his exceptional decency as well. In an unusual departure from contemporary German practice, Rommel treated the Allied prisoners under his control and the scattered civilians surrounding him with the same high degree of respect and humanity that he maintained for his own men. Foreign to his soldier's sense were the fashionable Nazi notions of concentration camps, mass executions, and systematic pillage. His ability and chivalry in the field had won him the esteem and admiration of even his fiercest opponents, and Winston Churchill, in a speech to the House of Commons during the dark, early days of 1942, said of Rommel that "we have a very daring and skillful opponent against us, and, may I say across the havoc of war, a great general."

Montgomery, though a brilliant commander and a gentleman, neither sought nor forged the intimate connections with his soldiers that came so naturally to Rommel. Even as Montgomery's slouchy beret and sweaters gave him the appearance of an approachable, jolly uncle, he still maintained a distance both emotionally and physically from the men under his command. For one thing, Montgomery felt that "Lili Marlene," as an enemy song, had no place in the hearts of proper English warriors. He hardly endeared himself to his troops when he decided to ban the tune. Luckily for the soldiers of the Eighth Army, that particular order proved difficult to enforce. The Allied servicemen out in the desert, indignant and in love with their dear Lili, continued to listen to Radio Belgrade in defiance of regulations and the halfhearted oversight of their officers, themselves too entranced by the charming bars of the song to force the men under their command into compliance with their commander's edict.

Another instance of Montgomery's aloofness unfolded while

his replenished and energized Eighth Army was pounding the comatose Afrika Korps at the end of August 1942. Churchill, then visiting the Egyptian front to assess the military situation first-hand, was sharing a lunch of tinned New Zealand oysters in a tent with some high-ranking officers. Over their steaming broths, the army men and the prime minister discussed plans and politics, the open desert, and their futures. Montgomery's participation in the meal had been expected. Upon his arrival, he was dutifully saluted and graciously invited in for shelter, food, and company. But the proud Monty, as he had already been nicknamed, refused. Out of a deep respect for himself and his rank, he held to his policy of never socializing with subordinates and chose instead to take a simple sandwich and lemonade into his car, where he ate, under the ferocious midday sun, dignified and alone.

Arrogance aside, by the end of the summer Montgomery's newly tuned Eighth Army was finally shaping up to be an able match for Rommel's forces. After a long series of skirmishes in August, the existence of the stalled, starving Afrika Korps was itself at risk, and the lack of fuel severely limited the options available to Rommel's men stranded in Egypt. All along the desert, the tension mounted as the dueling armies eyed one another across the thirty-five-mile-long Alamein line. The deliberate Montgomery consulted, plotted, considered, and waited. Then, on October 23, 1942, Churchill received an urgent message from his desert army: "Zip!"

With that solemn tiding, the prime minister was informed that the Second Battle of El Alamein had begun. For twenty loud and lengthy minutes, 1,000 Allied artillery pieces roared into action, belching shells across the sands and showering the Axis armies with precision and fear. The freshly painted tanks of the Eighth Army pulled forth from their starting gates and the rested Allies, for the first time in a long while, felt the momentum that carries along victorious armies.

For the Afrika Korps, the long-awaited offensive couldn't have come at a worse juncture. Rommel, who had fallen ill the previous month, was back home in Germany recuperating in a hospital room when the battle began. There, he learned that his able replacement, General Stumme, had died of a heart attack amid the first day's hostilities. The recovering Rommel rushed back to the desert on October 25 and faced a daunting task. Hitler would not allow a retreat, and, by the first week in November, the toothless Afrika Korps, with few options and nowhere to go, was soundly routed by Montgomery's reenergized Eighth Army. After their long, impressive run, Rommel's forces were spent. His men, their supply lines interdicted, their stomachs empty, had no choice but to retreat until their final surrender months later, in May of 1943.

The Second Battle of El Alamein, a disaster for Hitler, was the decisive engagement of the desert campaign. In its wake, the Allies steadily swept the German and Italian armies back and out of North Africa. By the end of the year, the Axis advance would be checked worldwide in climactic battles—most notably at Midway in the Pacific, where the Japanese Navy lost four aircraft carriers and 228 airplanes, and at Stalingrad in the Soviet Union, where the ruthless German advance into Russia was finally halted. The balance of the war, though fiercely fought and with some of its bloodiest contests still in store, would skew heavily in the Allies' favor.

While the matter may have been decided for history, to the soldiers on the ground there was still plenty of work to be done in the immediate aftermath of Alamein. Their positions radically realigned, commanders on both sides ordered their respective reconnaissance forces to gather intelligence about the enemy dispositions. For Montgomery, the immediate goal was to find new avenues of advance and openings to outflank the shattered Afrika Korps, while Rommel was desperately searching for lines of retreat and whatever supplies could be swiped from lost Allied convoys.

Both sides were seeking information, and traps were set across the empty desert for wayward scouts who could be captured and interrogated. Yet out in the field, far from their bases, the independent reconnaissance units fishing for captives would sometimes have to hold on to their prisoners for several days before they could turn them over to formations large enough to handle and process them efficiently. In the open deserts, an easy camaraderie between captor and captive grew out of the informality of their time in that equally foreign area and reinforced the reputation of the North African campaign as a gentleman's war. A daily tea-time truce was arranged each evening at five o'clock between these dueling reconnaissance groups. At that hour the English and German scouts would lay down their arms and raise one another on their wireless sets to politely call off the names of the soldiers they had captured during the day.

Eventually, trades were arranged and bargains for freedom secured with trinkets and antimalarial pills, delivered by jeeps flying white flags and meeting at prearranged points. It all began when an English lieutenant caught by the Germans was discovered to be a nephew of the man who owned Player's cigarettes. The lieutenant was approached by Colonel Hans von Luck, a close deputy of Rommel's, and asked if he would consider being traded back to his unit for tobacco, a commodity that von Luck's reconnaissance men were short of at the moment. Evaluating his value to the Allied cause, the prisoner coolly calculated his liberty to be worth no fewer than 1,000,000 cigarettes, and requested that the figure be relayed back to the Royal Dragoons if they wished to make a deal.

The amused German infantrymen, going along with what they must have thought was a gag, were caught off guard by the response of their English counterparts: "Sorry, we're a bit short ourselves, but we could offer 600,000 cigarettes. Reply, please." It was a crazy game to be playing in the middle of a war, but nothing could prepare the German soldiers for the response of the indignant English lieutenant, who, when asked if he would accept the adjusted offer, adamantly replied, "Not a single cigarette less than a million, that's final!" Needless to say, he remained in captivity, although in the future other prisoners seemed to take more of an interest in securing their freedom from enemy hands than this young lieutenant.

Von Luck, who generally got along well with his captives, recalled listening to the radio one evening in the presence of some newly snared English soldiers. After tuning into the day's wrap-up report, he switched the station to Radio Belgrade in time to catch the evening broadcast of "Lili Marlene." Soon he was surprised to hear the song in stereo as his English prisoners began singing backup for Lale Andersen. His captives, their choral exercise over as the song trailed off, informed the amused von Luck that, despite Montgomery's order, they still listened to "Lili Marlene" whenever they could. Something about the sentimental tune, they explained to the German officer, meant more to them than stuffy regulations. Later on, von Luck would find out that the Americans and the French were singing the song in the desert as well. For the reconnaissance men plucking each other off the sands and playing the alternating roles of captive and captor, "Lili Marlene" was common ground, something shared and sacred that men of all flags could appreciate and enjoy, whether freely in the cool evenings or bound and shackled in enemy hands.

Meanwhile, the Allies, busily driving Hitler and Mussolini out of Africa, forced their way across Libya, landed troops in Algeria and Morocco, and continued onward into Tunisia, where the initial assault was slowed by the heavy rains that made for tough going in the cold, soggy terrain.

Private Fred Hirst, then a young British infantryman with the quaintly named Sherwood Foresters, had arrived in North Africa in the January following the showdown at El Alamein. Now, out in Tunisia, Hirst and his unit were making their way through the hilly landscape, where they were seeing some scattered action and trying to cope with the unhelpful weather. In addition to the mud-soaked trenches and white morning frost of the chilly winter, Hirst, fresh to the field of battle, also had to get the hang of the whistling rush of the enemy's cannons and the cracking sounds of hostile rifles. It was a different life than the one that he was used to back home in Doncaster, but he was trying to make the best of it and hoping, in time, to become a useful asset to his unit.

In the middle of March 1943, Hirst and his unit were cut off and isolated on a Tunisian hilltop, where they were soon surrounded by German mortar and artillery fire. The section leader, sensing by the distant sounds of the barrage that the men were not in any immediate danger, asked for volunteers to head back fifty yards to retrieve a cache of food that had been left behind in a sheltered spot on the hill.

Hirst and another soldier, feeling helpful and brotherly, offered to trek out and retrieve the food for their comrades. Making their way through the vegetation toward the designated spot, the two men discovered a hidden cornucopia of tinned army rations. Without any corporal barking out orders, they were free to choose anything they wished from this ample, hillside pantry, and Hirst was suddenly struck by a strange, liberating sensation. Here, with no officers watching over him and confronted with piles of food, he found a welcome respite from the constant supervision and deprivation of army life. As he pondered this moment of bountiful freedom, he suddenly heard a burst of small arms fire nearby. Harsh, foreign voices called out to him, "Hands-up, Tommy!"

His hands were preoccupied with cans, though, so Hirst chose to ignore the command and instead dove into a shallow ditch where he tried to hide. But it was too late, and now he was being addressed directly: "Hands-up, Tommy! For you, the war is over!" It was a phrase that would come to haunt Hirst in the coming years, for his adventure had only just begun.

Before long, Hirst found himself delivered to the port of Bizerta in Tunisia by the Germans, where he was transferred to Italian custody. There he was loaded with a number of other Allied prisoners onto a ship for an unpleasant crossing of the Mediterranean Sea to Livorno, in the north of Italy. It was on this rickety ship, with its miserable cargo of depressed and defeated men, that Hirst first experienced the painful hunger that would become the hallmark of prison life. Every day, each captive was allotted a rusty tin of watery meat, a small biscuit invariably covered with green mold, and some drinking water. Needless to say, this meal did not reflect well on the high standard of gastronomy that Italians are famous for, and for some days of this sad journey, Hirst could not bear to eat anything at all. Famished, he would doze off, his head swelling with visions of cream cakes, sausages, Doncaster, and the company of his good friend Stan. Invariably, though, he would be awakened by either the throbbing hum of the vessel's pounding engines or the powerful stench of the unwashed bodies in the hold and reminded that he was, in fact, far from England and a prisoner of war.

After his arrival on the Italian mainland, Hirst's head was shaved. Then he was ferried to Campo di Concentramento P.G. 82 in Laterina. Thus detained, he was next enlisted by his Italian captors to help with the Axis war effort. He and a group of thirty other prisoners were trucked to a local farm, where they were instructed to clear rocks and rough ground from a hill so that it could be used for growing crops. His Italian guards, bored to tears by supervising the Allied servicemen, whittled the time away by singing songs. One of their favorite tunes, naturally, was "Lili Marlene," and it was here, in Italian, that Fred Hirst first heard the song:

Tutte le sere
sotto quel fanal . . .

As he shoveled, Hirst couldn't quite make out the meanings of the words he was hearing over the clanking of rocks and picks, since the only phrases he had learned during his forced Italian holiday related to the grueling and unpleasant experiences of camp life. He guessed, then, that between the heady, romantic texture of the lyrics and the vaguely martial air of the guards' melodic intonations, that this Lili Marlene was a famous prostitute serving some lonely soldiers. It was not exactly what Hans Leip had been thinking of when he set out to write his poem so many years ago, but, for someone who didn't speak the language, Hirst's first guess was nonetheless a respectable explanation, one that many people who had heard the song sung in tongues they did not speak had themselves assumed.

Over time, the prisoners and the guards developed an amicable coexistence, and, in the course of swapping stories and gossip, Hirst and other prisoners first learned of the Eighth Army's invasion of Italy following the successful completion of the desert campaign. On September 10, even bigger news spread throughout the camp: Italy had surrendered and joined the Allied side two days earlier. On September 11, then, the prisoners were taken to a nearby village by their Italian guards, who, happy to be finished with the war, feted their Allied charges with wine, song, and cheese.

The guards, expressing their disgust for the Fascists who had dragged them into this terrible endeavor, were soon joined in celebration by the local citizens, who, toasting the Allies in their midst, invited them into their homes for a long, fraternal evening of drinks and good cheer. The joy was short-lived, though, as the next day word began to spread that the Germans, resolved to regain control, were taking charge of the region and preparing to put up a stiff resistance against the advancing Allied armies. Hoping to avoid another encounter with the German army, on September 12, Hirst and his friends decided to head south and make their own way to the Allied forces.

Going from village to village on their trek toward the still-distant English and American formations, Hirst and the other freed inmates nervously approached the people and houses peppering their route through the hills and valleys of Italy. Avoiding conspicuous homes with flower boxes and manicured gardens, the fugitive Allied prisoners instead sought out humble dwellings that were more likely to house inhabitants resentful of the recently tumbled Fascist regime. Hirst made his way through caves and farms, over roads and mountains, and, by 1944, arrived at the small, isolated village of Castel di Ieri, the Castle of Yesterday, after a lengthy march across frozen ground.

Friendly local contacts led Hirst and his friends to the stone home of Signora Nobili, where they were introduced to a woman in her sixties or seventies whose three sons had all served with the Axis armies in North Africa. Even though one of the Nobili boys was still unaccounted for, a casualty of the Allied forces to which Hirst and his friends belonged, the elderly woman standing before the haggard young men on her doorstep nevertheless greeted them with open arms. Signora Nobili and her teenage daughter, Antoinette, quickly made Hirst and his comrades feel at home, welcome especially in the kitchen with its uneven floors and simple stove. In Castel di Ieri, as in other small hamlets where Hirst found refuge, the local residents chipped in to feed and protect the shivering Allied prisoners in their midst despite the very real fear of German retribution. Donations of food and supplies were taken from all the citizens of the village, and Hirst, cared for so well by people who had suffered so much under

Mussolini and who had, in fact, so little to give, developed in time a strong affection and respect for these brave Italians who were risking their lives and liberty to help young men in need. Hirst and his fellow soldiers would tease Antoinette, joke with her, and ask about her boyfriends. She, in turn, would invite others from the town over and the entire group, peasants and prisoners, would enjoy merry evenings of laughter and broken chats in loose translation. One of Hirst's fellow soldiers, sheltered elsewhere in the village, spoke fluent Italian and was able to entertain the Nobilis with his natural charm and singing ability. Over the family's table, he would regale his listeners with "Lili Marlene," and it was through these sessions of song and camaraderie that Hirst learned the song's lyrics in their Italian translation. This knowledge would prove useful on those cold evenings when the residents of Castel di Ieri, freezing in their humble homes, gathered in a barn, filled with hay and animals, for warmth and comfort. Under the warm glow of oil lamps, Hirst and his fellow soldiers bantered with the villagers in their limited Italian, understanding, at most, a quarter of what was said. Some things, however, needed little explanation, and among these was the time that the peasants and the prisoners they were protecting, at once, as if on cue, burst into a searing, heartfelt rendition of "Lili Marlene" to stave off the cold and isolation. While Hirst was far from home, the Sherwood Foresters, and safety, for now, at least, he was among decent people in a world gone mad with power and ambition. He was singing with people who he was led to believe months earlier were the enemy, and yet he now found himself completely dependent on their kindness and generosity. Still, though, the nagging question kept weighing on his mind: where were the Allied armies, and when would he find them?

As Hirst wondered when he would again make contact with his comrades, Harry Hudson, his days of driving in the desert long behind him, was working his way up the spine of Italy with the

Royal Army Service Corps and helping feed and ease the English advance toward the north. Here, on the European mainland, he was equipped with teams of mules in addition to the trucks he knew so well from North Africa and, luckily for his morale and humor, served alongside a former concert pianist. As Hudson's unit moved from town to town, the plucky pianist would scour houses in search of a working piano and, finding the occasional functioning instrument, would have it loaded onto the back of a truck, where he would play, for his fellow soldiers, hammy versions of none other than "Lili Marlene" in the evenings and during the odd hours of rest.

In Italy, however, the song would take a ribald and politicized turn when word spread that Lady Astor, a prominent politician and society lady, had referred to the English armies in Italy as the "D-Day Dodgers," a phrase that rankled the grizzled veterans of Alamein and the more recent hard-fought battles in Italy, at Anzio and elsewhere. Insulted by the suggestion that the Italian front was merely a sunny, clubby refuge from the brutal fighting on the beaches of Normandy where the Allies had launched their D-Day invasion on June 6, 1944, the men of the Eighth Army penned their own lyrics to "Lili Marlene" in a version seething with rage, resentment, and, ultimately, a quiet sense of pride and accomplishment:

We're the D-Day Dodgers out in Italy
Always on the vino, always on the spree.
Eighth Army scroungers and their tanks
We live in Rome—among the Yanks.
We are the D-Day Dodgers, over here in Italy.

We landed at Salerno, a holiday with pay,
Jerry brought the band down to cheer us on our way
We all sang the songs and the beer was free.

We kissed all the girls in Napoli.
For we are the D-Day Dodgers, over here in Italy.

The Volturno and Cassino were taken in our stride
We didn't have to fight there. We just went for the ride.
Anzio and Sangro were all forlorn.
We did not do a thing from dusk to dawn.
For we are the D-Day Dodgers, over here in Italy . . .

Now Lady Astor, get a load of this.
Don't stand up on a platform and talk a load of piss.
You're the nation's sweetheart, the nation's pride
But we think your bloody big mouth is far too wide.
For we are the D-Day Dodgers, out in Sunny Italy.

When you look 'round the mountains, through the mud and rain
You'll find the scattered crosses, some which bear no name.
Heartbreak and toil and suffering gone
The boys beneath them slumber on
They were the D-Day Dodgers, who'll stay in Italy . . .

By this late point in the war, "Lili Marlene" could no longer be said to be the property of any one army or country. It had become a truly ubiquitous tune on the battlefields of the Second World War, and on almost every front, in almost every campaign, versions of it were scribbled and sung.

Eventually, after the Allies had finished flushing Hitler's army out of Italy and completed the long, hard task of liberating the rest of Europe, "Lili Marlene" was reinvented once more. This time, it was the American armies occupying their de-Nazified zones in defeated Germany that tried their hands as songwriters. Their versions, a mixture of the vulgar and the heartfelt, captured both the joys and frustrations, the confused emotions and powerful urges that the soldiers of all sides had suppressed through the last few years of war and hardship:

Down by the bahnhoff, American soldat
Zie haben cigaretten and a beaucoup chocolat
Das ist prima, Das ist gut
A zwanzig mark for fumph minute
Vie fiehl, Lili Marlene?
Vie fiehl, Lili Marlene?

And, then, finally:

Oh Mister Truman, won't you send us home?
We have conquered Naples and we have conquered Rome
We have defeated the master race
Oh why won't you give us shipping space?
Oh why can't we go home?
Oh why can't we go home?

IX

"Your Train Is Going to Berlin"

ALTHOUGH by the war's end the fighting men of all armies on all fronts had taken so much comfort and solace in her song, Lale Andersen herself had succumbed to a growing depression that had begun to fester much earlier, in the fall of 1942. Her options for performing had been curtailed by Hinkel and his gang. Andersen, who found that she could no longer find work in Germany or abroad, felt trapped. For her, even a stroll down an avenue or a few idle hours wasted away in a café were too perilous. She had seen too many of her friends and colleagues ensnared by the Nazi punitive machinery and was certain, correctly, that somewhere, in an office not far away, some bureaucrats were setting in motion events that would likely take away her freedom, if not her life. The death of Joachim Gottschalk the year before was all the proof she needed that even the most revered of popular entertainers was not immune to the Nazis' murderous harassment: before they took their own lives, Gottschalk's wife and child were informed of their immediate deportation to a concentration camp, and the actor himself was served with papers informing him that he had been recruited to the military and assigned to the eastern front. If only she stayed out of the public's eye, Andersen thought, she might postpone a similar fate, as if by remaining invisible the Nazis might forget her existence. It was a terrible burden on someone who thrived on public admiration. On the rare occasions when she did go out, she would quickly glance at the distant, stately halls on whose stages, just a few months before, she was seen and adored. Back in her apartment, angry and afraid, she realized she had to leave as soon as she could, before the Nazis came and took her away.

There was only one destination she had in mind. In Switzerland, she had powerful friends who could help and protect her. Kurt Hirschfeld was a successful dramaturge and a man of means, and Rolf Liebermann, having somewhat matured and settled his financial woes, was becoming increasingly renowned and respected as a composer and director of opera. She would send Michael, her younger son, to her family in Bremerhaven to be with his siblings. She would cross the border clandestinely, get to Zurich, and wait there until Germany came back to its senses and the Nazis were gone. In doing so, she understood, she would no longer be able to travel freely, as the lion's share of Europe was under Nazi control. She would no longer be able to see her children, perhaps for many, many years. She would become, of her own free will, a prisoner in neutral Switzerland. But she knew that that was a fate far preferable to languishing in a concentration camp. She began making arrangements to escape.

By late in September of 1942, she had a plan in mind: Germany's border with Switzerland, she knew from her friends who had crossed that very border in order to escape the Nazis, was tightly controlled, as the German authorities were determined to prevent a mass wartime exodus. France's Swiss border was no better, as the Nazis guarded it closely to prevent resistance fighters from smuggling supplies and ammunition across the frontier. Italy, on the other hand, a German satellite state for all effects and purposes, was largely left to its own devices, and was considerably less concerned with maintaining an omnipresent security mechanism. This, she thought, is why she had always enjoyed performing there: elsewhere in Nazi-occupied Europe, she felt as if she were under the constant gaze of some well-concealed Gestapo informant, which she probably was. In Italy, however, she felt as if the shadows of surveillance were largely lifted; there, she could sip a cappuccino in an outdoor café or stroll through a park and not worry that some zealous official had assigned some unlucky grunt to watch and report her every move. Italy's border, she thought, would be the most porous. Although she had just returned from a tour of that country, and although it was becoming increasingly difficult to find venues that would accommodate her in her recent incarnation as persona non grata, she wrote to her contacts in Italy and informed them that she was coming once again, right away, for one more brief tour.

Studying the map as if searching for the location of hidden treasure, Andersen tried to decide which would be the best border crossing from which to slip into Switzerland unnoticed. She consulted with her friend and accompanying pianist Friedrich Pasche, often chuckling at the fact that here they were, two entertainers, poring over a map as if they were seasoned generals preparing for a military offensive. Even without much knowledge of topography, however, a basic strategy seemed to suggest itself: nothing too obvious, nothing too crowded, nothing too closely watched. Finally, an idea crept into Andersen's head: the best way to cross into Switzerland, she realized, was to pretend not to cross into Switzerland at all.

She would travel, she decided, to the Brenner Pass, the lowest and easiest of the Alpine passes between Italy and Austria. Even though the pass was an immensely popular point of transit, she did not think anyone would suspect her, a mere performer, of contemplating an escape. Once she crossed over to Austria, she would be in the Tyrol region, a few hours from the Swiss border, a crossing point too remote to merit any real scrutiny. Italy to Tyrol to Switzerland; she rehearsed the plan again and again in her mind. She made sure her tour took her to Italy's very north, a short distance away from the Brenner Pass. She packed as if going away for a few weeks, but paid extremely close attention to her choices. The clothes she was taking, she couldn't help but think, might be the only ones she'd have for a very long time.

In October of 1942, she embarked on the tour. She said her goodbyes to friends and family, and did her best to fight back tears and remain upbeat. It was just a short tour, she told everyone, and she'd be back in no time to celebrate Christmas and greet the new year. The first few concerts in Italy went by smoothly, but she was too preoccupied to enjoy the freedom she usually relished in that country. Now, with her escape looming, she hadn't a mind for open-air cafés or outdoor strolls. She was much too nervous, as if being the least bit imprudent might somehow foil her plans. She performed, thanked her hosts, and ran back to the hotel.

One morning in early October, she woke up, grabbed the suitcase she had packed the night before and rushed down to the hotel's lobby. There, she bumped into a few of the musicians who were accompanying her, and assured them that she was merely rushing to the train station, anxious to get on with the tour and to the next destination. This was not unusual; the musicians had accompanied Andersen several times during her visits to Italy, and knew of her propensity to be the first one on the train whenever they traveled.

But Andersen was headed for the Brenner Pass. She rushed over to the train station at the nearby small town of Bolzano; from there, it would be a matter of hours before she was safely in Tyrol.

Nervous as she was, standing there on the platform and waiting for her train, she still couldn't help but take a moment to take in the scenery: all around her, the Alps were protruding, regal and enchanting. She was born in a small seaside town, and never really understood the national German obsession with mountains, captured so faithfully in the Bergfilm, that genre of films that portrayed mountain climbing as a nearly transcendental experience. But standing there, at the foothills of the Alps, she felt a little bit of that almost religious feeling, as if the mountains were somehow a passageway to something a bit closer to the divine. There was no snow yet, and the countryside was still green. If nothing else, she thought to herself, Switzerland would bring with it a welcome change of scenery, a vast improvement over bombed and charred Berlin. She took a deep breath of autumnal air and looked at the scenery once again. So much like a postcard, she thought. It was enough to make even a fugitive relax for a few moments. She became calm.

Then, in the distance, she spotted two men moving in her direction.

The first and most distinct feature of the two was how indistinct they were, almost as if someone had paired them based on their capacity to blend in, to go by unnoticed. But in the train station in Bolzano, nearly empty just a few hours after dawn, it was hard even for two extraordinarily ordinary gentlemen not to stand out. Another glance raised more suspicions: the two were tall, their skin light, their hair fair—an unusual look for Italians, even in the north. One glance at their clothes further confirmed Andersen's hunch: boring suits, plainly cut. No Italian, she thought, would ever dress in such uninspired clothing.

Watching the two advance, she had more than enough time to devise a plan. They walked slowly and deliberately, obviously headed toward her, holding her in their gaze. She looked away, breathing deeply, doing her best to remain calm. She began to pace around, as if absentmindedly, looking at the men and at the scenery intermittently. Slowly, she began to make her way toward the two men. Maybe, she thought, she was just paranoid, and the two were just fellow travelers who meant her no harm. And maybe she could still run, run right past them and disappear into the Alps, finding her way into Switzerland on foot. Avoiding their gaze, she picked up her pace. She clutched her suitcase hard in her right hand. She was now walking right past them.

"Excuse me," one of them said suddenly, tipping his hat at her. "Do you speak German?"

Andersen had run out of time. She needed to do something, and do it quickly. Running seemed foolish. She was once an actress, she thought, and would try to act her way out of trouble.

"Excuse me?" she asked, looking up at the two men, doing her best to conjure an expression of utter confusion. She pretended she was lost in thought, awoken suddenly from a deep meditation and gradually reacquainting herself with her surroundings.

"Excuse me," she said again, hurriedly. "But I seem to be on the wrong track." With that, she began to move away from the two men, toward the station's exit, walking as briskly as she could without appearing to be actually on the run.

The two men followed her, catching up with her a moment or two later. One grabbed her arm.

"You are on the wrong track," he said, not impolitely but firmly. "Your train is going to Berlin."

Andersen went numb. She didn't cry, or try to reason with her captors, she didn't scream or even think much about what had just happened. She just stood there, now sandwiched between the two men, following them onto another track and aboard the train headed back to Germany. She was silent the whole way. She seemed incapable of thought. Now and then, she tried to think back to the elite artists' tour, and how uncanny it was that she was once again finding her travel plans interrupted by the Nazis. But mostly she just sat there, staring out of a window. Just a few hours earlier, she could almost sense freedom. Now she was a prisoner. Now she would be sent to a concentration camp. Now all hope was lost.

Despite her not mentioning it, her Gestapo guards assured her that was not the case. She was not a prisoner, they said, merely wanted for questioning back in Berlin. They said little else, but were altogether genial. She wondered if they were fans of hers, of "Lili Marlene." She wondered how long she had been under their surveillance. She wondered who it was back in Berlin who wanted to question her and why. When the train pulled into Munich, Andersen's guards, wishing to be civil, asked her if there was anyone she would like to call. Escorted to a nearby telephone, she called Friedrich Pasche.

He was thrilled to hear her voice. She tried to tell him what had happened, but he spoke quickly and exuberantly, not letting her get a word in. She was lucky, he said, lucky to have fled Berlin at just the right moment: a warrant had been issued for her arrest, her travel permit revoked, and insinuations had been made suggesting she might even be engaged in espionage. She wasn't allowed to perform in Germany anymore, Pasche continued on, and her songs were banned from the radio. He was so happy she was safely in Zurich, he added, finally letting her speak.

Andersen gasped. For the first time since being intercepted in Bolzano, she was overcome by emotion, every emotion, it seemed, at one and the same time. She burst into tears. Breathless and sobbing, she told her friend what had happened. She would be in Berlin that evening, she said, and would see him there.

Pasche, however, was not entirely correct. There was indeed a document boding great ill for Andersen, but it was not a warrant for her arrest. It was a letter, sent on October 19 by Hans Hinkel to a number of key officials in the Nazi cultural bureaucracy, ordering the eradication of Lale Andersen's career.

Andersen, read Hinkel's letter, had maintained "continuing correspondence with Jewish immigrants in Switzerland, particularly the infamous former dramaturge Dr. [Kurt] Hirschfeld. The last letter from Lale Andersen to Hirschfeld was secured by the SD [the SS's intelligence service] and forwarded to us." Hinkel was referring to Andersen's promise to hug her rotund friend with both her arms and legs and called the letter's content "politically unworthy and pornographic." Finally came Hinkel's *coup de grâce*: Andersen, he wrote, "was encouraging all of her acquaintants, famous artists and some innocent soldiers and unimportant diplomats, to intervene in her interest," an odd sentence lacking context that, given the nature of the rest of the letter, could only suggest that Andersen was involved in some form of espionage. Therefore, Hinkel decreed, Andersen was to be forbidden from leaving Germany and banned from performing. The radio was not to play her songs, and the newspapers were not to write about her. She was to be made invisible.

When she finally arrived in Berlin, Andersen quickly learned that Pasche had been mistaken, and that no warrant had ever been issued. But the very next morning, she knew, she had to report to questioning. It did not surprise her when her guards told her that the official requesting her presence was none other than her old acquaintance Hinkel. She dreaded their reunion. She kept thinking about their encounter in the hotel in Warsaw, about his creeping hands on her back and breasts, about the satisfaction, however short-lived, of slapping such a repellent man in the face. But now he was surely out for revenge, with the endless means at the disposal of the Nazi machinery, for not succumbing to his aggressive advances.

The truth, however, might have been more complex. While Hinkel certainly had a long history of abusing his authority to force sex on the women he desired, he was not, despite his high office as the head of the Culture Chamber, omnipotent. The firmament of Nazi propaganda had no brighter star than Goebbels, the light of whose will shone brightly upon the others. No matter, then, how great Hinkel's passion for abusing Andersen might have been, it was unlikely that any course of action in the matter of such a famous artist would have been taken without the consent, if not the direct order, of Goebbels.

Examining the Nazi regime's relationship to Lale Andersen, scholars remain uncertain on the precise nature of its dynamic. Some, titillated by the image of the brutish Hinkel forcing himself on the tall and elegant Andersen, see the Culture Chamber's campaign against the singer as little more than the personal vendetta of a spurned official. Why else, they claim, would Hinkel even mention, in his letter to his colleagues, Andersen's relationship with Hirschfeld? True, Hirschfeld was Jewish, a fact that surely served to undermine Andersen's credibility; but compared with the other allegations raised in the letter, particularly the intimations of espionage, an affair with a Jewish émigré seems a minor infraction, even for a Nazi. That Hinkel put so much emphasis on Andersen's personal life, goes the claim, and brought up the more serious accusations almost as an afterthought, is proof enough that his focus was intensely personal.

Other scholars, however, suggest that while Hinkel was certainly motivated by personal animosity, the Nazi policy toward Andersen was guided by far more cerebral considerations, stemming from the concerns not of Hinkel but of his superior. Goebbels, they suggest, saw Andersen as a battlefield on which to overpower Radio Belgrade. Miffed that the army's radio station, audible all across Europe, was surpassing his own civilian radio network in popularity, and unable, in the midst of war, to confront the army station directly, Goebbels targeted instead Radio Belgrade's most obvious asset, the singer responsible for its unofficial anthem, Lili Marlene herself. Whatever the Nazis' motivation for suppressing Andersen, however, they realized full well Andersen's stature as a superstar. Despite all the allegations against the singer, Hinkel signed off his letter by assuring his colleagues that "no official decision was made in the matter as of yet."

Andersen, getting ready to meet Hinkel on a frosty morning in late October of 1942, just a few days after her attempt to escape was botched, was far from reassured. She knew she wasn't under arrest, and was slightly relieved that her Gestapo guards had taken her back home rather than directly to a concentration camp. Now she stood in front of her wardrobe, trying to choose an outfit. Once again, she needed a strategy, some ploy to quell Hinkel's anger as much as possible. She could no longer do as she had done on the tour, pretending to be oblivious, flighty, and dumb. Hinkel's hotel room gambit had already exposed that to be an act. She decided it would be best to come across as somber and remorseful, to walk into Hinkel's office with her head bowed and hope that he finds in the ashen-faced and sullen person standing in front of him no trace of the willowy, beautiful woman who just a few months before slapped him across the face. She picked a dark, unflattering dress, one that hung loosely from her shoulders and concealed the contours of her body. She picked bulky black shoes, the most unfeminine pair she owned. Finally, she put on a small hat with a black, netted veil. It made her look like a woman in mourning, she thought. It would also hide her tears.

Once she was ready, she grabbed the fourteen-year-old Michael, her youngest son, by the hand, and took the train, one or two stops down the Kurfürstendamm, to Hinkel's office. She informed the secretary of their arrival. They waited a while, staring at the enormous wooden doors that separated Hinkel's chambers from the rest of the suite. Finally, the doors opened a crack. Andersen blurted out a few words to her son and went in.

All the boy could hear were shouts. He couldn't make out the words, just the muffled thunderbolts of sound emanating from Hinkel's throat. He had no idea what the man was saying, but was shocked by the viciousness of his voice. Not long thereafter, a new sound came into the mix. It was a much softer sound, like a whimper or a suppressed cough. It was, he realized, the sound of his mother crying. A few minutes later, the giant doors opened again, and Andersen walked out, giving a little jump as the doors slammed behind her. She grabbed Michael and hurried out of the office. Even through the black veil, he could clearly see her tears.

She said little to him of what happened inside Hinkel's office, of what he had said or of how she had responded. She left no account of the meeting anywhere—not in her diaries, not in her subsequent memoirs. The only thing she said was to Pasche, when she and Michael were safely back in the apartment: Forbidden from working as an entertainer. Indefinitely.

For a few days, Andersen sulked around the apartment, lamenting the loss of her career, seething silently, spending long hours locked away in her bedroom. Then, a more profound question rudely presented itself, that of income: with barely enough money to sustain her and her children until the end of the year, Andersen needed to find a job. She was thirty-seven years old and had never held a job in her life other than performing. She thought, at first, to ask her friends in the theaters and the concert halls for a job as a ticket-seller or an usher. However, the thought of showing people to their seats in the very halls she herself once filled up was more embarrassing than she could bear. Besides, she thought bitterly, Hinkel must have instructed anyone in the culture industry to avoid any contact with her, which meant no jobs whatsoever in the entertainment business, be it singing on stage or cleaning up the aisles. Other prospects were equally as grim. She had no formal education and was therefore ill suited to any prestigious or demanding jobs. She could work in the service industry—a shop clerk, perhaps, or a waitress—but in war-ravaged, hungry Berlin, most stores, bereft of both goods and customers, were merely hollow halls with little need for new, untrained employees. Any job for the city, the government, or the army was similarly out of the question. Such jobs necessitated the Nazi Party's stamp of approval, approval she would never get. She toyed briefly with the idea of trying once more to escape but dismissed it almost immediately. Her passport had been taken away, and she was under close surveillance. She wouldn't even make it as far as the border. She was at a loss.

The remainder of 1942 passed with little change. She made a few attempts to find work, but succeeded in none. She tried her best to be hopeful and strong. She reminded herself and her loved ones that her life was nothing if not a series of near-disasters followed by great surges of success. She would bounce up once more, she promised. But, increasingly, she believed less and less in her own words. Sometimes, she let herself unleash a torrent of white-hot fury: Who, she thought angrily, were these petty bureaucrats to tell her she couldn't perform? How dare they? And why? She was the soldiers' sweetheart, and the war wasn't going too well. Who better to lift the spirits than Lili Marlene? What better voice to soothe than her own? And yet, her voice was stifled. Even more insulting were the recordings that had sprung up, in just a few weeks, trying to steal her Lili away from her. Learning of Lale Andersen's misfortune, and realizing that her version of the hit song was now no longer allowed on civilian radio, a gaggle of lesser-known singers, from young women to elderly men, tried their hand at the tune, releasing their own versions of "Lili Marlene." The radio was dishing out a new interpretation of her song every day, it seemed. It was her fame, she thought, her glory, and it was being taken away from her.

Mostly, Andersen was hopeless. Survival in Berlin was a struggle, a daily tussle with empty shelves, Allied bombs, and the harrowing grind of losing brothers, husbands, and friends on the front lines of an all-consuming war. But to be unemployed and unemployable, too famous for one's own good, all that seemed like a death knell. Andersen ate less and less, spent more and more time in her bedroom, singing and sobbing to herself. She became less interested in her friends, even the doggedly faithful Pasche. With each day, she allowed another part of herself to shut down, another bit of her spirit to pass away.

Christmas brought with it no relief. Willing to spend a small portion of her rapidly dwindling funds on gifts for her children, Andersen forced herself to go shopping and was rendered even more despondent when she discovered there was truly nothing to buy. The stores did their best to decorate, to give the impression of business as usual, but inside one could find nothing of value. Even the *Schwarze Korps*, the SS's official publication, a vehemently chauvinistic paper that habitually took pleasure in dismissing those Germans complaining about the shortage in supplies as unpatriotic whiners, was now forced to admit that Berlin's stores stood entirely empty. "First floor junk," ran a description of one of the city's largest department stores. "Second floor junk, third floor junk, fourth floor junk. Sometimes in between one finds useful things, but they are not for sale, because they are only show pieces."

The crisis was far from being the personal lot of Berlin's unfortunate citizens; utilizing the enemy's shortages to score a propaganda victory, the British and American press carried no end of dispatches from Berlin, all describing the destitution in vivid terms. "The traditional toy-producing country of the world," ran a piece in the New York Times on Christmas Eve, "is this year incapable of gratifying even a fraction of the normal Christmas demand for toys and trinkets."

The economic situation, however, worked in Andersen's favor. With nothing to spend their money on, Berliners put it in the banks. Then, a rumor spread that the shortages were artificial, and that it was all part of a government ploy to force people to deposit cash into their accounts. Any moment now, many believed, the government will take over the banks and confiscate all the funds for the war effort. Out of the banks came the money. Berliners kept it in their apartments or gave it in envelopes in lieu of small gifts such as flowers. The papers began carrying more and more ads soliciting barter: a piece of jewelry for a child's toy, a dress for a pair of shoes, a used book for another one. It was an economic system Germans could trust, private and personal, away from the government's prying eyes. It was also very much to the benefit of those who, like Andersen, had no salary to speak of. She bartered away a few of her possessions, the valuable and glamorous goods of a former star, trading them for a few essentials. She got by. But the things she needed more than all others were nowhere to be had: her name in lights, her picture on the front pages of newspapers, the adulation of an adoring audience as she took the stage. It was, she was realizing gradually, all that she had ever really wanted, and she was convinced that she had lost it forever. Even if the war ended the following day, she was not young anymore. Even if she was permitted to retake the stage tomorrow, other, more attractive women would capture the audience's heart. Even if she survived, she would never be as famous as she'd once been.

One April morning, Andersen's son Michael sat down for breakfast at the usual hour. The pianist Pasche was there as well, stopping by, as he did often, to check on his struggling friend. The two sat down at the kitchen table, nibbled on what little food there was to be had, drank their weak coffee, and chatted. They were both accustomed to seeing Andersen's chair empty. With her depression, she would often fail to come out of her room until much later in the day. But after talking for nearly an hour, both were gripped by a deep unease. Andersen, they noticed, was quiet, too quiet. When she was in her room, she usually walked around, sat down and got up, wept and sang softly, sending faint signs of life to the people in the next room. Now, however, there were no such sounds. Perhaps, the two men told each other, perhaps she was still sleeping. But a few minutes later, they realized they could no longer just sit there and ignore the ominous silence. They got up and, knocking once or twice, opened the door to Andersen's bedroom.

There she was, lying on the bed, face down. She was wearing a ratty nightgown. Pasche noticed just how thin she really was: always trim and fit, she now looked gaunt and unwell. They took a step closer. Then, they saw that her head was drooped in an unnatural position, lying in a puddle of vomit. Pasche ran to her and shook her violently, but she did not respond. On the floor, he noticed an empty bottle of sleeping pills. Lili Marlene had decided to kill herself.

X

"The Gravity of the Situation"

PASCHE called an ambulance and rushed Andersen to the hospital. Her stomach was pumped, but the doctors were uncertain about her chances. She was out for a long time, they said. She was in a coma, they continued, and may never recover. Two days later, she awoke. Pasche and Michael, thrilled to see her regain consciousness, reassured her that it would be alright. Their words, however, did not comfort her. "Why?" she asked, smiling meekly. "Is the war over?" It wasn't, of course, and Andersen spent a few more days in the hospital before returning home, now having the indignity of a failed suicide attempt added to her already tattered resumé.

News of Lale Andersen's hospitalization spread rapidly. With the press forbidden from mentioning her name, news traveled from person to person, much as it did years earlier after the death of Joachim Gottschalk. This time, however, the story was rapidly altered, each listener adding his or her own flourish before passing it along. She tried to kill herself, one would say, and another added that it was the Gestapo that tried to kill her. A third claimed that there was nothing physically wrong with her at all, but that she was whisked away and imprisoned in a hospital, where she could be kept under control. A fourth added that it was not a hospital she was taken to but a concentration camp. This, apparently, was the version of the rumor that hit London a few days after Andersen's suicide attempt. Among its early recipients in Britain were a few old acquaintances of Andersen's, German artists who had fled Berlin in the 1930s. They had since followed her career, loved her signature song, and were distressed to learn of her problems. One of them went a step further: having made a few acquaintances at Bush House, the BBC headquarters, the man told his friends that the Nazis had outdone themselves, putting none other than Lili Marlene in a concentration camp.

As problematic as the BBC's relationship was with the German song that had become the favorite of British fighting men everywhere, the rumor was too good a propaganda opportunity to resist. In April of 1943, no more than two weeks after Andersen's release from the hospital, the BBC offered a special broadcast to inform its listeners inside Germany of their sweetheart's grim fate.

"Have you noticed," asked the broadcaster, "that you haven't heard the song lately. Could it perhaps be because Lale Andersen is in a concentration camp?" Besides, the broadcast continued, the song's lyrics were no longer up to date. A more faithful, modern version would go something like this, sung deliberately out of tune by Lucy Mannheim:

Führer, I thank and greet you
For you are good and wise
Widows and orphans greet you
With hollow, silent eyes . . .

The broadcast had a tremendous impact. Hundreds of letters poured into the BBC studios, expressing outrage about the murder of Lili Marlene. The letters poured into Radio Belgrade as well. They were soon also piling up on Goebbels's desk. He realized that the BBC broadcast was a nightmare, confirming the German people's worst fears and casting the Nazis as the ultimate villains, murderers of the one woman beloved by everyone around the world. Begrudgingly, and regardless of his dislike of the song and of Andersen, Goebbels knew it was necessary for her to make an appearance singing before German soldiers, looking healthy and happy, or else the Ministry for Popular Enlightenment and Propaganda would suffer a major blow.

It was as much a personal struggle for Goebbels as it was a national one. The first months of 1943 were the most crucial of his career, as he, almost entirely on his own, was struggling to grab control of Germany from the largely incompetent circle, spearheaded by Göring and Himmler, that surrounded Hitler and led Germany to one disaster after another. The latest debacle was the Battle of Stalingrad, which was imagined at first as a potential turning point in the largely staggering campaign against the Soviets. But now, a large portion of the German army found itself, a few months after laying siege to the city, surrounded by Russian forces. With nearly 250,000 German soldiers, the entire Sixth Army of the Wehrmacht, encircled by two Soviet armies, the battle, which had begun with swift German advances in August 1942, was by November of that year dissolving into a huge, cataclysmic defeat for the Nazis. Rather than allowing German soldiers to surrender or try to fight their way out of the siege, Hitler, acting on the poor advice of Göring and ignoring most of his senior officers, insisted that the Sixth Army await support from the air. However, when the Luftwaffe's planes neared the surrounded German pocket in December of 1942, Soviet gun batteries shot down scores of aircraft, severely depleting the already strained air force. The few pilots who did manage to land successfully were soon shocked by the condition of the men they were sent to assist. So malnourished, exhausted, and frostbitten were the men of the Sixth Army that they failed to muster even the energy required to unload the goods off the planes. The weakened soldiers, for their part, were shocked as well: thrilled, at first, with the sight of relief, they looked at the contents of the containers on the planes with disbelief. Rather than sending food, medicine, and other essentials, the planes carried such useless items as light summer uniforms, a bitter joke in the midst of the Russian winter's deep freeze, as well as twenty tons of vodka. When it became evident that the aerial rescue mission had failed, Hitler shrugged the battle off as a lost cause. On January 30, 1943, he promoted Friedrich von Paulus, the commander of the encircled Sixth Army, to the rank of general field marshal. His intention could not have been clearer: the promotion was a farewell gift, as von Paulus, now entirely unable to save himself and his men, was expected to take his own life and encourage his soldiers to do the same. Von Paulus refused. He had obeyed Hitler's commands faithfully, even when he personally thought that waiting for the air force was a far inferior tactic to attempting to break out of the siege through ground warfare. Now, however, he had lost his confidence in his Führer and felt betrayed. He gave the order to surrender. On February 2, 1943, the Soviets took 91,000 emaciated German soldiers, including twenty-two generals, as prisoners.

Hitler was shocked. Von Paulus, he raged, had committed the most heinous of treasons, being the first German general ever to surrender to the Soviets. Even worse, however, the defeat deeply shook the German population, who had been largely told that all was going well. Just a few months before, in an attempt to raise morale during the Christmas season, Goebbels launched a major propaganda offensive, sending emissaries to every sizable German town armed with nothing but reassuring words and optimistic prognoses, all but guaranteeing a swift victory in Russia. Instead came defeat on a massive scale, a defeat for the first time palpable to ordinary citizens. Outrage followed, a real howl of pain from a population that revolted at being told lies while their young men lost their lives in ill-planned, unjustifiable wars.

Amazed at the disconnect of Hitler and his close circle, Goebbels decided to do his best and wrestle control of as much power as he could from the hands of Göring and Himmler. If he could at least be in charge of the economy, he thought, he would be able to put an end to the two's uncritical spending and restore a modicum of stability to the lives of ordinary people. To do that, he realized, he needed to gather popular support, a tall order for a man as disliked as he was. There was one solution, he decided, which was to tell the German people the truth, or as close to the truth as a Nazi minister of propaganda could get.

He chose his timing carefully. On February 2, 1943, panicked by the defeat in Stalingrad, Himmler ordered 100,000 cafés and restaurants throughout Germany shut down, urging citizens instead to give whatever meager sums they would've spent on dining out to the war effort. The move was short-lived, perceived, as it was, as a new and considerably more oppressive step in the government's cascading incompetence. More military defeats followed. Emboldened by Stalingrad, the Soviets unleashed themselves on the remaining German invaders with great fury, taking back position after position.

On February 18, 1943, Goebbels filled Berlin's Sportpalast with throngs of carefully selected zealous fans and gave a speech. Known to history as "the Total War speech," it contained one admission previously unuttered by any Nazi official: the war was not going well. Goebbels blamed the defeat on a myriad of factors—first

and foremost the Jews—and stressed time and again the importance of the German people standing united, sacrificing their all
for the holy struggle against Bolshevism and international Jewry.
But the German people cared most of all for the few words Goebbels said at the very beginning of his speech: "I believe," he said,
"that the entire German people has a passionate interest in what
I have to say tonight. I will therefore speak with holy seriousness
and openness, as the hour demands. The German people, raised,
educated and disciplined by National Socialism, can bear the
whole truth. It knows the gravity of the situation. . . ."

The speech, carried on the radio and heard by millions, went
a long way to position Goebbels as a preferable and more capable
alternative to Himmler and Göring. He could little afford, then, a
massive propaganda blow, and it was just such a blow that the
BBC's broadcast announcing the incarceration of Lili Marlene
dealt him. Almost immediately, he called Hinkel and ordered him
to summon a press conference on the matter. Clenching his teeth,
the head of the Culture Chamber informed the gathered journalists that there was no truth to the rumors of Lale Andersen's arrest,
that she was, in fact alive and well, and that, eager to dismiss the
nasty rumors, she was getting ready to embark on a major tour to
entertain Germany's soldiers. But the public announcement wasn't
enough. Nazi officialdom thrived, after all, on propriety and order.
Hinkel had to put his decision in an official letter to Andersen.
On May 15, he wrote her saying: "Taking into consideration your
personal conditions, namely your oldest son being a soldier in the
east, I allow you, despite your evidently unworthy behavior as a
German artist, to be active as an artist in privately owned variety
or cabaret establishments. You are responsible that no print or oral
propaganda is published concerning your former broadcasts to
our soldiers on Radio Belgrade. Also, any connection of your
name with the soldiers' song 'Lili Marlene' is not allowed. You are

also not allowed to perform in front of soldiers, or government, or Nazi officials." The latter edict, of course, excluded her one propaganda tour for the soldiers, the one Hinkel himself had told the press was imminent.

Andersen was thrilled. She was forbidden to sing the one song that had made her famous, the one song that won the hearts of people across the ideological divide of Europe, but she could once again work, once again take the stage, once again hold her place in the public's eye. Her first concert was scheduled for the following month in Dresden, and she began practicing as if she had not been on a stage before.

The June concert was a triumphant return: packed to the hilt with soldiers, the small venue seemed to reverberate with energy. The men in attendance were all well aware, like most Germans, of Andersen's recent travails, and saw the concert as a historic heroine's welcome. She was the antidote, many thought, to the bumbling and heartless men who were running Germany's faltering war. Whereas they could do little but send men to their untimely deaths, she, Lili, was a clear and unequivocal voice yearning for the boys to come back home. The hall shook as she took the stage. The three or four hundred men in attendance stood up and flooded the aisles, clapping their hands in a frenzy, hooting, and stomping their feet. More than one later said that they felt the earth move, as if the small building might implode from the rapturous enthusiasm of Andersen's audience. Many minutes later, she began to sing, and each song was followed by cascading applause. She sang her classic repertoire, all songs but one.

The men in the audience, however, weren't about to give up. They began to chant and shout. They wanted Lili Marlene. Andersen stood there, looking at her fans, at a loss. She was expressly forbidden from singing the song and wanted nothing less than to reignite Hinkel's wrath. But these soldiers, moved to ecstasy by her presence, were demanding the song. She could not let them down. She motioned with her hand for the crowd to quiet down.

"I've sung that song so many times," she said, her voice quivering. "Why don't you now sing it for me?"

And with that, she nodded at Pasche, and he and the other band members began to play. Andersen stood on stage as all the men in the room jumped to their feet and, with their arms around the comrades standing beside them, began singing as loudly as they possibly could. The impromptu chorus, with no rehearsal, no harmony, and no training, resounded with an abundance of earnest fervor. For three or four minutes, a few hundred people sang the song like a religious hymn. From his seat at the piano, Pasche was the only one who could see the tears rolling down Andersen's cheeks.

Once Andersen was done with her short round of a dozen or so performances for the military, she was once again on the civilian circuit. She soon discovered, however, that much had changed in her year's absence from the stage. By now, in June 1943, Allied bombers were a staple in Berlin's skies, and many of the capital's stately halls of entertainment were eviscerated by their relentless, airborne assaults. The KadeKo, where Goebbels had been disgusted by the cosmopolitan comedy of so many years ago, had been destroyed in February and the Scala, where Andersen performed with Bianco, the King of Tango, would be flattened in the fall. Audiences were now far less likely to venture out of their houses and away from the safety of their nearest bomb shelters, regardless of a singer's fame or talent. Musicians were scarce, too: the reliable Pasche was always there with Andersen, but the other members of her band kept changing almost every month, some called away to the front while others preferred to stay at home with their families and prepare for the inevitable aerial bombardments. But despite her dwindling audiences, shrinking venues, and unreliable band-mates, Andersen remained fiercely committed to her craft, giving each performance her all, treating even the shabbiest of halls as if they were the grandest of palaces. Having spent all those months convinced that her career was over, she was determined never to be anything other than her best.

Goebbels kept a watchful eye over Andersen's resurrected career. And while there was little he could do to keep the singer out of the spotlight, "Lili Marlene," the song, could be more tightly controlled. Shortly after instructing Hinkel to inform the press of Andersen's return, he himself dispatched another curt order to Karl-Heinz Reintgen at Radio Belgrade. "From now on," read the order, "it is forbidden to play 'Lili Marlene' by Lale Andersen." It was a bold move, as the radio station, being part of the military, had lain outside the reach of Goebbels's propaganda network—which Reintgen knew very well. Especially now, with the power struggle for the heart of the regime in full throttle, any attempt by a civilian minister to try and assert his authority over a military entity could backfire, dealing Goebbels a blow. But he didn't care. He had yielded enough ground. He was the one who first admitted the grim realities of the war effort. He was the one who had to acquiesce on Andersen, even though her silly and sentimental song was interfering with his own carefully planned design to use the airwaves to bolster morale and steel the people's resolve. He needed a victory, however meaningless, to signal to his competitors at the top of the Nazi ladder that he was still the feared and obeyed man he had been a decade before. And "Lili Marlene" was an easy and highly visible target.

Back in Belgrade, Goebbels's communication was unhappily received. Reintgen and his men found it offensive that a civilian with no official foothold in the army should dispatch messages telling them how to do their jobs, especially when the men, the real soldiers fighting the real war, were so fond of the song. On the other hand, they were well aware that Goebbels was not a man it was advisable to cross. Reintgen called all his men into a room to debate the subject. Some said Lili should trump Goebbels, others that the minister, if refused, would simply exert greater pressure, stopping at nothing to get the song he so much reviled off the air. They were divided more or less evenly, and Reintgen had no choice but to break the tie. He took the Talmudic approach: Goebbels, he told his men, forbade us to play "Lili Marlene" by Lale Andersen; he said nothing of the song in any other version. They pulled an alternative version from the archives, this one performed by a young Austrian chanteuse. It went on the air at 9:57 P.M. one day in late August, the regular spot of "Lili Marlene." A day or two later, scores of letters came in from the front lines: this, the soldiers said, was not the original Lili, and wasn't nearly as good. Faced with a growing demand for the real Lili Marlene—Lale Andersen—Reintgen once again had a painful decision to make. Never one to shy away from conflict, he decided to go for broke and put Andersen's version back on the air. The following morning, his commanding officer called, screaming at him for defying Goebbels's direct orders. Reintgen apologized weakly and coyly promised that he had only played the song by accident and that it would not happen again. That very night, however, he played it again. He never heard another word about it from his superior, Goebbels, or the Propaganda Ministry, and Lale Andersen was, once more, back on Radio Belgrade.

Meanwhile, Andersen herself knew nothing of these squabbles. She continued to perform as often as she could, but venues were getting harder to find. More than once, she and her musicians would arrive at a given address at the designated time only to find themselves staring at a pile of rubble, the hall having been hit by British bombs the night before. Berlin was a city in distress. By late 1943, the dearth of even the most basic essentials, combined with the ever-increasing intensity of the British bombing, turned Berlin into an apocalyptic vision of some nightmare city. The *New York Times's* European correspondent, writing in the early days of January 1944, quoted a friend of his, a recent escapee from Berlin: "He said it was perfectly incredible that a living being should escape such fire, fumes, confusion and destruction. He saw people he knew coming out of shelters quite transformed—white hair, insane, indifferent, wandering about, running away, not knowing where to go. He saw others sitting in comfortable chairs in the middle of the large streets as if just waiting for some event. He saw animals in the Zoo being shot by the police as they were attacking the wounded. He saw houses crumbling down."

Increasingly, Andersen's thoughts were given less to performing and more to simply surviving. She was skeletally thin, often having sacrificed whatever little food she could find so that her teenaged son could eat a little more. By the end of January 1944, there were no venues left open in Berlin or elsewhere. Finally, Nicki Rummert, a longtime friend, came up with an idea. He had just returned from a visit to Langeoog, the tiny island in the North Sea where Andersen had some relatives. The island, he said, was peaceful. More importantly, food was plentiful there because of Langeoog's isolation. Early in February, Andersen and Michael left Berlin and made their way to the tiny landmass off Germany's northern shore. It was freezing outside, and the short boat ride from the coast, not far from Andersen's childhood home of Bremerhaven, to Langeoog was a constant battle with lacerating, icy gales. Finally, they arrived, and were greeted warmly by Andersen's excited relatives, happy to have their famous kin in their midst. That night, Andersen and Michael had their first full meal in more than a year.

Lale Andersen spent the rest of the war on Langeoog. No bigger than a few city blocks, the island offered little in the way of entertainment. When the weather was clement, which was rarely, one could stroll on the beach. The rest of the time, the islanders had to stay indoors to avoid the wrathful winds. A new sensation took over Andersen, one she hadn't felt before. It was neither ennui nor depression, and it was far from the viscous, paralyzing despair that followed her capture at the Italian border pass. This time, it was apathy. She was no longer forbidden to sing, but the universe, it seemed to her, made singing itself impossible. Everywhere was war and madness, everywhere hunger and firestorms. No room for beauty. No place for joy. No time for art. She was alive and well, better than she had been in Berlin. But absent her true passion, she felt little more than dull indifference.

XI

"My Sweet Lili, the War Is Over"

BUT WHEREAS Andersen felt apathetic, Hans Leip, the poet who had given birth to "Lili Marlene," was angry. Like Andersen, he too watched with futile rage as his life was torn apart by the Nazi ascent and the all-encompassing war. After the heady days of the 1920s, with costume parties and love triangles and instant literary fame, the 1930s were bleak. He struggled to find work, his celebrity working against him. Every artist who wished to retain a high profile had to join the Nazi party, and Leip would not do that.

"I said no," he told an interviewer many years after the war. "Me as a Hamburger, as a free Hamburger, you know, I do not become a party member."

His principles pushed Leip even further into a corner in 1938. Now earning his living almost entirely from writing brief cultural reviews for small newspapers, and forced to scrutinize every sentence he wrote and search for anything that might cause even the faintest displeasure to the bureaucrats of the Culture Chamber, Leip was offered a flattering and lucrative deal. One of his old acquaintances, remembering the poet in his golden days, was involved with Ufa and entrusted to produce a script for a new film. He offered Leip the job. An added incentive was the fact that the film was to star Emil Jannings, a revered actor who had gained international acclaim when he starred opposite Marlene Dietrich in *The Blue Angel*. Leip had always loved Jannings, was intrigued by the way the actor, who often portrayed men who had fallen from grace, managed to embody at once the searing hurt of being humiliated by his environment and the fundamental, perennial dignity that made life, even at its darkest hours, worth living. The theme of the film appealed to Leip as well. It was to be a nautical adventure, capturing the struggles of a German battleship fighting the British during the First World War. Leip saw the film as a chance to relive his childhood dreams of life on the high seas. If he wasn't fit to serve in the navy on board submarines, he could at least now live vicariously by creating a fictional world of sea battles, brave ensigns, and nautical drama aplenty. However, his enthusiasm soon faded. It being 1938, with Germany and Britain engaged in the tortuous power play that would shortly lead to war, the film's plot shifted dramatically as did world events: as soon as Britain ceased to be a friendly appeaser, Ufa's sovereigns were instructed by Goebbels to change their film from an innocuous story of peril at sea to a bombastic piece of anti-British propaganda. Instructions along these lines were conveyed to Leip, who was expected to amend the script accordingly. He, however, refused.

Bowing out of the film did little to tarnish the reputation of Jannings, but it took its toll on Leip. Already viewed with a jaundiced eye for refusing to pledge his allegiance to National Socialism, he was now an outcast, with all but a handful of courageous editors keeping their distance and refusing to publish his contributions. Having amassed some money as an author of best-selling work, Leip had enough funds to live in modest comfort for a few years. With a wife and two children in tow, he prepared for a few lean years. Optimistic by nature, he was certain that the impending war would turn out much like the one that preceded it, with the fanatical fires of nationalism burning furiously for a few years and then dying down, giving way to another Weimar, to another Renaissance of art and enlightenment. At least this time around, he told himself, he was too old to be sent to the front. He wrote sporadically, sketched from time to time, and did his best to ignore the world outside.

On February 8, 1939, however, Leip's life was shattered when his wife, Gretl, suddenly died. He was mad with grief. She had been not only his spouse and the mother of his two daughters but also a cherished companion. Together they had traveled around the world, from Tangiers to New York, immersing themselves in foreign cultures, reveling in the strange foods, the smells, and the music. And now that the world was closed and secretive, inhospitable to the traveler and dismissive of fraternal spirits, he had hoped to take comfort in the friendship of his wife, and had looked forward to spending his days reliving old adventures with her, as if the past could truly heal the present's pain. With Gretl gone, Leip felt like a prisoner in his spacious home. He had no one to talk to, no one, at least, who would see the world quite as Gretl did. He had always felt that he could handle anything, that no Nazi goon would ever manage to break down his spirit. With Gretl no longer beside him, he was no longer sure.

Sensing his great distress, Gretl's sister, Ilsa, moved into the house and assumed responsibility for the upbringing of Leip's young daughters. Nothing, after all, seemed more natural: Leip had always been close with both sisters and had flirted with Ilsa before marrying Gretl. And Ilsa had always loved Leip, had always imagined, however privately, what life might be like had the poet chosen her rather than her sister. Increasingly, she acted more and more like a surrogate wife. In May of the following year, 1940, Leip asked her to marry him.

Still, his second marriage was little like the first. He was fond of Ilsa, and was grateful for the affection and care she gave both him and his girls. But no matter how hard he tried, he just could not bring himself to once again exert the emotional effort required to craft an intimate relationship. He wanted to feel for Ilsa as he did for Gretl, but more often he just wanted to be alone. Shortly after their wedding, he sent Ilsa and the children to Tyrol, not far from the Brenner Pass, and booked himself a cruise to Madeira. He stood on the ship's deck night after night and tried to come up with new projects that would rescue him from the solitude he felt closing in on him. No matter how hard he tried, nothing came to mind.

He returned to Hamburg. The following summer, he took a small house on Lake Constance, located on the Rhine and bordering Germany, Austria, and Switzerland. It was quiet and pastoral, just the kind of place, he imagined, in which a poet was likely to find inspiration. By summer's end, however, Leip's hopes of winning the Muses' favor evaporated when he learned that a poem he had written many years before, a poem he considered too personal to publish, was set to music and was now, thanks to the military radio station in Belgrade, a hit all across Europe with soldiers and civilians alike. It was embarrassing for him to think of "Lili Marlene," to recall the two women who had captured his youthful imagination and propelled him to write the poem. It was awkward for him, now forty-eight years old, to relive the same sensations that stirred him as a much younger man. But more than anything, it was unbearable for him to think of how little had changed since he had given life to Lili Marlene in "Song of a Young Sentry." Back in 1915, he thought, he had imagined Lili as a promise: guarding the barracks, watching the invalid soldiers in the hospital and the oblivious men at the officers' quarters, he conjured Lili as a force stronger even than the madness that drove men to the battlefield. The war will be over, he thought, and the men will all return to their own Lili Marlenes. His Lili seemed to assure him, a young and anxious soldier about to be shipped to war, that love will triumph over death. But now, more than two decades later, here again were young men taking solace in his words, looking up to Lili as the embodiment of a brighter future. Here again were men marching en masse to their death, again fighting a gratuitous and pointless war. Leip found little comfort in the thought that millions of men looked forward to the song each night or that his words brought soldiers to tears, reminding them of loved ones left behind and of lives interrupted by the war. He was horrified to learn that a poem so personal, a poem he considered to be a strong statement against war, was put to march-like music and made popular by an army radio station. "Lili Marlene," he thought bitterly, would now forever be thought of as a soldiers' song, when he had imagined it to be everything but. And he, the song's lyricist, the poet and humanist, the bohemian intellectual and man of peace, was now linked in the popular imagination with the soundtrack to so many bloody battles. If that wasn't enough, his original poem was robbed of its male voice, the voice of a soldier pining for his sweetheart, and given a new, female voice instead. And what a woman's voice it was! That harsh tone, that strange diction, that literal interpretation that shied away from any vocal flourishes, all those maddened Leip even further. If the song had to be interpreted by a female singer, he thought, why not someone who could actually sing? And yet, there was little he could do about it. By early 1942, Leip, like Andersen, realized that the popularity of "Lili Marlene" was unstoppable.

Leip's opinion of Lale Andersen softened somewhat when, in

the first months of 1942, he met the singer after a matinee in Hamburg's Ufa Palace. Andersen had just returned to Germany after performing for soldiers across occupied Europe, and her popularity was at its peak. Hinkel and his harassments were months away, and she was thriving on her enormous success. After a spirited performance, Andersen bowed to her audience and stepped offstage, meeting some friends in the cloakroom. One friend pointed out to her a striking gaunt man with a large bald head and an intense gaze; that, he said, was the man who had written "Lili Marlene." Andersen needed no further incentive. She walked up to Leip and, without introducing herself, kissed him. Then she walked away. Leip might have been disappointed with Andersen's appropriation of his Lili, but he could not remain indifferent to the singer's charms: the blue eyes, the blond hair, the pleasing lips. He was always enchanted by beautiful women and became an admirer of Lale Andersen's from that moment on.

Her song, however, he still disliked. He came to dislike it even more when its immense success on Radio Belgrade propelled the Nazis to put everyone involved in its creation under tighter watch. With Andersen recruited by Hinkel for his elite artists' tour and Schultze a registered member of the Nazi Party and a prolific tunesmith in service of the army, Leip was the next logical target. Pressures increased on him to join the party. He continued to refuse. Veiled threats were made, but he wouldn't budge. He did not believe in anything the Nazis represented and would not declare himself one of their ranks merely for expediency's sake. One day, sometime in 1943, he received a telephone call; it was a Nazi high official, a key player in the Culture Chamber's division for writers and poets. Curtly, the man said that while he was a patriotic German, he couldn't stand to see the way the Chamber was persecuting anyone who did not succumb to its will. And Leip, he said, was about to be its next target, having incurred Hinkel's anger.

"My dear Hans Leip," said the man, "you have to see to it that you get away a little bit so you are not drawing attention, because they want to interrogate you by the SS and, as I know, you will tell them exactly how you feel. And then you are finished. You know, then you will be imprisoned." Stunned by the man's unexpected candor, Leip took his advice. He bid Ilsa and the girls farewell and moved to his summer house on Lake Constance. There, he sank back into a routine of artistic infertility. Over the course of the following two years, he wrote only eleven poems, a meager outcome for the once-prolific man of letters. He devoted most of his time to his drawings, which grew darker and more chaotic as time went by.

As both Hans Leip and Lale Andersen suffered from harassment, depression, and despair, Norbert Schultze was thriving. Of the three artists who had breathed life into "Lili Marlene," the composer alone spent the war years in relative comfort. A member of the Nazi Party since 1940, his name safely on the Führer's List, that coveted roster of artists deemed too valuable to be sent away to the front, Schultze had as pleasant a time in Berlin as was possible for anyone during the taxing war years. After composing many soundtracks for propaganda films commissioned by the army's various branches, Schultze emerged as the movie industry's most sought-after musician. He was the perfect man for the job. Films in Nazi-controlled Germany fell either under the category of propaganda or under that of light entertainment, both demanding a composer who, like Schultze, had a natural proclivity toward the sweet, the sentimental, and the stirring. He was on board, for example, to lend a violin-heavy, nearly overbearing score to *Ich klage an* (I Accuse), a chillingly effective drama produced largely as an argument for euthanasia. He composed crescendo-laden soundtracks, rich with thundering pianos, to the only two propaganda films written by Joseph Goebbels. But most curious, perhaps, of all his wartime cinematic efforts was a movie called *Eine kleine Sommermelodie* (A Small Summer Song). A doomed wedding between musical comedy and propaganda, the film tells the tale of a young German petty officer, an aspiring musician moved by patriotism to enlist in the army and go to war. Shortly before being shipped to the eastern front, he meets a young woman, Eva Maria. They have a brief but passionate affair, and the officer, saddened by his imminent departure, composes a sentimental song for his sweetheart. After many scenes featuring the front line as a fun, friendly place, the officer and his girl are unexpectedly reunited, after the song he had written her becomes a runaway hit with German soldiers the world over. It didn't take too long for Schultze to recognize the plot as a thinly veiled incarnation of "Lili Marlene."

Despite *Eine kleine Sommermelodie* being a small and unimportant film, never released for public screening, it gave Schultze an opportunity to reflect on his part in creating what was now the unofficial anthem for men on all the fronts and in all of the armies. Like Andersen and Leip, Schultze too was surprised to see his song become an international hit and was delighted to see it bring so much comfort to soldiers. A part of him had always felt a dull pang of guilt for having avoided the front lines, and "Lili Marlene," much more than his bombastic work for the army, seemed to him a genuine and valuable contribution to military morale. He was also secretly happy to learn that his song was beloved on both sides of the trenches. Despite being a part of the Nazi mechanism, he felt little animosity toward the British or the Americans and was proud that they, too, despite not understanding its lyrics, found his tune captivating.

But he was still a Nazi and, at that, one who had close and continuing ties with Goebbels. He spoke little of "Lili Marlene," neither distancing himself from the song nor taking any pride in it. Lili's success had little effect on him. Unlike Andersen and Leip, who found the song's popularity to be both a blessing and a burden, Schultze was on the safe side of the political divide. As a party member and valued musical propagandist, he was invited to all the right parties, knew all the right people, enjoyed all the right privileges. He was well fed when all around him slowly starved. He was well entertained when no others were. He was, from the Culture Chamber's viewpoint, that most desired of all artists, famous and efficient and entirely acquiescent. There was therefore no need for browbeating, as had been the case with Andersen, or veiled threats, as there had been with Leip. There was no sudden change in status, no reversal of fortune. Norbert Schultze was a famous, privileged, and compliant artist before Radio Belgrade began its broadcasts, and he remained one thereafter.

His success and his contacts allowed for a satisfying personal life as well. Spending most of his days on movie sets, he indulged in his love of women, rolling from romance to romance, from actress to actress. In 1941, he met Bulgarian film star Iva Vanja on Ufa's lot and, two years later, married her. Settled down once again, and with a strong salary to support him, he returned to his true passion and composed an opera, *Das kalte Herz* (The Cold Heart), commissioned by the city of Leipzig and based on a popular fairy tale. Like his previous endeavor, *Schwarzer Peter*, this one, too, enjoyed tremendous success: light, amusing, and approachable, it was the perfect distraction for a nation increasingly mired in war.

But while all accounts from that time, including Schultze's own, portray a content, unreflective man, one work stands out. It was an experimental film, released in 1943, titled *Symphonie eines Lebens*, a symphony of life. Four symphonies accompany four lengthy flashback scenes to tell the story of a popular composer whose life slowly unravels. The score, a clear tribute to late Romanticism, was emotionally raw, considerably darker, and significantly more mature than Schultze's usual simple sentimentality. It suggests, however, subtly, that there might have been a more troubled, unseen side to the composer, something deeper underneath his perpetually wide smile.

Whatever it might have been, it did not again surface until the end of the war. The Allied armies, beginning their liberation of western Europe with the D-Day landings at Normandy on June 6, 1944, advanced rapidly, mostly finding an overwhelmed, under-supplied, and desperate Wehrmacht. By April 1945, with the Soviet army having completed a long and arduous battle against the remnants of the German military, Berlin fell. On April 29, Adolf Hitler married Eva Braun in a brief civil ceremony. Joseph Goebbels and Nazi party boss Martin Bormann served as witnesses. The bride wore a black dress, and, a day later, Braun and Hitler committed suicide in the depths of their Berlin bunker. On May 1, Goebbels followed suit; he asked an SS doctor to inject each of his six small children with morphine. When they were unconscious, he crushed an ampule of cyanide into each of their mouths. Then, he put on his hat, coat, and gloves, took his wife's hand, and went up to the bunker's garden. A minute later, he shot Magda and then himself. He would never have to hear "Lili Marlene" again. The remaining occupants of the bunker tried to burn the bodies, wishing to leave no evidence of the Nazi defeat behind. They didn't have sufficient fuel, however, and the Allied soldiers who later stormed the bunker could easily identify Goebbels's half-charred body by the metal brace on its deformed right leg. The following morning, May 2, Grand Admiral Karl Dönitz, signed Germany's surrender to the Soviet Union.

These were ambiguous times for Schultze. He was relieved to see the war come to its end, relieved by the thought of wasting no more young lives in futile imperialist efforts, and relieved also by the inevitable rebuilding efforts that would improve the quality of life in Germany. But the Americans and the Soviets, he knew, were likely to settle in Germany for a good, long period, and when they did, he thought, they would first seek to rid the country of anyone who had actively partaken in the Nazi madness. And there he was, a party member, the composer of inflammatory propaganda songs, the man who so effectively put the Nazis' ideology to music, the man who wrote "Bombs over England." He was bound to be arrested, he thought, bound to pay the price for his political acquiescence. He moved through Allied-controlled Berlin like a wraith. Cut off from the Nazi mechanism that had kept him well fed and warm throughout the war, he now had to play for his living, pounding the keyboard in small, lesser-known clubs for little money and a few drinks. The Allied forces had rapidly stabilized the economy, which began its climb back to normalcy. Schultze needed a job but was terrified that applying for a position would remind the Allied administrators that there was a prominent Nazi they had neglected to arrest. He couldn't just march back to Ufa and get in touch with his old acquaintances. If anything, he realized, most of Goebbels's underlings at the movie studio were probably already being questioned. Even if they weren't, it was highly unlikely that they would employ him in the current climate, not a man whose nickname was Bomber Schultze. Even the larger clubs might prove dangerous. The only ones who could afford them were the American soldiers—a terrible audience for a tainted pianist trying to stay undetected. Need, however, triumphed over reason, and in the summer of 1945, Schultze, hitting up an old friend for a favor, got a job at an upscale club, making his living mostly off tips. It wasn't long before one of the waiters recognized the famous composer.

The Ausschuss zur Ausschaltung von Nationalsozialisten, or the Committee to Extinguish National Socialists, defined Schultze as a "fellow traveler." It meant that he was a Nazi sympathizer, a participant even, but not a hardened ideologue. The good news, Schultze soon learned, was that he was spared a prison sentence, deemed too inconsequential to punish severely. But he would not be allowed, his interrogators told him, to practice his art. He was forbidden from performing, in any capacity and in front of any audience, until further notice.

It was a terrible blow, worse even, perhaps, than imprisonment. Music had always been his passion, fame the currency he cared about most. Now both were taken away. He was thirty-four years old, had no other skills or profession and had a family to support. Around him, fellow musicians who resisted the Nazis were being hailed. He was well aware that that made him a villain. And he didn't feel like one: all he did, he thought, was make music. Regardless of the master he was serving, he couldn't see that as a crime.

To eke out a living, he took on a string of jobs. For a few months, he joined a construction crew making road repairs just outside of Berlin; for a few others he worked as a landscaper in the private gardens of the postwar wealthy. Almost overnight, he had undergone a physical transformation as well: once a rotund man with blushed cheeks and a general air of well-being, he was now lean and ashen-faced. The skin of his former self hung on his frame like an ill-fitting shirt. His pianist's fingers, long and manicured and used to nothing but the smooth touch of the piano keys and the soft skin of beautiful women, were now calloused, dried, and cut.

He worked at such jobs for three years. In 1948, he was finally allowed to perform again, mostly in small clubs and for audiences who took some pleasure in demeaning the once-celebrated Nazi composer. A reporter, witnessing him play in a bar late that year, recalled Schultze, in the middle of a Chopin waltz, interrupted by someone in the audience.

"Play 'Lili Marlene' and sing it for us, will you, Norbert?" the man shouted, disrespectfully referring to Schultze by his first name. The reporter recounted what happened next: "A pained expression crossed his face, but he said, 'as you wish.' Turning back to the piano, he broke into the haunting love song, the favorite of nearly every army during the last war."

Schultze now hated "Lili Marlene." Speaking with an interviewer many years later, he claimed to have altogether suppressed the song from memory. "I forgot that it was my creation," he said. "I forgot it. Because it was for me depressing to listen to all that stuff. . . . It was like the song of another person, a folksong."

He never said anything else about "Lili," nothing that would help determine why the song, easily his most celebrated work, caused him so much consternation. It is easy to speculate: as he worked by the side of the road or in some muddy bed of flowers, the last thing Schultze wanted to remember was "Lili Marlene," the song that had come to represent humanism, hope, and everything else his fellow partisans sought to destroy. But Schultze himself never spoke of it again.

One night shortly after the war, General Dwight Eisenhower, visiting one of his divisions in Innsbruck, not far from Hans Leip's home near Lake Constance, learned that the poet who had written "Lili Marlene" was living nearby. Intrigued, he asked a soldier to go to Leip's house and invite him over for a late dinner. The soldier arrived at the darkened home a while later and found its shutters locked. He knocked on the door several times, but no one answered. Leip, wishing to avoid even an accidental snippet of "Lili Marlene" from one of his neighbors' radios during the 9:57 broadcast, not only made sure to be in bed before the song was aired but also locked his windows and, often, placed a pillow over his head. He did not hear Eisenhower's emissary. The soldier returned to base and told the general that Leip appeared to be sleeping.

"Let him sleep, then," Eisenhower said, "because he's the only German who has given pleasure to the world during the war."

A few months later, Leip left Lake Constance and returned to

Hamburg. He had heard it had been completely ravaged by the war. He was told that Blankenese, the wealthy neighborhood in which his house stood, was destroyed. But he found the neighborhood intact, Ilsa and his daughters both safe, having hidden in a bomb shelter and with relatives out of town for the last, and most bitter, months of the war. The Leips' house, however, was now commandeered by an English officer.

One day in September 1945, Leip and Ilsa knocked politely on the door of their old home. They understood, they told the officer, that houses were confiscated, and wished to offer no resistance. They would just like to go over their belongings and take a few things of sentimental value. The British officer cordially agreed, and, chatting with the couple as they surveyed their belongings, learned that Leip was the lyricist of "Lili Marlene."

The British officer smiled, called his assistant and ordered him to pack up and prepare for departure. He did not wish, he told Leip, to occupy the house of a man who had brought him so much comfort during the war. With each such case of admiration, with each confession—from the enemy, no less—of Lili's healing powers, Leip grew to like the song more and more.

Lale Andersen, on the other hand, no longer had any feeling for it. Unlike Schultze or Leip, "Lili Marlene" neither gave her consternation nor resuscitated faded memories she would rather forget. It simply seemed irrelevant. She was on Langeoog, where the winds were cold and radio reception was barely possible. There was some food and a few family members, and time, lots of time. Tempted to dive into her memories, she kept her mind in the present. Anything else, she thought, would make her cry.

She didn't follow the progress of the war. She no longer cared. She knew that her son, fighting on the eastern front, was safe, and it was all the military news she needed. Music, too, made her sad, reminded her of too many things. Along with her son Michael, she continued to take long walks on the beach and continued to avoid her memories.

One afternoon, in the early summer of 1945, Michael was walking alone on the beach when he saw a tall figure walking toward him. A few more feet, and Michael could see the man clearly: he was a uniformed Canadian soldier. He looked friendly enough. Michael struck up a conversation, and the soldier, in his broken German, did his best to respond. He asked Michael where his family was, and Michael replied that he was on Langeoog with his mother. She was, he said with pride, none other than Lale Andersen, Lili Marlene herself.

The soldier grew pale.

Please, he asked Michael, bring her to me.

A few moments later, a woman materialized. She looked nothing like the Lili of the song, far from the paragon of youth and promise men across the world had come to imagine and adore. She was bony, her features hard, her cheekbones jutting out from her face. But more than anything, her eyes seemed dark. Was this, the Canadian solider wondered to himself, the right woman? Politely, he asked her to sing a few lines, just a bar or two of her famous song.

Lale Andersen began:

Vor der Kaserne
Vor dem grossen Tor . . .

There was no doubt: she was Lili Marlene. That voice, that harsh voice, had sung him to sleep every night. It made him think of his own girl back home. It made him feel that everything was going to be alright. He fell to his knees. Weeping, he hugged Lale Andersen's legs.

"My sweet Lili," he told her, "the war is over."

Epilogue

ON OCTOBER 19, 1944, a few days before a combined force of Yugoslav Communists and Red Army divisions closed in on occupied Belgrade, Karl-Heinz Reintgen, the commander of Radio Belgrade, called his men into his office. The city would fall any day now, he said, and the Wehrmacht was thrust into a desperate, hasty retreat. There was no panic in Reintgen's voice, no fear. He spoke calmly and matter-of-factly, ordering his men to grab the transmitter, a few records, and prepare for months of constant redeployment, running from the Russians alongside Hitler's broken army. That night, the men of Radio Belgrade broadcast from the hills surrounding the city. They did the same the following night, and the night after that, moving around nimbly, avoiding detection. And every night at 9:57 P.M., without fail, Reintgen would play "Lili Marlene." He listened to the song's bugle call and looked up at the sky: It was filled with British supplies being dropped from Allied planes in the heavens to the Communist partisans in the mountains. The bright white nylon parachutes glistened against the backdrop of an ink-dark sky like so many luminous, white whales in the ocean.

Soon, Reintgen could broadcast only sparsely throughout the day. There was little time, in retreat, for him to properly set up the transmitter. Wherever he was, however, and whatever the situation, one thing was inviolable: shortly before ten, all activity would stop, the transmitter would be set up, and at the ritual moment, Lale Andersen's voice would pour out across the Balkans, across Europe. Reintgen's station was now—as it had been, perhaps, throughout the entire war—solely the voice of "Lili Marlene."

With the Communists closing in, Reintgen gathered his men on October 19. It was 9:50 P.M., and he asked them all to stand in a circle around the transmitter. His voice quivered a bit as he thanked them for being such a dedicated crew. He continued, saying that he looked forward to seeing them all back home, where they might finally be free of the war and its tolls. He then put Lale Andersen's record on the portable record player, turned the transmitter on, and bowed his head. His men did the same. It was to be the last broadcast of the German Army's Radio Belgrade. A few hours later, Reintgen and his men were captured by Communists.

Not far away, Fitzroy Maclean and his men were listening, as they did every night, to Radio Belgrade. Maclean had traveled from the Libyan deserts to the mountains and villages of Yugoslavia, where he was now attached to the headquarters of the partisan leader known as Marshal Tito and witnessing the Wehrmacht's retreat with glee. And yet, there was one German for whom Maclean and his small group of men were feeling some affection: "We would turn our wireless set in the evenings to Radio Belgrade, and night after night, always at the same time, would come, throbbing lingeringly over the ether, the cheap, sugary and yet almost painfully nostalgic melody, the sex-laden, intimate, heart-rending accents of Lili Marlene. 'Not gone yet,' we would say to each other. 'I wonder if we'll find her when we get there.' "After Reintgen, his men, and their transmitter were captured, Maclean tuned in to find Lili vanished: "At the accustomed time, there was silence. 'Gone Away,' we said."

But even with Radio Belgrade no more, "Lili Marlene" was far from finished. In Berlin, it soon became a tool in yet another propaganda war. After East Germany defiantly built the Berlin Wall, it enlisted "Lili Marlene." The government-run radio station, which hailed itself as the "voice of the free world," made its central broadcast a daily show entitled *Lili Still Lives*, suggesting, not so subtly, that the message of "Lili Marlene," one of universalism and hope, compelled all Germans to unite under socialism and the red flag of proletarian revolution.

Hans Leip, in his house in Hamburg, was then living in what had become West Germany. He was furious to learn about the East German appropriation of his creation and, on June 23, 1964, fired off an angry letter to the Communist radio station, demanding that they cease to abuse his words by setting them in the context of political propaganda. He was bursting into an open door, though: for much as the Nazis did two decades before, the totalitarian barons of the German Democratic Republic had, in time, come to despise "Lili Marlene." Despite their initial attempt to use the song for their own purposes, the tune, the East Germans claimed nonsensically, had revealed itself to be nothing but a bit of western frivolity—an American, imperialistic song unfit for consumption by the enlightened and ideologically committed East Germans. It was, in other words, too sweet and sentimental, and not at all conducive to stoking the dogmatic fires they wanted to incite in the hearts of the people. Soon after Leip's letter was sent, the song was banned throughout East Germany.

In Yugoslavia, Marshal Tito, the partisan turned political leader, took a similarly dim view of "Lili Marlene." While fighting the German occupiers from his mountainous hideouts during the war, aided by Fitzroy Maclean, Tito had delighted in the broadcasts of Radio Belgrade and was quite fond of its legendary sign-off song. Coming to power, though, changed his mind. The Communist Tito soon saw the composition in much the same light as the Soviet puppets in East Germany did, denouncing it as empty pop at best or a vessel of American cultural colonialism at worst. By 1963, Yugoslavia, the former home of Karl-Heinz Reintgen's Radio Belgrade, banned "Lili Marlene" as well.

In the West, meanwhile, "Lili Marlene" fell victim to the ideology of capitalism, harder to resist, perhaps, than even the oppressive ones enforced in East Berlin and Belgrade. Being the most popular song of a war perceived by many as democracy's finest hour, "Lili Marlene" quickly became something it had never been before: a commodity. By the early 1970s alone, "Lili Marlene" served as the inspiration for more than thirty-nine different movies and television programs. American entertainers, including Mel Tormé, Perry Como, and Frank Sinatra, served up more than two hundred renditions of the song. Moving further afield, the song was a big hit during the 1970s in Japan's karaoke clubs, and marched, at one time or another and well into the 1980s, in hit parades in various countries in Europe, North America, and Asia.

But this Lili, while every bit as popular as her wartime doppelgänger, was a very different creature. Hans Leip had written the poem under the shadow of the First World War, and Andersen and Schultze recorded it on the precipice of the Second. It always had a hard kernel amid the soft tune that resisted ideology, that transcended borders, that spoke of what we had in common. But while love in a time of war is a powerful balm, love in the time of peace runs the risk of turning into a sweet nothing. In the mouths of so many of its subsequent performers, sung on the stages of Las

Vegas, Los Angeles, and Tokyo, "Lili Marlene" turned into a saccharine ballad sung with a half-smile, signifying nothing.

In some cases, however, Lili was able to retain her original meaning. She once again became a soldiers' sweetheart as American troops marched into Korea under the auspices of the United Nations in 1950. The following decade, in Vietnam, she emerged as an inspiration, not so much in her original form but as a muse guiding young poets feeling much as Hans Leip had in 1915. South Vietnam's most popular song in the first years of the war was "A Rainy Evening on the Frontier," written by a young Vietnamese petty officer. It is nearly identical to "Lili Marlene," a credited source of inspiration, in its simple and sentimental treatment of a young soldier pining for his love back home. It became a huge hit with South Vietnamese and American military men alike. Unsurprisingly, the South Vietnamese government banned the song, claiming its sad lyrics failed to inspire sufficient anti-Communist zeal.

But while Lili went on to fight in other conflicts, those who were entranced by her during the Second World War had a hard time letting her go. After the war, a flood of memoirs, popular histories, and works of reportage washed across the United States and Western Europe. Despite the momentousness of the battle that had just ended, it was "Lili Marlene"—a song, after all—that appeared and reappeared in the recollections of everyone from privates to authors.

"If the contest had been decided on musical merits," wrote General Mark W. Clark, commander of the renowned American Fifth Army, in his memoir, "I feel no doubt that the Germans would have a walkover with 'Lili Marlene.' Our men soon picked up the enemy song and it was often heard where they gathered. In fact, at a later date in the campaign, our arrival in Florence, where a considerable number of American or former American citizens had been in residence throughout the war, resulted in a touch of panic because the American soldiers were singing 'Lili Marlene' as they marched along the streets. 'What can this mean?' the American-born wife of an Italian asked me urgently. 'We have been sitting here listening to the Germans sing that song for months, and now the Americans arrive singing it too.' "

While Clark was in Italy, John Steinbeck was trekking across Europe as a war correspondent. In an article for the *Washington Post*, the writer summed up the song's great irony: "It would be amusing," he wrote, "if, after all the fuss and heiling, all the marching and indoctrination, the only contribution to the world by the Nazis was 'Lili Marlene.' "

Above all, however, the most tireless keepers of Lili's postwar flame were the three who gave her life: Lale Andersen, Hans Leip, and Norbert Schultze. Despite their travails in the immediate aftermath of the war, all three found Lili to be a springboard to further fame and fortune.

First and foremost was Andersen. After being discovered by the Canadian soldier, she found her way back to Berlin. There, to her dismay, she was summoned by the de-Nazification committee. While she suffered at the hands of the Nazis, she did participate in numerous of their cultural exhibitions, from Hinkel's elite artists' tour in 1942 to her heavily publicized reemergence following the BBC's broadcast of her imprisonment a year later. Was she, then, asked the committee, on romantic terms with Hinkel?

Such allegations, Andersen responded, were grotesque. "Everyone in the area around Hinkel," she replied angrily, "felt the dangerous tension that existed from our first encounter onwards."

And what, asked the committee, about "Lili Marlene"? Wasn't the song itself a staple of militarism, a soundtrack to war?

Here, too, Andersen distanced herself. "The domestic and foreign armies loved a woman, or a voice, which according to Goebbels and Hinkel was absolutely unworthy of the success," she replied, stressing that being Lili, if anything, was an enormous burden on her, drawing, as it did, the unrelenting attention of the Nazi elite.

Finally, commenting on her letters to Hinkel, the ones she was forced to write in order to save her career, she said it was her duty as a mother to do whatever she could to continue supporting her children. "Only the hard duty and responsibility towards my children," she told the committee, "for whom I had to care alone, was the reason why I had to embarrassingly humiliate myself and write these letters full of lies."

The committee exonerated her of any blame. Soon after, she was once again an international superstar, this time around revered by a world unburdened by global war. She reveled in her new-found fame and freedom, traveled widely across Europe and North America, filling the largest venues with audiences, mostly comprised of recent veterans, eager to meet in person the woman whose voice had come to symbolize their wartime experience. When she married her lover, the Swiss composer Arthur Beul, in June of 1949, newspapers from Chicago to Catalonia carried the news, along with photographs of the glamorous Andersen, on their front pages. As a wedding gift to the woman whose voice he was commissioned to silence, Tommie Connor, the lyricist who had penned the English version of "Lili Marlene," wrote another song, this one aptly titled "The Wedding of Lili Marlene." Set to a new tune by British composer Johnny Reine, Connor's words closed a circle:

As she knelt where the candle-lights were gleaming,
It seemed the choir sang soft and low,
"Farewell my angel of the lamplight,
We'll always love you so."

Happy decades followed. She continued to travel extensively and met with the most idolized stars of her day. She befriended Marlene Dietrich, whose rendition of "Lili Marlene" was equally famous as her own. Even more exhilarating was the fact that on the numerous occasions when the two met, Andersen did not feel a bit inferior to Hollywood's celebrated leading woman. With satisfaction, she noted that, just a few years before, she had looked at Dietrich as a goddess, and now here they were, dressed in chic clothes, sharing laughs and wartime anecdotes. Although she never said or wrote anything to this effect, it couldn't have been altogether unpleasant for Andersen to note that as Dietrich's postwar career was stagnating, her own was soaring. A television special and a best-selling autobiography further cemented her status as a canonic figure of contemporary German popular culture.

On Monday, August 28, 1972, after a sold-out tour of Austria, Andersen was at the Vienna airport, waiting for a flight back to Berlin. She suddenly began to feel unwell, and her oldest son, Björn Wilke, who had accompanied her on tour, rushed her to the hospital. She died there, of a hemorrhage, at the age of sixty-seven. As per her last request, she was cremated and her ashes buried in the small cemetery in Langeoog. The vessel that transported her remains to the tiny island was named, appropriately enough, "Lili Marlene." Some years later, the island's municipal council erected a statue of Andersen in her honor not far from the lighthouse; in it, she is young and smiling, and leaning on a lamppost.

Good fortune smiled, too, on Leip and Schultze. The two met several times after the war and found they had many things in common, not the least among them a shared concern over lost royalties. During the war, all earnings generated by "Lili Marlene" in the United States were collected by the U.S. Alien Property Custodian, and placed into a general war-claims fund to which all eligible enemy artists were entitled to stake a claim. This, of course, was wildly unfair to Schultze and Leip, whose financial reward for their hit song, objectively considered, should have been immense. Still, as the years progressed, the two began enjoying a steadily growing stream of royalties. Writing in the *Sunday Times* of London in 1967, journalist Derek Jewell stated that for that year alone, royalty checks for "Lili Marlene" came in from the United States, Canada, Austria, Australia, Japan, New Zealand, France, Denmark, Norway, Belgium, Spain, Greece, Italy, Switzerland, Sweden, Peru, West Germany, and the United Kingdom, not to mention a payment of 17 pfennigs from Egypt. Jewell also interviewed Schultze, who estimated his total earnings from the song at that point to be $140,000, approximately $850,000 in today's dollars. Even considering the fact that Schultze and Leip evenly divided all their earnings, both men made a handsome profit from "Lili Marlene."

Hans Leip passed away in 1983. He was ninety years old. He spent his final years doing what he had done his entire life: writing poems and sketching. Untainted by any connection to the Nazis, he was widely acclaimed as a paragon of nobility and morality and awarded an assortment of honors and medals.

Things were a bit more difficult for Norbert Schultze. After three years of menial labor mandated by the de-Nazification committee and a few more years as a petty pianist exposed to the scorn of unfriendly audiences, he again emerged, in the early 1950s, as one of Germany's most prolific film composers. His were mainly feathery-light compositions, with titles such as "Take Me on a Journey, Captain" and "Little White Seagull," and he was far from uncritical of his creations: "Seen in the cold light of day, of the 25 films for which I wrote the music within a period of ten years, only a few are worth mentioning." To assuage his soul, he continued composing operettas based on fairy tales. To his repertoire were added adaptations of "The Princess and the Pea," "Snow

White," and "The Brave Little Tailor." In 1980, a German radio station reworked Schultze's first hit, *Schwarzer Peter*, and a few years later, in 1984, his wartime success, *Das kalte Herz*. Schultze himself conducted the orchestra on both recordings. He composed a large number of popular songs and was involved in various professional musicians' associations. After the death of his wife, the actress Iva Vanja, he married a younger woman, Brigitt Salvatori, whom he called his "evening sunlight." He moved to Mallorca and spent most of his days with his six children, eighteen grandchildren, and four great-grandchildren. He died in 2002, aged ninety-one, seemingly free, at least internally, of his past sins.

But those who knew him well suggest that more than having simply overcome his past, Schultze had never come to terms with it in the first place. Karl Heinz Wahren, one of Germany's most celebrated contemporary composers and a protégée of Schultze's, recalled a telling conversation, sometime in the 1980s, with his mentor. A German magazine had just published pictures of a man they both knew, an esteemed composer and educator, having tea with Adolf Hitler. The pictures were an embarrassment to their colleague, who had spent the postwar years vigorously downplaying the extent of his involvement with the Nazis. Schultze, Wahren recalls, sighed.

"Hitler never invited me for tea," he sadly told his friend. "And I wrote such beautiful music for him."

This, Wahren said, was Schultze, both during the war and in the years after: naïve to a fault, utterly oblivious of all but his own simple pleasures, a childlike man who went to his death never entirely understanding the furor over his complicity when all he wanted to do was to compose music.

But more than the illustrious lives of its creators, more even than the men and women who clung to it in desperate times, it is the song itself that remains in the popular imagination, impossible to forget and difficult to understand.

There are many plausible explanations for the popularity of "Lili Marlene." Most of them are obvious and come back to the same basic point: as the war divided the world into different ideologies, different nationalities, different visions of the future, the song reminded the young men at the front and their dear ones back home of the one virtue that, ultimately, binds the entire world together, the one virtue that travels across time and trenches, the one virtue that matters most of all—love.

But these explanations, we believe, are missing a large part of the point, and ignore the very thing that made "Lili Marlene" popular and that keeps her popular still. The best war songs, John Steinbeck noted in his observations, are not about war at all; instead, they are about the things that make war bearable, the things that await at its end, the mundane and wonderful little pleasures of the everyday. These pleasures—a sweetheart's kiss, say, or a country sunset—are too elusive for ordinary speech. They evade even the most sensitive of writers. Put them in a sentence and they sit listlessly, deflated of all meaning. But put them in a song and they glow. The music charges the words, guiding the simple images to those compartments of the mind that store wild emotion. It is there that a song's significance and its potency lie. As Lale Andersen herself witnessed when she toyed with alternative compositions to "Lili Marlene," it was only Norbert Schultze's music that made the song a crowd-pleaser, only his tune, a wedding of folk songs, military marches, and a children's ditty, that managed to capture the true spirit of the poem. Hans Leip's words alone weren't enough; "Lili Marlene" needed a melody and a memorable voice to translate its essence from the private language of one man to the international idiom that captured the hearts and minds of men of all cultures and tongues. This is the true essence of every great song, and it is certainly true in the case of "Lili Marlene." The secret of the song's universal appeal, then, may lie just there, in its bars, stating its case in a sublime musical language that transcends the artificial constructs that men have built to separate themselves from other men. Beethoven, quoting from Schiller, addressed this pleasant joy directly in the choral finale of his Ninth Symphony: "Thou shining spark of God . . . / your magic reunites those / Whom stern custom has parted / All men will become brothers / Under your protective wing."

This is why, perhaps, "Lili Marlene" often retains its strong imprint in the minds of old soldiers, even long after details of battles fought and friends lost fade away. Every year, the veterans of the North African campaign—the English Eighth Army and the German Afrika Korps alike—get together to reminisce about their years in the desert. They've been meeting annually since 1952, only seven years after the war ended, when the physical and emotional scars they carried were still fresh. Theirs, now, are odd meetings. To a table full of elderly German gentlemen shuffles a hunched Englishman, himself grayed, and asking if, per chance, any of them happened to be fighting on a certain hill at a certain date, more than six decades ago. Yes, comes the quiet reply of two or three of the Germans, we were. And the British man, without a hint of anger, informs them that it was probably they who took the life of his best friends, who wiped out his platoon, who maimed his arm or burned his leg. The men nod, as if the Englishman had just reminisced about a pleasant time they all miss. In turn, they will scan the room for past opponents, asking questions, showing scars.

Rudolph Schneider, Rommel's onetime driver, has attended these meetings regularly, at least since the collapse of the Berlin Wall in 1989 freed him to travel from his home in East Germany to meet his colleagues and former foes living on the other side of the Cold War's divide. Fred Hirst is usually there, too, traveling from his home in a small village not far from Manchester. The elderly veterans chat with each other and marvel at how much alike their war experiences had truly been: Schneider tells of his imprisonment by the English, Hirst of his by the Germans. They speak of the same fears, the same hopes. They genuinely enjoy one another's company and still keep in touch long after their meetings conclude.

But there is one bit of ceremony they take as solemnly as possible. Before each meeting begins, before the dinner is served and conversation commences, the men take their places at the table and rise to their feet. It doesn't matter if the annual meeting is held in Germany or in England. It doesn't matter if the men at the table took their orders from Montgomery or Rommel. They all await the same signal. When it is given, they begin to sing. They sing the song that brings tears to their eyes. They sing the song they listened to every day of the war. They sing the song that carried them every night, if only for a brief moment, back home, to their girlfriends or wives, back to the promise of a quiet, happy life. They sing "Lili Marlene."

Notes

Prologue

3 Fitzroy Maclean brought his vehicle to a stop: The account of Maclean's adventures during World War II, and his affinity for "Lili Marlene," is taken from *Eastern Approaches*, his memoir.

4 Undertaking long-range raids: In *Eastern Approaches*, pp. 207–8.

5 "husky, sensuous, nostalgic": Ibid., p. 208.

5 "Belgrade": Ibid., p. 208.

1 Underneath the Lantern

7 For the first time in his short and unhappy military career: The account of Hans Leip's night guarding at the barracks, as well as the pages about his life before and after the First World War, are taken from three sources. The first is Carlton Jackson's *The Great Lili*, pp. 5–17. Mr. Jackson interviewed Mr. Leip a few years before the latter's death; the account of the events that led up to his writing of "Song of a Young Sentry" are Leip's. A second source is *Hans Leip: Schriftsteller, Maler, Graphiker*, the catalogue of a Hans Leip tribute

exhibition presented by the Hamburg Art Museum (Kunsthalle) in September–November 1983, particularly pp. 3–12.

Finally, a 1972 documentary, produced by ARD Television and entitled *Wenn Sich die Spaten Nebel drehen*, includes lengthy interviews with Leip, as well as others related to the success of "Lili Marlene."

12 "Lili was the first that I loved deeply": Quoted in Emil Ludwig's *Goethe: Geschicte eines Menschen*, p. 441.

17 He wrote the first verse: The translation is the authors' own.

20 These fourteen years, however, were the most eventful: In addition to the three aforementioned sources, further details about Hans Leip's life between the two world wars were retrieved from an interview in December 2006 with Dr. Ortwin Pelc, the director of the Museum of Hamburg History and the author and editor of several museum-produced catalogues dedicated to Leip's life and art. These catalogues include *Hans Leip und die Revolution 1918 in Hamburg*, *Entwürfe zur "Hafenorgel,"* and *Hans Leip in Amerika*.

II A Harsh, Primitive Voice

25 As the day dawned: Lale Andersen left behind extensive documentation of her life, including, most notably, a detailed diary she kept from her arrival in Berlin until her death. The diary is reproduced, almost in its entirety, in a book edited by her daughter, Litta Magnus Andersen, and entitled *Lale Andersen: Die Lili Marleen: D. Lebensbild e. Kunstlerin: Mit Auszugen aus bisher unveröffentlichten Tagebüchern*. In addition, Dr. Gisela Lehrke, the cultural commissioner of the city of Bremerhaven, has collected all archival material available on Andersen, including personal letters and official documents, in *Wie einst Lili Marleen: Das Leben der Lale Andersen*. Andersen herself wrote an autobiography, focused mainly on her role in bringing "Lili Marlene" to life, entitled *Der Himmel hat viele Farben: Leben mit einem Lied*. She is also prominently featured in the documentary *Wenn Sich die Spaten Nebel drehen*, in which she thoroughly recounts her life and

career between 1938 and 1945. Additional information came from interviews in April 2006 with Litta Magnus Andersen, who still lives in Germany. In addition, *Lili Marleen an allen Fronten: Das Lied, seine Zeit, seine Interpreten, seine Botschafen,* a four-CD compilation of various renditions of "Lili Marlene," was published in Germany by Bear Family Records and is accompanied by a voluminous catalogue including documents pertaining to Andersen and the others involved in the creation of the song. The authors also interviewed one of the catalogue's researchers and authors, Volker Kühn, in December 2006.

27 "A blond, north German girl": A photocopy of the review appears in Lehrke's book, p. 39.

30 As early as 1926: Kurt Robitschek's essay is quoted in Alan Lareau's *The German Cabaret Movement During the Weimer Republic,* p. 482.

31 Despite being so strongly associated: The description of Berlin's Weimar-era cabaret scene that follows relies mostly on Lareau's comprehensive study.

31 "In those early years": The quote by Walter Benjamin appears in Peter Jelavich's *Berlin Cabaret,* p. 16.

32 "A great deal of champagne is consumed": Quoted in Lareau, p. 473.

32 "artless, without poetry, castrated": Erich Mühsam is quoted in Lareau, p. 474.

34 Hans Heinz Stuckenschmidt put forth a disparaging picture: Ibid., p. 479.

38 "No matter what the viewpoint": Ibid., p. 482.

III Song of a Young Sentry

42 In 1932, Norbert Schultze decided: Like his two colleagues in the creation of "Lili Marlene," Norbert Schultze, too, left behind extensive records of his life. Primary among these is his autobiography, *Mit dir, Lili Marleen: Die Lebenserinnerungen des Komponisten Norbert Schultze.* Schultze also gave interviews to Carlton Jackson, recap-

tured in the latter's book *The Great Lili*. Finally, Schultze, too, appears
at length in the documentary film *Wenn Sich die Spaten Nebel drehen*.
In addition, the authors interviewed Karl Heinz Wahren, Schultze's
protégé and close friend, in December 2006.

44 As the evening eventually narrowed to a close: The account of
Schultze and Andersen's night of passion is somewhat controversial.
Andersen herself, despite being the fastidious diarist, never men-
tions having been romantically involved with Schultze. The com-
poser himself speaks of the affair in *Lili Marleen: Ein Lied uber
Verlangen*, a Dutch television documentary. Wahren, too, con-
firmed having heard Schultze refer to having had a brief affair with
Andersen.

45 "a totally Jewish affair": Quoted in Jelavich's *Berlin Cabaret*, p. 230.
The rest of the chapter's description of the Berlin cabaret scene in
the early years of the Nazi regime is taken from Jelavich as well.

46 "Against decadence and moral decay!": Ibid., p. 230.

47 "2,000 years ago the Catacombs were the refuge": Ibid., p. 236.

48 "Berliner, German, Christian": The exchange between Hinkel and
Hesterberg is quoted in Jelavich, pp. 230–36.

50 "once more into a popular cabaret": Ibid., p. 235.

IV "Bombs! Bombs! Bombs!"

63 "Mob law ruled in Berlin": Hugh Carlton Greene, "A Black Day
for Germany," *Daily Telegraph*, November 11, 1938, p. 1.

64 "No foreign propagandist bent upon blackening Germany": Editorial, *Times* of London, November 11, 1938.

64 "I suppose that it is Goebbels' megalomania": Quoted in Saul
Friedländer's *Nazi Germany and the Jews, Vol. 1: The Years of Persecution, 1933–1939*, p. 272. The account of the Nazi leadership's actions
during *Kristallnacht* is taken from Friedländer.

65 "To be a soldier!": Quoted in Joachim Fest's *The Face of the Third
Reich*, p. 88. Goebbels's brief biographical profile is taken from Fest's
account, as well as from the Nazi minister's own diaries.

66 Fest wrote of Goebbels: Quoted in Fest, p. 87.

67 "with us in the west, there can be no doubt": Quoted in Joseph Goebbels's *The Early Goebbels Diaries*, p. 34.

67 as historian Richard F. Hamilton noted: Quoted in Richard F. Hamilton's *Who Voted for Hitler?* p. 84.

68 "I no longer fully believe in Hitler": Quoted in Richard John Evans's *The Coming of the Third Reich*, p. 205.

68 "I love him": Quoted in Ian Kershaw's *Hitler: 1889–1936 Hubris*, p. 277.

68 From that moment on, Goebbels strove: The account of Goebbels's rise to power is taken from the Goebbels diaries.

75 "the Führer has decided": Quoted in Friedländer, p. 268.

75 MEASURES AGAINST JEWS TONIGHT: Reinhard Heydrich's telegram is available online through the Museum of Tolerance Learning Center's Web site, at http://motlc.wiesenthal.com/site/pp.asp?c=gvKV LcMVIuG&b=394829.

V Radio Belgrade

89 "an enemy of Germany": Quoted in Jo Fox's *Filming Women in the Third Reich*, p. 16.

91 Karl-Heinz Reintgen, a young lieutenant: The account of Karl-Heinz Reintgen's involvement with Radio Belgrade and "Lili Marlene" is taken from two separate interviews with him. The first appeared in Johannes Steinhoff, Dennis E. Showalter, and Peter Pechel's *Voices from the Third Reich*, pp. 88–90. The other, and more extensive, one appeared on a CD dedicated to Radio Belgrade, entitled *Heimat deine Sterne, Vol. 4: Lili Marleen und der Soldatensender Belgrad*.

92 "On no account present political opinion": Quoted in Peter Wicke and Richard Deveson's "Sentimentality and High Pathos: Popular Music in Fascist Germany," p. 154.

93 "Gone," he wrote: Ibid., p. 150.

98 Kistenmacher was to travel to Vienna: The soldier, R. Kistenmacher,

is interviewed on *Heimat deine Sterne, Vol. 4: Lili Marleen und der Soldatensender Belgrad.*

102 "soldiers can die": Quoted in Carlton Jackson, *The Great Lili,* p. 23.

105 Speaking many years later: Klimkeit is interviewed in the documentary film *Lili Marleen: Ein Lied über Verlangen.*

107 Werner Hoffmeister, a soldier in North Africa: Hoffmeister is interviewed in *Lili Marleen: Ein Lied über Verlangen.*

VI "A Small Piece of Home"

109 Howard K. Smith, an American journalist: Quoted in Samuel Hynes, et al., *Reporting World War II,* p. 71.

110 Near those crumbling buildings: The account of Rudolph Schneider's experience during World War II was compiled from an interview by the authors with Mr. Schneider in December 2006.

111 But Schneider didn't lack for words very long: The English lyrics of "Lili Marlene" used throughout the text are taken from Tommie Connor's wartime translation, found in Horst Bergmeier, Rainer E. Lotz, and Volker Kühn, *Lili Marleen an allen Fronten,* p. 169.

113 For the first two days of the battle: The account of the desert warfare is taken from Maj. Gen. F. W. Von Mellenthin's classic *Panzer Battles,* as well as from Derek Jewell, ed., *Alamein and the Desert War.*

114 "Deluges of sand and dust kicked up": Quoted in Robert Crisp, *Brazen Chariots,* p. 93.

115 "defeat is one thing, disgrace is another": Quoted in Winston Churchill's *The Second World War, Vol. 4: The Hinge of Fate,* p. 344.

115 "We lay a few kilometers in front of Tobruk": Quoted in Carlton Jackson, *The Great Lili,* p. 23.

116 In a different corner of that same vast landscape: The account of Harry Hudson's experience during World War II was compiled from an interview by the authors with Mr. Hudson in December 2006.

118 In London, however, "Lili Marlene": The account of the BBC's Patrick Morley, *"This is the American Forces Network:" The Anglo-American Battle of the Airwaves in World War II*, p.6.; John Bierman and Colin Smith, *War Without Hate: The Desert Campaign of 1940–1943*, p. 85; and Carlton Jackson, *The Great Lili*, pp. 41–62. The same story was also recapped in a 1943 British Crown Film Unit documentary, *The True Story of Lili Marlene*.

VII "Can the Wind Explain Why It Becomes a Storm?"

126 "She steps into the room in bewitching dresses": The reviews from the German and Italian newspapers that follow are reprinted in Gisela Lehrke, *Wie einst Lili Marleen*, pp. 78–79.

133 The elements colluded in this shortage: Quoted in Dagens Nyheter, "Finds German Cities Short of Potatoes," *New York Times*, January 28, 1942, p. 5.

133 In March, with the situation deteriorating: Quoted in the Associated Press's "Germany Reduces Civilian Rations," printed in *New York Times*, March 20, 1942, p. 8.

136 She didn't have to wait for long: This remains one of the more obscure chapters in Lale Andersen's history. Unlike the other events of the tour, which she documented in detail in her diary, the nocturnal meeting with Hinkel is glaringly absent. An account of it appears only in her autobiography, *Der Himmel hat viele Farben: Leben mit einem Lied*. Several subsequent scholars claimed that the scene's absence from the diary, and its dramatic appearance at a much later date, indicate a possible fabrication on Andersen's part. Certainly, being forced to testify before the de-Nazification committee and asked about her relationship with Hinkel, Andersen had a sturdy motive to embellish the account of her relationship with the Nazi official, making it sound more horrid than it was. However, since no concrete evidence exists to the contrary, the authors opted to go with Andersen's account.

139 "I hope all of this will finish one day": Andersen's letters to Lieber-

mann and Hirschfeld are quoted in Carlton Jackson, *The Great Lili*, p. 30, as well as in Gisela Lehrke's *Wie einst Lili Marleen*, pp. 83–97.

VIII "We're the D-Day Dodgers"

142 "Destiny has offered us a chance": Quoted in Winston Churchill's *The Second World War, Vol. IV: The Hinge of Fate*, p. 377.

145 "we have a very daring and skillful opponent": Quoted in David Jablonsky, *Churchill and Hitler*, p. 25.

145 Montgomery, though a brilliant commander: This account of Montgomery is taken from Churchill, *The Second World War, Vol. IV: The Hinge of Fate*, pp. 464–66.

148 Eventually, trades were arranged: The account of prisoner exchanges that follows is taken from Hans von Luck's *Panzer Commander: The Memoirs of Colonel Hans von Luck*, pp. 124–128.

149 Private Fred Hirst, then a young infantryman: The account of Fred Hirst's experience during World War II was compiled from a December 2006 interview by the authors with Mr. Hirst. Further information was retrieved from *A Green Hill Far Away*, Mr. Hirst's memoir of his war years.

151 One of their favorite tunes, naturally: This Italian translation of "Lili Marlene," attributed to Nino Rastelli, is taken from Horst Bergmeier, Rainer E. Lotz, and Volker Kühn, *Lili Marleen an allen Fronten*, p. 171.

155 In Italy, however, the song would take: The lyrics for the "D-Day Dodgers" are quoted in ibid., p. 177.

157 Eventually, after the Allies had finished: The lyrics for the two following versions of "Lili Marlene" are taken from Carlton Jackson, *The Great Lili*, p. 75.

IX "Your Train Is Going to Berlin"

159 Although by the war's end: The account of Andersen's escape is constructed here from two complementary sources: Andersen's

autobiographical *Der Himmel hat viele Farben: Leben mit einem Lied,* and Litta Magnus Andersen's *Lale Andersen: Die Lili Marleen.* Each source curiously lacks several minor details mentioned by the other, but neither source negates the other. The combined account also matches the one given by Carlton Jackson in *The Great Lili,* p. 30.

165 It was a letter, sent on October 19: The letter is reprinted in Gisela Lehrke's *Wie einst Lili Marleen,* p. 90.

167 Once she was ready, she grabbed: The account of Lale Andersen's meeting with Hinkel comes from Michael Wilke, her son, who accompanied her that day. While Wilke himself was not available to the authors, he was interviewed several times by Mathias Deinert, the proprietor of the most exhaustive Web site devoted to Lale Andersen, http://www.lale-andersen.de. The authors interviewed Mr. Deinert several times between December 2006 and June of 2007, and had access to his audiovisual recordings and extensive physical archives.

170 Even the *Schwarze Korps:* Quoted in the Associated Press's "Morale Builders Stump the Reich," printed in the *New York Times,* December 23, 1942, p. 3.

171 "The traditional toy-producing country: Quoted in Anon., "Bleak Christmas Looms for the Reich," *New York Times,* December 24, 1942, p. 6.

171 One April morning, Andersen's son Michael: The account of Lale Andersen's suicide attempt is comprised both of Mathias Deinert's interviews with Michael Wilke as well as from the other sources pertaining to Andersen, including her autobiography, her diary, and Gisela Lehrke's *Wie einst Lili Marleen.*

8 "The Gravity of the Situation"

173 Pasche called an ambulance: This account, too, is taken both from Mathias Deinert's interviews with Michael Wilke, as well as Andersen's autobiography and diary. Her dialogue with Pasche and Michael is quoted in Carlton Jackson, *The Great Lili,* p. 31.

174 "Have you noticed," asked the broadcaster: The account of the BBC's broadcast, and the lyrics to their grim version, is taken from Gisela Lehrke, *Wie einst Lili Marleen*, pp. 92–93. The translation is the authors' own.

174 sung deliberately out of tune by Lucy Mannheim: The lyrics for Lucy Mannheim's "Lili Marlene" are taken from Rainer E. Lotz and Volker Kühn, *Lili Marleen an allen Fronten*, p. 174.

175 It was as much a personal struggle: The account of the Battle of Stalingrad is taken from William Craig's *Enemy at the Gates: The Battle for Stalingrad*.

177 He chose his timing carefully: Goebbels's "Total War" speech is available online at http://www.calvin.edu/academic/cas/gpa/ goeb36.htm.

178 On May 15, he wrote her saying: Hinkel's letter is reprinted in Gisela Lehrke, *Wie einst Lili Marleen*, p. 94.

180 The KadeKo, where Goebbels had been disgusted: The dates of the destruction of Berlin's entertainment halls are mentioned in Jelavich, *Berlin Cabaret*, p. 257.

181 And while there was little he could do: The account of Radio Belgrade and its stormy relationship with Goebbels is provided by Karl-Heinz Reintgen and others on *Heimat deine Sterne, Vol. 4: Lili Marleen und der Soldatensender Belgrad*.

183 The *New York Times*'s European correspondent: Quoted in Anon., "Berlin Chaos Described," *New York Times*, January 9, 1944, p. 25.

XI "My Sweet Lili, the War Is Over"

185 But whereas Andersen felt apathetic: The account of Leip that follows, and his comments, are quoted in Carlton Jackson, *The Great Lili*, p. 33.

186 However, his enthusiasm soon faded: Quoted in ibid., p. 31.

189 Leip's opinion of Lale Andersen: Quoted in ibid., pp. 31–32.

191 "My Dear Hans Leip": Ibid., pp. 33–34.

193 But while all accounts from that time: Karl Heinz Wahren,

Schultze's friend and protégé, suggested, in a December 2006 interview with the authors, that *Symphonie eines Lebens* was the one work of which the composer was most proud, or certainly the piece toward which he felt most sentimental.

194 By April 1945, with the Soviet army: The following account of the last hours of the Third Reich is taken from Joachim Fest's *Inside Hitler's Bunker*.

194 These were ambiguous times for Schultze: The account of Norbert Schultze's postwar woes, and of his performance in Berlin, is taken from *Newsweek*'s "Lili's Composer Frets Under His Nazi Cloud," published March 11, 1946, p. 78.

197 Schultze now hated "Lili Marlene": Quoted in Carlton Jackson, *The Great Lili*, p. 33.

197 General Dwight Eisenhower, visiting: The incident involving Eisenhower and Leip is recounted in George Forty's *Afrika Korps at War*, p. 49.

198 Lale Andersen, on the other hand: The account of Andersen that follows, including the meeting with the Canadian soldier in Langeoog, is taken both from Mathias Deinert's interviews with Michael Wilke and from Andersen's autobiography and diary. Additional details were retrieved from the authors' May 2006 interview with Andersen's daughter, Litta Magnus Andersen.

Epilogue

201 On October 19, 1944, a few days before: The account that follows is Karl-Heinz Reintgen's, and is taken from Johannes Steinhoff, Dennis E. Showalter, and Peter Pechel's *Voices from the Third Reich*, pp. 88–90.

202 Not far away, Fitzroy Maclean: In Fitzroy Maclean's *Eastern Approaches*, p. 504.

203 But even with Radio Belgrade no more: The account of the song's postwar fate in East Germany and Yugoslavia is taken from Carlton Jackson, *The Great Lili*, p. 95.

205 The following decade, in Vietnam: Quoted in Anon., "Ban on Love Song Saddens Vietnam," in the *New York Times*, February 8, 1963, p. 3.

205 "If the contest had been decided on musical merits": Quoted in Mark W. Clark's *Calculated Risk*, p. 355.

206 While Clark was in Italy, John Steinbeck: Quoted in John Steinbeck, "Steinbeck Tells How Nazi Song, 'Lilli Marlene,' Got Out of Hand," *Washington Post*, July 5, 1943, p. 9.

206 First and foremost was Andersen: The account of Lale Andersen's appearance before the de-Nazification committee is taken from Gisela Lehrke's *Wie einst Lili Marleen*, pp. 91–97.

208 Good fortune smiled, too, on Leip and Schultze: The account of the song's royalties is taken from Derek Jewell's "Lili Marlene: A Song for All Armies."

210 But those who knew him well suggest: Authors' interview with Karl Heinz Wahren in December 2006.

212 Beethoven, quoting from Schiller: The translation provided for the finale of Beethoven's Ninth Symphony is drawn from Edward Downes *The New York Philharmonic Guide to the Symphony*, p. 111.

212 This is why, perhaps, "Lili Marlene": The account of the veterans' meetings is taken from the authors' December 2006 interviews with Rudolph Schneider, Fred Hirst, and Harry Hudson, all of whom are active and frequent participants in these meetings.

Bibliography

Andersen, Lale. *Der Himmel hat viele Farben: Leben mit einem Lied.* Munich: Deutsche Verlags-Anstalt, 1984.

Anonymous. "Ban on Love Songs Saddens Vietnam." *New York Times,* February 8, 1963.

———. "Berlin Chaos Described." *New York Times,* January 9, 1944.

———. "Bleak Christmas Looms for the Reich." *New York Times,* December 24, 1942.

———. "Lili's Composer Frets Under His Nazi Cloud." *Newsweek,* March 11, 1946, p. 78.

ARD Television. *Wenn Sich die Spaten Nebel drehen.* Germany, April 1972.

Associated Press. "Germany Reduces Civilian Rations." *New York Times,* March 20, 1942.

Bergmeier, Horst; Rainer E. Lotz; and Volker Kühn. *Lili Marleen an Allen Fronten: Das Lied, seine Zeit, seine Interpreten, seine Botschafen.* Hambergen: Bear Family Records, 2005.

Bierman, John, and Colin Smith. *War Without Hate: The Desert Campaign of 1940–1943.* New York: Penguin, 2004.

Churchill, Winston S. *The Second World War.* Vol. 4: *The Hinge of Fate.* London: Reprint Society, 1953.

Clark, Mark W. *Calculated Risk*. New York: Harper & Brothers, 1950.

Craig, William. *Enemy at the Gates: The Battle for Stalingrad*. New York: Barnes & Noble Books, 2003.

Crisp, Robert. *Brazen Chariots: An Account of Tank Warfare in the Western Desert, November–December 1941*. New York: W. W. Norton, 1959.

Deinert, Mathias. *Lale Andersen*. 2003. (September 2006). http://www.lale-andersen.de.

Downes, Edward. *The New York Philharmonic Guide to the Symphony*. New York: Walker & Co., 1976.

Editorial. "Unnamed." *Times* (London), November 11, 1938.

Evans, Richard J. *The Coming of the Third Reich*. New York: Penguin, 2005.

Fest, Joachim. *Inside Hitler's Bunker: The Last Days of the Third Reich*. Translated by Margot Dembo. New York: Picador Books, 2005.

———. *The Face of the Third Reich: Portraits of the Nazi Leadership*. New York: Da Capo Press, 1999.

Forty, George. *Afrika Korps at War*. New York: Scribner, 1979.

Fox, Jo. *Filming Women in the Third Reich*. Oxford, UK: Berg Publishers, 2000.

Friedländer, Saul. *Nazi Germany and the Jews*. Vol. 1: *The Years of Persecution, 1933–1939*. New York: Harper Perennial, 1998.

Glagla, Helmut. *Hans Leip: Schriftsteller, Maler, Graphiker*. Hamburg: Museum für Hamburgische Geschichte, 1983.

Goebbels, Joseph. *The Early Goebbels Diaries: The Journal of Joseph Goebbels from 1925–1926*. New York: Weidenfeld & Nicolson, 1962.

———. "Goebbels' 1943 Speech on Total War." *German Propaganda Archive*: 1998. (April 2006). http://www.calvin.edu/academic/cas/gpa/goeb36.htm.

Greene, Hugh Carlton. "A Black Day for Germany." *Daily Telegraph*, November 11, 1938.

Hamilton, Richard F. *Who Voted for Hitler?* Princeton, NJ: Princeton University Press, 1982.

Heimat deine Sterne. Vol. 4: *Lili Marleen und der Soldatensender Belgrad*. Carinco AG, 2007.

Heydrich, Reinhard. "Measures Against Jews Tonight." *Museum of Tolerance Online Learning Center*, 1997. (April 2006). http://motlc .wiesenthal.com/site/pp.asp?c=gvKVLcMVIuG&b=394829.

Hirst, Fred. *A Green Hill Far Away*. Wakefield, UK: A Lane Publishers, 1998.

Hynes, Samuel (adv.), et al. *Reporting World War II: American Journalism, 1938–1946*. New York: Library of America. 2001.

Jablonsky, David. *Churchill and Hitler: Essays on the Political-Military Direction of Total War*. London: Routledge, 1994.

Jackson, Carlton. *The Great Lili*. San Francisco: Strawberry Hill Press, 1979.

Jelavich, Peter. *Berlin Cabaret*. Cambridge, MA: Harvard University Press, 1996.

Jennings, Humphrey. *The True Story of Lili Marlene*. British Crown Film Unit, 1943.

Jewell, Derek. "Lili Marlene: A Song for All Armies." *Sunday Times*, September 1967.

———, ed. *Alamein and the Desert War: A Dramatic Account of Victory in Africa by Field Marshal Bernard Montgomery and Others*. New York: Ballantine, 1968.

Jones, John Bush. *The Songs That Fought the War: Popular Music and the Home Front, 1939–1945*. Waltham, MA: Brandeis University Press, 2006.

Kershaw, Ian. *Hitler: 1889–1936 Hubris*. New York: W. W. Norton, 2000.

Langemann, Irene. *Lale Andersen: Die Stimme der Lili Marleen*. A coproduction of NDR, WDR, and Arte.

Lareau, Alan, ed. "*The German Cabaret Movement During the Weimar Republic*." *Theatre Journal* 43, no. 4 (1991): 471–90.

Lehrke, Gisela. *Wie einst Lili Marleen: Das Leben der Lale Andersen*. Berlin: Henschel Verlag, 2002.

Ludwig, Emil. *Goethe: Geschichte eines Menschen*. Stuttgart: J. G. Cotta, 1920.

Maclean, Fitzroy. *Eastern Approaches*. New York: Penguin, 1991.

Magnus Andersen, Litta. *Lale Andersen: Die Lili Marleen: D. Lebensbild e. Künstlerin: Mit Auszügen aus bisher unveröffentlichten Tagebüchern*. Berlin: Universitas, 1981.

Morley, Patrick. *"This Is the American Forces Network": The Anglo-American Battle of the Airwaves in World War II.* Westport, CT: Praeger/ Greenwood, 2001.

Nyheter, Dagens. "Finds German Cities Short of Potatoes." *New York Times,* January 28, 1942.

Palmer, Torsten, and Hendrik Neubauer. *The Weimar Republic Through the Lens of the Press.* Cologne: Könemann, 2000.

Pelc, Ortwin. *Entwürfe zur "Hafenorgel."* Hamburg: Museum für Hamburgische Geschichte, 1998.

———. *Hans Leip in Amerika.* Hamburg: Museum für Hamburgische Geschichte, 1999.

———. *Hans Leip und die Revolution 1918 in Hamburg.* Hamburg: Museum für Hamburgische Geschichte, 2003.

———. "Morale Builders Stump the Reich." *New York Times,* December 23, 1942.

Schultze, Norbert. *Mit dir, Lili Marleen: Die Lebenserinnerungen des Komponisten Norbert Schultze.* Zurich: Atlantis Musikbuch, 1995.

Steinbeck, John. "Steinbeck Tells How Nazi Song, 'Lilli Marlene,' Got out of Hand." *Washington Post,* July 5, 1943.

Steinhoff, Johannes; Dennis E. Showalter; and Peter Pechel. *Voices from the Third Reich: An Oral History.* New York: Da Capo Press, 1994.

Van Waveren, Guus, and Henk Van Gelder. *Lili Marleen: Ein Lied über Verlangen.* Netherlands: Avro, 2003.

Von Luck, Hans. *Panzer Commander. The Memoirs of Colonel Hans Von Luck.* New York: Dell, 1991.

Von Mellenthin, F. W. *Panzer Battles: The Classic German Account of Tank Warfare in World War II.* Translated by H. Betzler. New York: Ballantine, 1971.

Wahren, Karl Heinz. "On the Death of Norbert Schultze: 1911–2002." *GEMA,* November 2002 (November 2006). http://www .gema.de/engl/press/news/n166/schulze.shtml.

Wicke, Peter, and Richard Deveson. "Sentimentality and High Pathos: Popular Music in Fascist Germany." *Popular Music* 5 (1985): 149–58.

List of Interviews

All interviews conducted in person unless otherwise indicated:

Deinert, Mathias. Potsdam, Germany, December 2006; subsequent interviews via e-mail, January–June 2007.

Hirst, Fred. Poynton, England, December 2006.

Hudson, Harry. Poynton, England, December 2006.

Kühn, Volker. Berlin, Germany, December 2006.

Magnus Andersen, Litta. Telephone. May 2006.

Pelc, Ortwin. Hamburg, Germany, December 2006.

Schneider, Rudolph. Stauchitz, Germany, December 2006.

Wahren, Karl Heinz. Berlin, Germany, December 2006.

Acknowledgments

Liel Leibovitz and Matthew Miller wish to acknowledge the following people:

Anne Edelstein, our fearless agent, we are deeply grateful for your faith, your taste, your grace, and your wisdom. The attentiveness, support, and guidance you shared with us on this project helped take it from the simple spark of an idea into the book it is today. We look forward to many more years of collaboration with you and, we hope, your friendship.

Amy Cherry, our incomparable editor, provided us with insightful observations, acute comments, and perceptive suggestions in addition to tea and cupcakes. Every page in this book is a testament to your talent.

Timm Baur's translations and Tamara Rosenberg's transcriptions were both immensely helpful in trying to find our way through the tricky thicket of German grammar, and for that, *Danke schön*.

In England and Germany we had the honor of meeting with three extraordinary men: Fred Hirst, Harry Hudson, and Rudolph Schneider. Their courage and kindness not only illuminated our understanding of their experiences in World War II but also strengthened our faith in the ability of man's decency to carry him through even the most troubled times.

Volker Kühn, a critic and an authority on all-things "Lili Marlene," was generous with his time, coffee, and knowledge. Karl Heinz Wahren informed and delighted us with stories about his late friend and teacher, Norbert Schultze. Dr. Ortwin Pelc, the director of the Museum for Hamburg History, opened his vast archives to us, and helped us portray a more accurate picture of Hans Leip. Litta Magnus Andersen, Lale Andersen's daughter, and Jackie Mileham, the singer's granddaughter, kindly shared with us their recollections of their famous relative. The staff at the Deutschen Musikarchiv in Berlin showed us remarkable hospitality, giving us access to many useful documents. For the Hotel de Rome, which provided us with shelter and luxury, we are still grateful.

Mathias Deinert, whose unparalleled collection of newspaper clippings, recordings, and television documentaries about Lale Andersen and "Lili Marlene" was a trove of information and insight, helped us at every stage of the way, from the first stirrings of our research to the final vetting of the manuscript. His sharp eye and infectious enthusiasm gave us comfort and encouragement.

Finally, we would like to acknowledge those mentors at Columbia University's Graduate School of Journalism who helped us train whatever talent we have into a disciplined craft. Kevin Coyne, for teaching us style; David Hajdu, for teaching us that the thought comes before the word; Samuel Freedman, for his gift of story and structure; Todd Gitlin, for his unaffected brilliance and uncommon warmth; and Dale Maharidge, who once drank the remnants of a spilled martini out of his leather cap, for giving us a taste of the requisite spirit. In time, may we prove to be apt pupils to you all.

LIEL LEIBOVITZ:

To my parents, Iris Mindlin and Rony Leibovitz, and my grandmother, Rivkah Greller, for their love and support.

To the Gehl clan—Edna, Zorach, Roy, Amir, Erez, and Nicole—for their unending friendship.

To Molly, for her sweet and unending gift of companionship and affection.

And, as always, to Lisa, my true love and inspiration, for the world entire.

MATTHEW MILLER:

Of the many people who helped me to rally on all those grisly mornings of labor and revision, I would like to thank Mehmet Guner for his smiles and skill with tricky stripes and natural shoulders, Dominic Casey and George Glasgow for ensuring that even my missteps could be made in style, and Raphael Raffaelli for the beauty of his creations, the rich hues of his expression, and the kindness he extends to a young curmudgeon.

For his friendship and assistance with this project, I would like to thank Sean Corcoran, alpha team leader, not only for reading half a page out of the hundred or so he was sent to review but also for teaching me that there is always a kinder, gentler approach. Adam Marelli kept me from kicking a goose and, over bottomless cups of green tea, shared with me his thoughtful reflections on art, aesthetics, and life. Todd Estrin, whose mother long ago predicted that I would one day write a book, has guided me with patience, consideration, and wise counsel to that distant goal. For that strange alignment of our stars, for all the inspiration, I thank him.

To Julie Masciandaro I will always be indebted for the kindness shown to me, so long ago, when I was alone. And to Annamaria Bisazza, Mark Bratt, Tom Conigliaro, Brandon Frank, Rob Morse, Richard Nesi,

Michael Peyser, Matt Safaii, John Simunek, and Amparo Vergara: where would we be without the laughter, the misadventures, the long drives and lazy afternoons? We are shaped by our friends—thank you for being mine. I would also like to thank Arthur and Judy Bernhang for introducing me to the breadth and adventure of the world, for telling interesting stories of faraway places and opening my eyes.

Of the unlucky bunch tasked with teaching me, I am especially grateful to Terry Price for seeing past all the misbehavior and sloppy, half-finished homework. For paying attention to me and threatening, every once in a while, to fail me for the whole semester, I belatedly thank him with everything that I have.

To my aunt, who gave me my education, my sensibilities, my approach—in short, everything, I am deeply indebted. I thank my mother for allowing me to grow a Mohawk and wear incendiary T-shirts to elementary school, and my grandmother for sharing with me her oatmeal, wisdom, and the occasional piece of furniture. My father, whose support and understanding means the world to me, has given me the ability to explore. I thank him for the freedom, for being my advocate, and, above all, for his patience. And I note that my sister, who serenely endures it all, is always appreciated.

My dear lily, Marlene: this book was born the moment I saw you through the window of the bookstore. It is yours, keep it always and every so often please think of me.

To my grandfather: there are no words. The approximations of language are, like the tea you loved, far too weak, much too pale. May I still be worthy of your esteem.

Photograph Credits

Frontispiece: Courtesy of the 352nd Fighter Group.

1. Hans Leip Gesellschaft, Hamburg, Germany.
2. *Lili Marleen an allen Fronten: Das Lied, seine Interpreten, seine Botschaften,* by Horst Bergmeier, Rainer Lotz, and Volker Kühn. Published by Bear Family Records, Berlin, 2005.
3. Hans Leip Gesellschaft, Hamburg, Germany.
4. Hans Leip Gesellschaft, Hamburg, Germany.
5. *Wie einst Lili Marleen: Das Leben der Lale Andersen,* by Gisela Lehrke. Published by Henschel Verlag, Berlin, 2002.
6. *Wie einst Lili Marleen: Das Leben der Lale Andersen,* by Gisela Lehrke. Published by Henschel Verlag, Berlin, 2002.
7. *Wie einst Lili Marleen: Das Leben der Lale Andersen,* by Gisela Lehrke. Published by Henschel Verlag, Berlin, 2002.
8. *Lili Marleen an allen Fronten: Das Lied, seine Interpreten, seine Botschaften,* by Horst Bergmeier, Rainer Lotz, and Volker Kühn. Published by Bear Family Records, Berlin, 2005.
9. *Wie einst Lili Marleen: Das Leben der Lale Andersen,* by Gisela Lehrke. Published by Henschel Verlag, Berlin, 2002.

10. *Lili Marleen an allen Fronten: Das Lied, seine Interpreten, seine Botschaften*, by Horst Bergmeier, Rainer Lotz, and Volker Kühn. Published by Bear Family Records, Berlin, 2005.

11. *Lili Marleen an allen Fronten: Das Lied, seine Interpreten, seine Botschaften*, by Horst Bergmeier, Rainer Lotz, and Volker Kühn. Published by Bear Family Records, Berlin, 2005.

12. Courtesy of Dr. John McClane III.

13. *Lili Marleen an allen Fronten: Das Lied, seine Interpreten, seine Botschaften*, by Horst Bergmeier, Rainer Lotz, and Volker Kühn. Published by Bear Family Records, Berlin, 2005.

Index